All PR is Local

By Jack J. Prather

The science of Public Relations is making things *sell* better,

the art of Public Relations is making things *seem* better.

ALL PR IS LOCAL

a 275-page guidebook for businesses, non-profit organizations, professionals and students.

Copyright 2002 by Future Now Publishing / Jack J. Prather

I S B N # 0-9720847-0-3. Library of Congress Number pending

Ordering Direct from Future Now Publishing:

Single Copy: $38 plus $5.50 postage-handling.

Multiple Copies: $34.20 per book (10% discount) plus $3.00 postage-handling per book.

Bookstore/Library Copies: $26.60 (30% discount) plus $3.75 postage-handling any size order. *NJ orders add 6% sales tax.*

How to Order:

By Mail -
Send request with check or Visa/MC/Amex information to:
All PR is Local
c/o The Prather Group
Suite 301, 93 Spring Street
PO Box 3087
Newton NJ 07860-3087

Online -
www.allprislocal.com
(Available in hardcopy, or by electronic download in whole or in part)

By Telephone -
Call 973-300-0665.
(Leave message for callback if unanswered.)

By e-Mail -
Visit Prathergroup@aol.com
State request with full credit card information.

By Catalog -
Available from Bowker's Books in Print powered by BookSurge.

Other productions from the Future Now Publishing division of The Prather Group:
The Public Relations BLUEBOOK (@1981/reprinted 1986)
The Power of Public Relations and Advertising (@video 1991)

Reviews of All PR is Local

NJ Association of Chambers Executive (former) and President Sussex County Chamber Tammie Horsfield:

"Small businesses can greatly benefit from Prather's guidelines and tips whether they do their own public relations and marketing or work with an agency."

New Jersey City University Public Relations Associate Professor and author of 21 books, Dr. Bruce Chadwick:

"All PR is Local will help students prepare for careers in public relations and communications. It intelligently demonstrates that tactics and techniques used at the national and local levels are virtually the same."

President NJ Chapter of the Public Relations Society of America (PRSA) Irene Maslowski:

"This book is worth many hours of consultation with a PR pro. Prather's reflections on 30 years in public relations includes case profiles, action plans and proposals, all valuable resources for the PR practitioner. Small businesses, non-profits, PR professionals and students can all benefit."

Three-term New Jersey Assemblyman and health care company CFO Donald J. Albanese:

"If you need crisis-problem management and public relations-marketing consultation, Jack Prather is the go-to guy. His insightful new publication, All PR is Local, is a must read."

Owner 3-P Promotions and Kittatinny Recreation Association founder Doug Laird:

"Prather's new book is even better than his Public Relations Bluebook, and I found that very useful."

President Sussex County Community College and published author, Dr. Bradley Gottfried:

"This book offers a wonderful approach to public relations that can be effectively used by individuals at all educational and business levels."

Past Reviews of The Public Relations BLUEBOOK

New York Daily News:

"Did you ever wonder how to start your own public relations business? Jack Prather is ready to tell you everything you would ever want to know. The Bluebook serves as a kind of seminar in print."

The Ragan Report:

"The Bluebook offers do-it-yourself instruction for novices wishing to begin a career in public relations. The book contains narrative, instruction, tips, samples, vignettes and case histories."

The New Jersey Herald:

"A great concept for businesses, organizations or individuals who wish to do their own or begin a PR career."

The Middletown N.Y. Times-Herald-Record:

"It's a do-it-yourself PR guidebook for organizations, hospitals, businesses, politicians, careerists, schools, churches, etc. It will pay for itself many times over if one follows the key steps on how to deal with the media."

Table of Contents

Note: Chapters in <u>All PR is Local</u> have numbered sub-titles for easy reference to facilitate group or classroom discussion.

Continued on next page . . .

Table of Contents-page 2

Continued on next page . . .

Table of Contents-page 3

Continued on next page . . .

Table of Contents-page 4

PR Tip: Each public relations practitioner should learn the techniques, tactics, tools and methods of the trade and equally importantly learn to develop and trust his or her own instincts.

Author's Note:

A New Jersey City University public relations student asked this question during a lecture in 2001:

"How do you in good conscience represent a client that you disagree with?"

We answered:

"First you put yourself in his shoes. Then you put yourself in his brain. Then you fight for your point-of-view to the level of your belief in it. Then, unless it is illegal, immoral or unethical, you fulfill the client's wishes and mission to the best of your ability. His satisfaction will be your satisfaction; his success will be your success. Remember, you are there for your client or employer and not the other way around."

Foreword

Whoever described public relations as "selling the sizzle, not the steak" would not have made that declarative if he or she had first studied this most insightful and comprehensive guidebook, All PR is Local. This is the first book I have read that focuses on PR at the local level and demonstrates that the same basic public relations principles apply regardless of the size of a company or organization.

As vice president of one of the world's largest advertising agencies in New York for 20 years I was primarily charged with conceiving and executing marketing strategies for dozens of products and services, including the placement of hundreds of millions of dollars in advertising expenditures. Although dozens of professionals were involved in planning the creative and marketing strategies, it was not until fairly recently that advertising professionals began to fully comprehend the actual and potential importance of public relations to the process.

For too many years, public relations was an enigma within the advertising profession, but no longer. PR is a profession worthy of respect, as you will discover through the wisdom imparted by strategist Jack Prather whose varied clients have included the winner of the 1993 Malcolm Baldrige National Total Quality Award presented by President Bill Clinton and the late Commerce Secretary Ron Brown, Playboy Clubs Inc., Sprint, a U.S. Congressman, two manufacturers for whom The Prather Group won National Communicator Awards, and a host of regional and local businesses, organizations and entrepreneurs.

Today, we live in an age of advocacy and special interest groups. Even "Mom's apple pie" has detractors. Now, the way in which the public perceives a product, service or company is likely to be of equal importance to the more traditional advertising and marketing activities thanks to PR.

Until recently, I operated a suburban New York-New Jersey radio and television station, WSUS Channel 8 in New Jersey – "the Jersey Giant". There, we received literally thousands of press releases and other requests for news, public service, or public affairs airtime. Regrettably, the majority of these mailings were so poorly prepared that few gained exposure. The Prather releases were always on target and in proper format.

"All PR is Local" demystifies public relations and helps put it into perspective. Public relations is both a science that cannot be fully quantified and an art that can be qualified. With effective public relations, two plus two will almost always equal more than four and this creates *synergy*. Happily, the days when PR practitioners were perceived as tub-thumping extroverts are long over and they are now rightfully considered as true professionals.

Most medium and small businesses and organizations understand that PR can be the catalyst in establishing, improving, or revising that elusive but essential commodity known as image. Every product or service and every firm or local organization has an image to develop and protect. The key question remains: is the desired image best reached through PR? You bet!

As demonstrated in this book, effective public relations can take many and diverse forms. Knowing which buttons to push when (never the panic button) will be apparent after you understand the how and the why. In essence, that's what this book is about and probably the reason you purchased it. I urge you to pay particular attention to the valuable insights in the case profiles section and to study Jack Prather's take on the creative process. Whether you use this book as a refresher or as a daily guide, good results will follow.

This foreword was written by Peter Michael Bardach, former owner and president of WSUS radio and cable-TV stations in Franklin, N.J. Mr. Bardach is also a former senior vice president of Foote, Cone & Belding Advertising Agency in New York City. He currently operates the Sussex Bay Foundation in Panama City, Florida where he hosts a radio show and is active in various civic and charitable causes.

Acknowledgements

This book is dedicated to Pam, my wife, the string for my kite and soul mate whose profound love, support and friendship allow me to know happy thoughts and enjoy beautiful things.

Heartfelt thanks to the many clients, associates, relatives and friends who helped this public relations strategist along his career and life paths, especially nationally known college fundraising professional and brother Dr. Robert F. Prather and non-profit expert and sister-in-law Monica Prather, M.E. for their valuable contributions to this book.

Special thanks to former advertising executive and radio-TV station owner Peter Michael Bardach who wrote the foreword, and to New Jersey City University Associate Professor and author of 21 books Dr. Bruce Chadwick who wrote a positive review. Thanks also to the other professionals who took time to review this book and lend their good names to it.

Deep gratitude to former President and CEO of Ames Rubber Corporation Joel Marvil for the opportunity to be part of the team that received the coveted Malcolm Baldrige National Quality Award from President Bill Clinton and the late Secretary of Commerce Ron Brown in Washington D.C. in 1993.

Thanks for the contributions of effective PR, a high level of professionalism and good cheer to my partner of five years, Irene Maslowski.

Good luck to all readers of this book from the business, non-profit, academic or PR worlds who will hopefully benefit from my vision and experience. I hope they enjoy the wonderful world of PR as much as I do.

The Journey to Now: Author's Notes

The effort to impart essential lessons in PR began with The Public Relations BLUEBOOK presented through Future Now Publishing in 1981 and reprinted in 1986. That first guidebook was marketed to colleges and universities, small businesses and non-profit organizations. Reviews of The Bluebook accompany testimonials about this current volume on a previous page.

That debut instructional book was followed in 1991 by a two-hour video, The Power of Public Relations, targeted to the same audiences. The video included interviews with clients from a diverse range of business and industry, with instruction, sample cases and commentary.

In 2002, yet another decade later, this latest volume titled All PR is Local is presented as a compendium of 30 years on the front lines and in the trenches of consulting. It is written for businesses, non-profit organizations, current or potential PR practitioners, and students.

Three decades and counting in PR has proven to the author's satisfaction that virtually all businesses and organizations can benefit from effective public relations and that those who provide it can have fruitful and enjoyable careers.

PR Thought: *A creative idea not implemented is a waste of time.*

About The Author

Prior to becoming a consulting strategist in public relations and marketing, Jack Prather was sports editor and crime reporter at the Dover Advance and court reporter, sports editor and editorial columnist at The New Jersey Herald. He also freelanced as a stringer and covered a major murder trial and local news for UPI and the Easton, Pa. Express. Jack had majored in public relations journalism at Ohio University in Athens.

Prather has been published as a freelance fact, fiction and poetry writer in magazines, newspapers and literary publications, and for clients in specialty newspapers and trade publications.

Awards and recognitions for public relations, advertising, journalism and community service have included:

- The Award of Distinction from the National Communicator Awards in 1996 for a new kit of marketing materials produced for an injection-molding manufacturer of plastic caps and closures for a variety of industries.

- Honorable Mention from the National Communicator Awards in 1997 for a portfolio produced for a manufacturer of plastic and glass ampoules for the healthcare industry.

- Top-Ten Advertising Award from *Jobber Topics Magazine* for a series of editorial columns ghost written to promote a client's interest in an auto parts store and an auto after-care computer software company, as well as his longtime interest in being elected to local office.

- National recognition for a speech written for political client county Freeholder who delivered it at a local VFW Veteran's Day event.

- Best Column-All Divisions for *In The Jackpot* sports column that appeared daily in The New Jersey Herald from the New Jersey Press Association (NJPA).

- Second Place and Honorable Mention awards for *In The Jackpot* and *The Observer* Sunday editorial column from the NJPA.

- Best-Editing of a sports section twice in successive years for competing newspapers from the NJPA.

- Second place and a cash-prize for fact-based fiction in competition conducted by *Listen Magazine.*

- Fourth place and a cash-prize for poetry in a contest run by *Explorer Magazine.*

- The Newton NJ Jaycees' Distinguished Service Award, their only non-member winner, and other recognitions for community charitable and civic service.

- Jack Prather was part of the Ames Rubber Corporation team that was presented the coveted Malcolm Baldrige National Quality Award by President Bill Clinton and the late Commerce Secretary Ron Brown on December 14, 1993 in historic Mellon Hall in Washington D.C. The Baldrige Award is considered the top business honor in the world. Prather served as public relations consultant and corporate newsletter editor-publisher for Ames Rubber for five years.

PR Thought: *Communications is the body of PR, creativity the soul.*

A Bit of History

Writing has been the lifeblood of our two careers, first in journalism and then a lengthier one in public relations, and has provided more thrills in return than we can document here. If you pay the price to become a proficient writer or journalist and evolve into a PR professional, many rewards can and will come your way.

Among the prized personal rewards was connecting with three lifelong heroes by first writing newspaper columns about them: Brooklyn Dodger first baseman and Mets Manager Gil Hodges, cartoonist icon Charles Schultz, and Senator and Presidential Candidate Hubert H. Humphrey. Here is a bit of history about our exciting encounters with these three diverse and wonderful personal heroes:

We had followed Hodges' Dodger career as a young baseball fan growing up in Brooklyn, and had honored him by wearing his number 14 through eight years of amateur baseball.

We interviewed our boyhood hero while he was recuperating from an operation in the coverage area of the newspaper where I was sports editor. The result was a column titled "The Quiet Man" that chronicled Gil Hodges' dignity and grace as a player and manager.

Shortly after the article appeared, he sent a thank you note and an invitation to share the night in his honor at the old Polo Grounds! It was a magical evening.

A Peanuts nut, we extolled the comedic and life-sensitive virtues Charles Schultz portrayed through his Peanuts gang in our editorial-page column *The Observer*.

Soon after we received a canary-yellow envelope from One Snoopy Lane in which the famed cartoonist wrote: "Thanks for the article, Jack. Cartoonists rarely get recognition such as you gave me in your column. Sincerely, Charles Schultz." We were overwhelmed with *good* grief.

We considered Hubert H. Humphrey a political hero for his stand on Civil Rights and for his basic decency. After we endorsed his 1968 presidential bid in a column, we met the Senator at a political forum and presented him with a copy (presuming he hadn't read it). He promptly stuffed it in his jacket pocket.

However, we soon received a letter on U.S. Senate stationery that said, "I read your column on the plane back to Minnesota. What a wonderful endorsement and tribute to me. Thank you. Senator Hubert H. Humphrey"

Hodges' invitation and the Schultz and Humphrey letters remain treasured mementoes of our journalism career.

Notes: During our 10 years with Playboy and later for Warner Bros. Jungle Habitat, we promoted almost every major performing star of the 1970s and 1980s including Bill Cosby, Jay Leno, Kenny Rogers, Bob Hope, Johnny Mathis, Tony Bennett, Vic Damone, Andy Kaufman, Neal Sedaka, Al Martino, Pat Boone, Natalie Cole, Enzo Stuarti, Liberace, The Oak Ridge Boys, Doc Severinsen, Freddie Prinz, Ed McMahon, *et al*.

We served as the main contact to dozens of stars, arranging media interviews and show reviews, and got to know top marquee performers quite well in the process. It was a gig to kill for, as many of my contemporaries in PR said. Access to the stars provided terrific material for grateful columnists and reporters and benefited all concerned.

For this writer, it was exciting, rewarding and sheer fun.

Chapter One

The Prather Method of PR

1. How The Prather Group Operates

Each public relations practitioner should determine his or her unique and personal method of practicing the art of PR: as an employee for a business or organization, an account representative for an agency, an independent consultant, or ultimately as an agency owner.

Jack Prather made the choice to launch The Prather Strategic Public Relations and Marketing Group as an independent consultancy in 1972. It operates the same way to this day.

The Group consists of affiliated professionals who provide expertise as needed in graphics and printing, promotion and special events, research and technical writing, direct mail and Internet venues, *et al.*

This method provides multiple paybacks: eliminating the necessities of maintaining a staff and large office space and maximizing return-on-investment (ROI) of marketing and PR dollars for the client. It also allows for control and peace-of-mind that is of special importance to the founder.

The complex format required for a practitioner to become a full-service public relations consultant or to eventually start an agency is not suited to those who prefer and are more suited to work for someone else within a business, organization or agency. In short, it is not for everyone.

Practitioners who are employed by a business or organization can enhance their value by developing an in-house agency for their employer and save up to 17 percent on advertising: 15 percent in commissions and two percent in pre-payment where applicable by following the detailed steps outlined in the section devoted to this subject later in this book.

PR professionals who wish to start their own fulltime consulting business or agency can do so through the instructions in much the same manner.

The key is for each practitioner is to determine a direction and then pursue a career within that format *if* it is both compatible and comfortable. However, it is important to remain flexible because a career may start in one direction and then an opportunity may present itself that can lead in a lucrative and fulfilling new direction.

Each practitioner should think like a computer: new information in and new answers out when making choices.

Many times random opportunity or simple chance will put you in the right place at the right time. If you fully know when that happens you can consider a career shift, if you don't the opportunity will pass you by.

The smart and tuned-in practitioner will evaluate each career opportunity and either vigorously pursue or reject it. At least he or she will be in the game. The important thing is to enjoy options rather than missing opportunities because of timidity, lack of confidence or fear of the unknown.

Good luck in making good career choices!

2. *Phases of the Journey*

The first decade of our public relations activity was captured in a manual of guidelines, tips and case histories titled The Public Relations Bluebook@, published in 1981 and reprinted in 1986.

The next 10-year phase was reflected in personal commentary, instructions and first-hand testimony from six clients in a two-hour video titled The Power of Public Relations produced in 1991.

Both the book and video were marketed to small businesses and organizations, colleges and universities, and novice PR practitioners. Both self-produced items are being updated and targeted for re-release in 2003.

The last 10-year phase is reflected in this palindrome year of 2002, All PR is Local, a compendium of lessons learned and cumulative knowledge gained during three decades of practicing strategic public relations. It is presented with the ardent hope that it will help guide current and future public relations practitioners to fully respect their chosen career path, observe professional standards and do their jobs better than ever.

After serving entities in such diverse industries as small business and manufacturing, leisure and tourism, healthcare and rehabilitation, chambers of commerce and economic development, non-profit and governmental organizations, legal and environmental professional firms, entrepreneurs and elected officials, *et al,* we finally have the comforting feeling that we have just about paid our dues - although we aren't planning to retire for at least another 10 years.

3. *Fortunate Along the Way*

Along the way we have been fortunate to serve dozens of wonderful clients and enjoy hundreds of enriching professional and personal experiences. Every client and experience was valuable to our learning process.

As a payback for that good fortune we have seized this opportunity to share our journey with promising young practitioners and students who are at the dawn of their careers within the wonderful world of PR.

Through the years consulting with dozens of diverse clients we crafted most of the action plans, from isolating the mission(s) to the *post mortem*, providing whatever was required for the client in the areas of public relations, marketing, communications, development and special projects.

All of this was done on a consulting basis, with the scope of services, fees and commissions hammered out in concert with the individual client and all support provided by affiliated outside professionals as needed.

When appropriate for the success of the mission we assumed the title of director to increase our internal and external clout, expand our access to all concerned, and enhance our real and perceived status to all concerned.

So it can be with the observant and dedicated public relations practitioner willing to pay the price to hone skills, gain confidence and reach for the brass ring.

Besides surviving for three decades as an independent consultant, we also served for stints as public relations director for two advertising agencies and as senior vice president for a major public relations agency. Those contracts were right for us at the time but we always returned to our roots as an independent full-service strategic public relations and marketing consultant.

The varied challenges of serving a highly diverse cross-section of clients have been interesting, rewarding and sometimes vexing. But overall it has been a great ride so far.

4. Dealing with Tough Clients

There are always going to be tough clients.

Although the vast majority of clients we've served over the years have been professional, fair and nice, there were a couple that proved to be extremely difficult and who challenged our minimum standards – but they failed to win those tugs of war.

The Prather Group believes it is the professional's job is to advise the client on how to fulfill the mission with as much enthusiasm as is warranted by his or her own belief system. If we are certain about a conflicting point of view, we go to the wall before finally yielding to the client's wishes. We battle in lesser degrees, depending on our own faith in the strength of our position.

Throughout the process of building a PR action plan we try to remain pliable, flexible and reasonable in order to influence the client toward our way of thinking through persuasion and information.

After all is said and done, it is our job to implement the plan that will accomplish the mission for the client full speed ahead, sublimating our own personal feelings or viewpoints. We are, after all, an agent for the client: he or she is our boss.

The Prather Group's inviolate standards are twofold: never go below the high minimum standards established in 1972 and never do anything that is or appears to be illegal, immoral or unethical.

Beyond that we stand by the use of good old common sense to handle difficult - tough - clients.

5. Team-Building

Always remember that if you do not yet possess the necessary personal or technical resources to fulfill your public relations missions, you *can* and should learn how to locate and cultivate outside professionals to work with you on an as-needed basis as The Prather Group does.

Teambuilding for success is the proven and cost-efficient method employed by the author for the length of his career. This method can create a pathway for you: the business owner, the organization president or the PR practitioner to effectively fulfill your missions.

The PR practitioner should search for, evaluate, cultivate and work with the best available *local* professionals who can and will provide a needed service whenever appropriate and cost-effective.

Help may be needed from many outside professionals including graphics designers, printers, writers, media buyers, photographers, video and sound production specialists, researchers, technical advisers, Internet consultants or other professional resources.

As part of the process, the PR practitioner should visit the office or studio of an allied professional to meet and interview all of the key people who will be involved in providing a service before retaining that resource. Samples should be reviewed. References should be checked. A comfort level and trust should be established.

Once the PR practitioner and the outside professional complete the 'vetting' process, mutually rewarding and fair agreements can successfully be hammered out.

The practitioner should attempt to obtain the best available service for the lowest possible price, calling for professional discounts or commissions where appropriate and applicable. However, it is more important to get a quality resource in place than an inexpensive one. The successful consultant will learn how to evaluate quality and cost to make proper selections of support professionals.

In turn, the practitioner should fulfill his or her end of the bargain and pay the affiliated professional promptly and according to standards set in advance by both parties.

Putting the right team in place and continuing to work together will result in experience, a better flow of service and a synergy that will benefit the practitioner, the service supplier and ultimately the client or employer.

6. *Fees and Commissions – How to Charge*

Among the most difficult challenges for novice public relations practitioners are: what fee or hourly rate to charge a client, what level of mark-up to apply to collateral materials, and how and when to collect monies due?

The answers are best worked out by the individual practitioner who can determine what the traffic will bear and examine the client's ability to pay.

It is especially important to charge fairly - never too little and never too much. Figuring that out can be tough but practitioners should remember that 'part of something is better than all of nothing', and to be flexible. You can legitimately increase fees and mark-ups as your PR success mounts and your value increases.

Obviously, the PR practitioner who is an employee of a business, organization or agency is paid a salary that is contingent on his or her skill set and whether or not she or he is capable of fulfilling *strategic* (proactive) rather than *traditional* (reactive) public relations roles.

The PR consultant can become part of the early development of a business or organization and become indispensable to the process. He/she can then grow with the client and earn increased dollars in the process.

For new projects or clients The Prather Group has a policy of requiring advance payment of the initial monthly fee with monthly payments thereafter and the right to cancel for either party with one-month's notice. We also require advance payment of one-third of the projected costs for printed materials, followed by one-third at sign off by the client and the final one-third upon delivery, with the same payment schedule for advertising production, and advance payment in full for ad placement.

These policies may seem too tough to fulfill and, to some PR pros, virtually undoable. However, it has worked for three decades for The Prather Group. And nobody gets hurt financially this way, practitioner or client.

The collection in advance policy was initiated for two equally valid and important reasons:

1) To prevent breakage (loss) to the agency of its fees or payment for collateral materials
   and
2) To eliminate anxiety over any monies due.

The key to obtaining approval on the advance-payment policies is to explain at the initial meeting in a low-key and lucid manner why this is advantageous to the client:

1) Prather Group consulting fees are lower because we suffer no losses (breakage) from non-payment
   and
2) Prather creativity will not be negatively impacted because of anxieties over non-payment of monies due.

The Prather Group for 30 years has operated on three levels of public relations consulting fees, depending on the status and potential of the client:

Level One – PR On A Shoestring.
This level provides PR and marketing services to a new or struggling business or organization that has potential and enough funding to get started. The practitioner will assist this type of client by providing marketing and PR assistance vital to fulfilling the short-run mission at a very reasonable rate. As the client grows so to does the practitioner's value and earning ability. This type of client can occasionally turn out to be the most lucrative over time depending on the success of the program.

Level Two – PR To Make Things Better.
This level provides PR and marketing services to an existing business or organization that is doing all right but wishes to do better and has adequate funding. The practitioner becomes part of the team and grows with the client, too. Compensation at this level is decided by what the practitioner must bring to the table, the potential and actual returns-on-investment, and most importantly what the traffic will bear. This type of client can turn out to be the most long-term and stable for a consultant.

Level Three – Go for It.
This level provides PR and marketing services for successful and relatively secure businesses or organizations that can afford the necessary budget dollars to fulfill the missions and are prepared to pay top dollar for consulting services. This is the most competitive type of client and requires the utmost of professionalism and consistent success or the contract will be short-lived.

Important Constant:
No matter the level of client or the amount of the fee, once you have agreed to serve do the best you can and treat each one fairly and equally.

7. *10 Tips On Public Relations Billing*

1. Make sure the value accomplished for the client or employer equals the value of compensation.

2. Keep records of all time spent on a project and use your best judgment re your fee or hourly rate

3. Keep records of all appropriate expense items and include in final billing and justification.

4. Present easy to understand and comprehensive invoices and expense justification.

5. Mark up advertising costs at 17.65 percent or deduct payment to the publication by 15 percent for the same final amount, and mark up printed materials in a fair and appropriate manner.

6. Do a full justification to the client with detailed billings.

7. Keep your fees and charges as high as justifiable but within the client's ability to pay.

8. Do not compare yourself in charging to a larger or more prestigious agency or individual.

9. When you are providing outside services, be fair to vendors and allied professionals.

10. Be ethical in your financial dealings with a client and vendors.

Note About collecting: As in any business venture, there will be a time when you cannot collect monies due despite your best efforts and precautions. When your time is at stake, the burden is not as great and you may be more flexible about advance payments. However, when you are asked to lay out your own cash for printed materials or advertisements, unless you *know* the client or employer is certain to pay, you should obtain at least 1/3 or 1/2 of the initial investment in advance or you may get stuck with the bills.

8. Acquiring Clients

The route to obtaining a client begins with the cultivation process.

One of the Prather Group methods proven over the years to cultivate a potential client has been to strike up a meaningful conversation at a business or civic organization meeting or any forum where professionals gather. Without being obvious or overly aggressive, we generally inquire about the business or organization that she/he heads or works for and learn as much as we can about its current status. If appropriate, we share our knowledge of important subjects of mutual interest and mention contacts and friends we may have in common and share interesting and pertinent information about The Prather Group. This is all geared to lead the person to suggest that we continue the discussion in the near future to see if there is possible mutual interest. If they don't we do.

Another method is to scour the newspapers for information about potential clients and then call or write offering your specific public relations services. If a chemical company is having a pollution problem, offer to discuss crisis-problem communications management. If a local politician is announcing a run for higher office, offer your publicity services. If an organization is identified as being in need of funds, offer your fundraising or special event expertise. You will identify the need and your ability to fulfill it as you scour the printed pages. Follow the same method with contacts you have made and leads that you have uncovered from other sources.

There is some value to a carefully conceived targeted direct mail campaign to potential clients. Although The Prather Group has only done this a few times in 30 years, it has resulted in some significant contracts, including a large catering hall, a major communications company and a prestigious strategic public relations agency.

Remember that word-of-mouth can be the best and the worst form of advertising. If you earn a solid reputation and image in the field, then the single best form of acquiring clients will be yours: *referrals.*

9. All PR Is Local!

The similarities among the various strategies that have been employed for 30 years by the author for a diverse range of clients regardless of size or budget clearly demonstrate the essence of truth that permeates our theme: *all PR is local.*

Whether it is local client like the entrepreneurs we serve that own funeral homes, or a nationally known one like Playboy Clubs Inc., the same basic tactics, tools, techniques, standards, rules and attitudes apply. All clients receive equal dedication from Prather Group and its affiliated professionals regardless of fee or profit levels. The only difference in service is the commitment of time. Once signed on as a client, all are treated equally.

The strategies will be custom to each client but the tactics, tools and techniques remain virtually symmetrical when applied for any size business or organization, from crisis management to publicity, from promotion to support advertising, from image building to rumor control, from print materials to speech writing, *et al*.

What will differ is *creativity*, perhaps the most important element in any action plan.

The disciplines practiced within the PR world work best and in synergy when one additional constant thread is present: common sense.

The discussions and references within this volume illustrate a cross-section of strategies that were developed for such diverse and financially disparate clients as:

- Ames Rubber Corporation, winner of the coveted Malcolm Baldrige National Quality Award in 1993
- Playboy Clubs Inc. Great Gorge Resort, a 10-year client that we positioned as a 'family resort'
- Sprint-United Telephone Company for whom we completed a comprehensive survey and analysis
- Assemblyman Scott Garrett, a client of 11 years who led NJ in voting percentage four times
- Sunrise House Rehabilitation Center that recently began adolescent inpatient and outpatient care
- MicroNet Inc. Satellite Corporation that expanded three times despite stern opposition in the 1990's
- The Karen Ann Quinlan Center of Hope that provides priceless services to terminally ill patients.
- Health Choice Inc. that has become a leading third-party administrator of health plans in just five years

The instructions demonstrate how to create, implement and manage traditional and strategic public relations programs, projects and activities for virtually any employer or client within any industry or profession.

Equally important, the book instructs the practitioner how to select and work with an external public relations or advertising agency, or to form and manage an in-house PR agency with savings to 17 percent on ad costs, or to start his or her own consulting agency.

The book is offered as a roadmap for the novice public relations practitioner operating on a local, regional or national scope to better serve a client, employer, agency or self.

10. Crafting the PR Role and Title

When crafting the role for strategic public relations or marketing for a potential client, The Prather Group first figures what is best for that client and secondly what is best for the agency. The recommendation is then presented to that client with a full explanation of why it is the wise course of action and that is memorialized in the final proposal and action plan. The recommendation for the most appropriate and practical title for the role The Prather Group will fulfill must be mutually agreed upon in advance of beginning any activities.

Prather Group agreements are generally sealed with a handshake, followed by the action plan with an informal signed agreement designed to spell out the areas of responsibilities for both the consultant and the client that spells out policies and procedures, including payment schedules. This eliminates confusion or guesswork if the client decision-makers change in mid-stream.

Titles can be a positive element in your PR efforts if they are appropriate and fit. A title should not overly impress the practitioner who is really just crafting it for the benefit of the client. The only thing that should impress the PR professional is the ultimate success realized for the client or employer.

That said, proper use of titles can accomplish the following positive results:

- Enhance the practitioner's perceived status externally
- Enhance the practitioner's perceived status internally
- Improve the potential for responses from the media
- Help open doors to and communication with outside resources

Five distinct examples of various strategic public relations and marketing titles and roles fulfilled by The Prather Group include:

Title:	Public Relations Consultant
Client:	Warner Bros. Jungle Habitat
Role:	Publicity, traditional PR consulting
Duties:	Publicity-wrote and serviced media releases and features, media relations Created, managed and promoted special events Consulted with the manager and marketing director
Results:	Consistent media exposure including major article/photo in VIP magazine

Title:	Strategic Public Relations Consultant
Client:	Sprint-United Telephone Company
Role:	Designing/implementing attitude surveys of five publics of interest
Duties:	Advised and collaborated with eight-man task force Hired and oversaw survey manager and 23 survey callers Analyzed data/submitted 200-page report with extensive charts/graphs
Results:	The report was accepted and used as a company-wide model

Title:	Strategic Public Relations and Marketing Director
Client:	A Health Care Company
Role:	Director of PR and marketing, consulting
Duties:	Manage internal marketing team, advertising, sales materials, management consulting
Results:	The company became a leading administrator of health care plans in five years of operation

Title:	Lobbyist
Client:	A major ski area and a development company
Role:	Lobbying members of the New Jersey State Legislature
Duties:	Tracking and influencing key legislation regarding skiing
Results:	Confidential

Title:	Communications Director/Political Adviser/PR Consultant
Client:	Numerous elected-officials at state, county and municipal levels (Democrats and Republicans)
Role:	Media relations, publicity, political advice, crisis-problem management
Duties:	Articles, op-ed columns, print-broadcast interviews, event promotion, advertising, consulting
Results:	Long-term clients, 90 percent election and re-election success

11. *Fuel the Passion for PR*

There is probably not a lot of passion aroused from being an accountant, a lawyer, a bus driver, or in most professions or jobs, for that matter. Job satisfaction, career fulfillment and success, certainly, but passion – doubtful.

However, passion can and should be an emotion involved in the practice of public relations. It will help an advocate be the best she or he can be. After all, the primary role in PR is to make things *sell* better or *seem* better, services to others that can and should evoke strong feelings.

Without overly sounding like Pollyanna or Mr. Nice Guy, and with the full knowledge that no one can instill passion in another person, we believe passion can be inspired. So go for it! Fuel your passion by identifying and promoting the positives in any situation, and believing that negatives do not exist in the world of PR, only *positive-negatives.*

Put forth the best scenario possible for your client or employer in the face of a crisis or problem. The techniques necessary to mitigate or neutralize a problem or crisis will become clear after you evaluate the situation. You can then carefully implement solutions that will take your employer or client off the hook.

For example, by publicizing already established positives while you cope with the crisis or problem you will remind publics of interest that your client or employer is of good reputation and character.

These established positives include such valuable current and past community services as:

- Charitable monetary support
- Participation in civic causes
- Amount of taxes paid
- Number of employees on payroll
- Amount of purchases from local vendors
- Commitment in executive time to the community

12. *Making Things Sell Better or Seem Better*

Operating in the world of PR consulting for 30 years has been mostly a joy. It has allowed interaction with a wide diversity of clients with personalities that range from Type A to easy-going, and power styles that register on the barometer from semi-ruthless to persuasive. We prefer the latter category in both instances.

We believe that our primary job is to make things *sell* better and make things *seem* better. In order to do that we must first discover and then cultivate the very best within each client so we can do the most for that client. The PR practitioner can and must deal with and influence the varied and complex client personalities and styles in a professional manner and with high minimum standards. In the end the only thing that will matter is the result.

13. *Affirmation*

The New Jersey Chapter of the Public Relations Society of America (PRSA) sponsored a very special event for member practitioners at the Somerset Marriott Hotel on December 12, 2001.

The luncheon event featured 13 guest speakers from the print and broadcast media. Their brief presentations were followed by question-and-answer session.

The impressive array of media included the director of communications and an on-air anchor for WCBS-TV, the New Jersey Editor of the Philadelphia Inquirer, the news director of radio station WBGO-FM, the editor and publisher of Whitaker's Newsletters, an associate editor of Business News New Jersey magazine, the senior editor of New Jersey Business magazine, the assignment editor of Bloomberg News, a veteran reporter for WWOR-TV, the managing editor of The Hudson Reporter weekly group, the assistant editorial page editor of the Courier-Post, and the technology editor of The Wall Street Journal.

They encouraged PR professionals to pitch or query them with newsworthy, unique or interesting material and that much of their material is indeed generated by public relations professionals.

Many said they would accept advance telephone contact about submitting an article or suggesting an interview, or with a tip or news lead.

Almost all agreed that e-mail was a solid form of contact, and to a lesser-degree fax submissions.

They were unanimous in dissuading communications by mail, especially in light of the September 11 tragedy just three months before.

The unanimous standards among the broadcast pros were that PR practitioners should understand the radio and television news cycles and the best times to telephone or otherwise contact them.

They agreed that persistence – "we all have our jobs to do" - is fine but undue pressure is not, and that most professional public relations practitioners do know and respect the difference between the two.

The unanimous standards among the print pros were that PR practitioners should obtain the standards for each publication, including length, deadlines, names/ titles of who to target and calendars for special themed issues. All emphasized that they appreciated the professionalism of the PR practitioners of today and that most were courteous and respectful.

One asked that the public relations practitioners should operate with respect and courtesy and those traits will be extended back to them in return.

Another suggested that each audience member understand and allow for terseness when the editor or reporter is under the extreme pressure of deadline.

The sub-title on this segment is "affirmation". The reason for this claim is that the 13 professional media speakers affirmed many of the lessons offered in this volume: All PR is Local.

That this event occurred during the writing of the final chapters, that we attended and that we were able to use it to validate many of our PR points proves a key Prather Group philosophy: *it is important to be in the right place at the right time and know it.* One of our favorite words also comes to mind: *serendipity.*

14. Self-Promotion

A low-key but dynamic approach to self-promotion can benefit the PR practitioner and work wonders to enhance her or his image and reputation.

The main function of PR is to provide these benefits to a client or employer but why not utilize the techniques to build your own credibility and client roster?

We enhanced our standing within the communities and state we serve by getting involved in Chambers of Commerce, charity organizations and civic activities where we earned respect and recognition, and that led to bonding, networking, access to potential clients and a career.

We also wrote articles on crisis-problem management (sample in this book) and strategic public relations, and lectured at area colleges and high schools and to business groups about PR and marketing. All of that positioned us locally as an expert in the field of public relations.

Another credibility booster is serving in the legitimate role of spokesperson for a client or employer. When appropriate, this serves three main purposes:

1) It ensures that correct and carefully crafted messaging is conveyed through the PR strategist

2) It serves to protect the client or employer from possibly sensitive questions from the media

3) It puts the public relations pro in the spotlight

Perhaps the most complimentary words the author has ever heard were made by a former client, Kevin Kelly, Esq. who referred The Prather Group to Assemblyman Scott Garrett by saying: "When Jack's around good things happen".

PR Thought: *Public Relations is Truth Well Told.*

Chapter Two

The Basics of Public Relations

1. You Can Do It

You too can do it, yes you can!

You can become a fully qualified public relations practitioner, begin the process of evolving into a public relations strategist or do your own PR with some relevant guidance from this instructional volume.

The title of this book, All PR is Local, comes with a tip of the tam to the late Speaker of the House, Thomas "Tip" O'Neill, who coined the phrase "All politics is local".

All PR is local in the sense that the basic principles and standards, tools and techniques, and requisite skills and knowledge remain the same regardless of the size of the employer or client, the type of industry or profession, or the scope of the challenge.

Most PR missions share a common thread. For example, making things *seem better* or making things *sell better* requires creative ideas well implemented on any playing field. And positioning a client or employer in a positive light and as a unique industry leader requires strategic techniques administered with professional tools.

Through it all, the PR professional at any level must remember that effective communications is truth well told.

The practitioner must and should continuously polish personal skills and knowledge, image and reputation, and value and marketability to reach the pinnacle of his or her PR career.

Public relations is a profession best served by those who are ethical and moral, knowledgeable and studious, and positive and fair. Those who develop these attributes will deserve the financial rewards, respect and personal growth that a public relations career can provide. Those who do not won't.

This material is designed to promote understanding and observance of the professional standards, ethics and principles required of the public relations strategist as much as it is to impart instruction on how to operate within the industry.

The aim is to help provide purpose, direction and motivation to public relations practitioners and students. By learning and developing all of the professional requirements needed to do the job correctly, the PR practitioner can eventually aspire to and fulfill virtually any traditional or strategic public relations role and in an effective and cost-effective manner that will maximize the return-on-investment (ROI) of PR dollars for virtually any employer or client.

Public relations practitioners can greatly benefit from many sources other to attain their goals: from mentors, from under-graduate and advanced studies, from published books and manuals, from colleagues and experts in the field, and even from employers and clients.

However, it is ultimately up the public relations practitioners in the trenches to shore up their skills and knowledge, call on their inherent talents and guts, and learn from their failures and successes to well serve their employer or clients.

To each public relations practitioner or student who hears an inner voice about his or her career, let this be the message:

"I can do it, yes I can!"

2. *Important Elements of PR*

There are many important elements that the public relations practitioner must understand, embrace and develop if she or he wishes to have a successful career in traditional or strategic public relations.

Each PR element is important in its own right, and collectively they combine to show the enormous depth and intricacies of the profession.

Practicing strategic public relations is difficult, to be sure, but it is eminently doable by bright and aspiring practitioners who are willing to pay the price in study and effort to get to that high level.

PR practitioners should review each of the elements in this kit, from the various tools and techniques to the strategies to the use of the forms, and then sit back and do what is perhaps the most important function of the strategic public relations professional: *think.* Your own insights will follow.

The material is designed to help train, direct and motivate practitioners and those wishing to do their own PR to realize their full potential in such traditional or strategic public relations venues as:

- Internal public relations manager or PR representative of a business or organization
- Account manager or junior executive of a public relations or advertising agency
- Novice public relations consultant or novice independent PR agency owner
- Students of public relations, communications and marketing
- Business owners or none-profit organization executives who wish to do their own PR

Actual strategic PR case profiles and proposals, vignettes of unusual and hopefully interesting occurrences, tips, forms and basic philosophy have been drawn from the author's files and memory bank. They are presented in capsule form in this book to focus on the highlights and avoid the tedium of lengthy dissertations.

The material is a cross-section of examples of the creativity, insight, planning, implementation and *post mortem* analysis that resulted in synergy and ultimately in success for the client in the main but not always. We'll share some setbacks, too.

3. *PR Career Choices*

We've been doing things our way for most of the past 30 years: not better than, not worse than, merely different than the majority of our colleagues and competitors. This is as much a reflection on our personality, approach to life and need to be individualistic as it is a rejection of a boiler plate career path or simply not wishing to work for someone else.

Although an analysis of our PR journey forms the basis of this book, one of its basic lessons is to suggest the many career opportunities open to the practitioner or student. Here are five professional PR career options:

1. Employee of a business or organization
2. Employee of a public relations or advertising agency
3. Independent consultant
4. Owner of a consulting firm
5. Owner of an agency.

The past, present and future are inter-twined: the analysis and then an understanding of where you have been and where you are at now can lead you to determine the best place to go in the future. Understanding all this can provide enhanced thought and action and the resulting synergy.

That synergy will provide a strong base for you to launch or validate your PR career.

As previously noted, our public relations career began in 1972 with Playboy Clubs Inc. based at the $50 million 714-room Great Gorge Resort & Country Club at Great Gorge. We formed The Prather Group, continuing to serve Playboy until it was sold 10 years later and adding significant and numerous clients along the way. Over the next 20 years, we merged into the agency world on three occasions but always matriculated back to the world of independent consulting, retaining our original clients in the process. This is where we remain today.

4. The Essence of PR is Truth Well Told

Every public relations practitioner has heard the mostly casual but often serious charge from 'outsiders' that he or she is a flack, a *spin-meister* or some other euphemism for shill, inferring that we provide the sizzle and not the steak, partial truth, propaganda or worse.

These mischaracterizations ignore the essence of PR and the record of most professionals in the industry.

It is indisputable that PR has emerged into a highly disciplined profession that requires strict observation of the standards and principles published in this book. That is important for any practitioner to understand and follow. Ask most PR professionals and they will agree that any intentional lapse in integrity by a fellow practitioner will be quickly and soundly discovered and rebuked by contemporaries, and especially by competitors.

Moreover, if the media uncovers a release or information piece that is deceptive, the line of communication will evaporate.

It is inescapable: credibility is a must for the PR pro!

5. Creating Something from Nothing

Another important element for the successful practice of strategic public relations is the ability to create something where nothing exists. It is called vision.

The ability to develop this trait has been invaluable throughout the author's career in public relations.

A vignette: Lee Gottlieb, corporate director of Public Relations for Playboy Enterprises, reviewed more than 100 resumes and interviewed five applicants including Jack Prather for the position of director of public relations and regional advertising for the new Great Gorge Resort in New Jersey. Hugh Hefner and the Playboy team were in the midst of strategizing methods to gain approval for a gaming casino and this made the position at the resort vitally important in the scheme of things.

During a lengthy interview at the Plaza Hotel in New York City Gottlieb declared: "I want someone who can create something from nothing for this position". Prather handed him an *In the Jackpot* newspaper column titled "Ah, Snow" that had earned first-place honors in all divisions of the best-column competition sponsored by the New Jersey Press Association. Gottlieb read the column and said, "That's what I mean". Prather got the job on a fulltime consulting basis.

During an exciting 10-year stint, Prather studied gaming in Great Britain and lectured throughout New Jersey and in the media on the subject, created the local Playboy Foundation that raised or donated more than a million dollars to charities, hosted celebrity and sports events like the Bunny of the Year Pageant, televised boxing matches and entertainment spectaculars, and handled media publicity, conferences and relations. It was a dream come true for a young practitioner who was in the right place at the right time and took advantage of it.

6. *Public Relations Premises*

A creative idea that is not implemented is a waste of time!

That was the initial premise that motivated the launch of The Prather Strategic Public Relations Group in executive offices at the Playboy Great Gorge Resort three decades ago.

That simple idea about ideas fueled our journey into the world of public relations that has provided a wealth of experience and helped frame the following 10 additional premises that define the profession:

- Ideas are the essence of public relations and all PR activities are essentially those *ideas in action*.

- A version of the old sales axiom that "nothing happens until somebody sells something" applies to public relations because the effort will mean little unless PR helps to sell a product, service, point of view, crisis resolution, *et al*.

- PR often needs to create something where nothing exists (marketing and nature hate a void).

- PR implementation is intricate and involved: to build or repair an image or reputation, to publicize and promote a product or service, to solve a crisis or problem, and to provide advice and confidential counsel - all complex tasks.

- Publicity is a more effective tool than advertising to get a message across because it is more believable, relatively less expensive and placement timing can be controlled to some extent.

- PR synergy within a company or organization will result when the mission is determined, a creative action plan is developed and implemented, an appropriate budget is established, a solid internal team is assembled, needed outside marketing and advertising entities are cultivated, and a *post mortem* is held.

- The public relations budget for a client or an employer can be cost-effectively fulfilled by the practitioner who cultivates and hires outside consulting professionals and uses external resources only as needed to maximize return-on-investment (ROI), the ultimate goal of any marketing or PR effort.

- Traditional (basic) public relations is primarily *reactive* in nature and basically requires a keen knowledge of the techniques and tools of the trade and allegiance to principles and standards.

- Strategic public relations is pro-active in nature and advances the practice of PR to the ultimate level, requiring practitioners to possess deeply held convictions about the value of PR, the skill to convey its benefits to a client or employer, and the innate common sense and skill to put forth the best possible scenario to all publics of interest without misleading or misinforming anyone at anytime about anything.

- Public Relations practices, principles and standards are basically identical regardless of the size of the client or employer or the scope of the mission, proving that indeed, All PR is Local!

An understanding of the power of PR and its many tangibles and intangibles will enable the practitioner to summon enough will, confidence and diligence to sell the concepts, ideas and action to the client or employer.

7. *Experience is the Best Teacher*

For the traditional or strategic public relations practitioner, as it is in virtually every career path, experience is the best teacher. The successful PR professional will learn from his or her mistakes and become better for it.

The author has done learned from his mistakes and is committed to share the mostly positive but some negative experiences of a lengthy career in hopes it will help practitioners attain being the best they can be for their clients or employer while avoiding some of the inevitable pitfalls along the way.

As the practitioner prepares to handle his or her own clients or employer, he or she must gain the experience to fully understand and embrace the following basic marketing elements necessary for development of a public relations action plan, including learning how to:

- Evaluate and fully understand the client or employer product lines or services.

- Analyze available and new challenges and opportunities for sales growth and potential.

- Determine missions in sales or increased exposure.

- Propose solutions that will fulfill the missions.

- Determine the budget necessary to succeed.

- Implement the plan in a cost-efficient and professional manner.

- Conduct the *post mortem* to build on success and remedy failure.

Each of these elements is discussed in the various case profiles and guidelines throughout this book. The PR practitioner should not only learn how to deal with the technical expertise required to become a strategist but how to develop the common sense and instinct that can bring creativity and personal touches into the equation.

8. *Diverse and Complex Tasks*

In this new millennium, employers are increasingly calling on the strategic public relations practitioner to handle a wide variety of general and complex tasks, including:

- Publicizing and promoting a business or organization.

- Developing and nurturing a positive perspective for board members and shareholders.

- Fashioning innovative methods to meet competition head-on.

- Supporting the sales force in attracting and retaining customers or clients.

- Helping to deal with and solve problems and crises.

- Serving as executive team member and management advisor – and much more.

The case profiles, guidelines, tips and custom forms will help simplify the process, including handling such diverse and specific public relations tasks as:

- Planning and budgeting.

- Generating publicity.

- Maximizing clout.

- Enhancing an image or reputation.

- Creating newsletters and promotional materials.

- Designing an advertising support campaign.

- Creating a public relations kit – and much more.

9. *Active Roles for the Strategist*

Every professional public relations practitioner should strive to become a *strategist*, who by definition is an integral part of the management team and a significant player in the design, development and fulfillment of all missions.   Strategists are decision-makers and not just followers.

The public relations strategist will take active roles in:

- Defining missions.

- Creating and managing action plans.

- Determining tasking assignments.

- Implementing tactics and techniques.

- Developing and managing timelines.

- Determining and overseeing budgets.

- Conducting *post mortem* analyses.

The case profiles and proposal samples in this kit provide many examples of the elements listed above.   The practitioner should as a test create an action plan with those elements for a current employer or client.

The successful strategist intrinsically realizes that in the world of public relations good ideas are born from a free exchange of opinions and open-mindedness among those involved. It is easier to do when all concerned share the same basic agenda: to fulfill the mission in the most effective and cost-efficient manner possible.

The budding strategist can create a positive edge by honing skills, developing a keen sense of observation and listening before speaking or acting, especially in a sensitive crisis mode. Those who do not observe or listen well tend to knee-jerk their reactions and end up simply tossing enough mud against the wall until some sticks.

It is imperative that those entrusted with crafting solutions do so with the utmost professionalism, avoiding any action or activity that seems like grandstanding or trying to impress the boss - the client or the employer.

If the public relations strategy seems not to be working then shore it up or change it, don't doggedly pursue a faulty and failing idea or plan.

It is up to the PR strategist to provide input, direction and management of the process of public relations to the client or employer, and that is best done by truthfully evaluating each step of the way and changing direction when and if needed.

10. Standards and Ethics

Strategic Public relations should be viewed and practiced by insiders as a high-level profession with standards and ethics similar to that espoused by lawyers, by CPAs, by architects, by engineers, *et al,* because this is the right thing to do *and* so that PR will ultimately be viewed and evaluated in that manner by the public.

Practitioners should therefore read and abide by:

- The Declaration of Principles and Code of Standards of the Public Relations Society of America that requires from its members professional conduct, truth, accuracy, fairness and responsibility.

It is also important for PR practitioners to cultivate and utilize the media for a wide variety of communications missions. It follows that PR practitioners should understand the ethics and standards that credible editors and reporters follow and consider vital to their profession. They are succinctly presented in:

- The American Society of Newspaper Editors 'A Statement of Principles' that speaks of the integrity, responsibility, freedom of the press, independence, truth, accuracy, fair play and impartiality that are hallmarks of The Fourth Estate.

PR practitioners should develop a keen perspective of what matters to both sides of the professional equation: public relations *and* journalism.

Both the PRSA and ASNE documents are printed in full at the end of this book. Practitioners should read, understand and abide by each of them. As a member of the New Jersey Chapter of the Public Relations Society of America and a former San Diego chapter member, we have become familiar with and embrace the standards espoused in both documents.

11. Philosophy and Public Relations

To evolve and develop into a professional public relations strategist, the practitioner must develop his or her own philosophy and then abide by it in all situations, especially when under pressure. PR professionals should embrace The Prather Group concept that is worth repeating: *the essence of public relations is truth well told.*

The PR practitioner can develop a personal philosophy by being studious and diligent, confident and professional, reliant on instincts and common sense, aware and accepting of his or her own limitations, and determined to fulfill missions and challenges regardless of obstacles.

To operate under the tenets of a personal philosophy is to pay homage to one's profession and that demonstration of faith and integrity in what you do will engender proper respect from your employer or client.

Consider your profession and its standards as worthy as those of attorneys, CPAs, engineers, *et al,* and act accordingly.

Practitioner philosophy should include abiding by the standards and ethics of the Public Relations Society of America previously referred to and to never mislead, misinform or lie to anybody about anything at any time.

Your philosophy should extend to your dealings with members of the media within your world of PR. No one in the media will abide the statements: "I'll get back to you with the facts" or "Sorry, I can't comment at this time". And they will cut you off forever if you dissemble of the facts or deceit. Truth objectively and fairly told is an objective you should embrace in all PR communications.

The PR strategist who can put forth the best possible scenario to the media and publics of interest or who can limit the scope of damage by controlling the message without violating any ethical standards will be doing his or her philosophical job well.

It is important that the PR rep, consultant or agency owner treat each and every client with equal deference and with an effort that fulfills the agreed-upon mission regardless of the fees and commissions involved or the size or scope of the client. That is not just good philosophy it is good common sense.

Once the responsibilities, fees and commissions have been agreed-to with the client, the PR pro must and should abide by all facets of the bargain. This is required by public relations industry standards, is important to the image and reputation of the practitioner and is the right thing to do ethically and philosophically.

Public relations practitioners should understand and remember that proffering to the media and public a sincere *mea culpa* from a client or employer who wishes to set the record straight, atone for a misdeed or mistake or simply apologize will show strength of character that will be appealing to the publics of interest and the right thing to do. A sincere attempt to set the record straight and make things right should be tendered to the media and to the public at an appropriate time and in a professional manner by the public relations practitioner.

Developing the ability to make things right should become a major part of the public relations strategist's philosophical toolbox.

12. Defining the PR Mission

The process of defining the strategic public relations mission can be effectively accomplished only after the public relations strategist intensively brainstorms with all concerned to gain an overview of current status, an historical perspective of past successes and failures, real clues as to exactly what the client or employer is seeking to accomplish in the short and long runs, and an idea of the budget dollars available.

It then becomes the responsibility of the creative strategist to capture the mission in understandable, doable and more importantly in affordable terms. The return-on-investment (ROI) of public relations dollars is as important as any other bottom line within a business or organization.

Public relations successes will fuel future PR activities while failures will crimp the plans for any future PR projects unless the practitioner can demonstrate an improved *modus operandi*.

Defining the mission is important to the traditional Action Plan that development of effective tools and techniques needed to get the job done. The ultimate goals are to gain the maximum benefit to the client or employer in increased sales or sales potential, in better exposure and image building, in skilled crisis or problem management, or in fulfilling whatever mission is at stake.

Once the mission and the Action Plan are crafted and gain the full support and financial backing from the client or employer, the battle can be waged.

Fulfilling the missions of the plan – whether they are to solve a problem, promote a product or service, or enhance an image or reputation – will require an effective combination of activities that are designed to take the employer or client wherever they want to go.

During this activity, the PR practitioner is the general of the troops and must work with all concerned to protect, defend and fulfill the mission. Remember that in many cases the PR professional must convince others of the viability, credibility and necessity of the programs or they will stall because of misunderstanding their value.

13. PR Plans and Tasking

It is important to determine the chain-of-command and areas of responsibility for all involved in public relations programs and projects in order to increase the efficiency of the efforts and to position PR with the relative importance that this important discipline deserves.

Remember that it is generally accepted that public relations is primarily a management function that also works in conjunction with marketing and sales.

Internal or external *strategic* public relations activities are basically considered management functions while the implementation of *standard* PR and advertising activities are basically considered marketing functions, although they often intertwine and vary greatly.

The PR command structure will be required to make important decision-making calls before the implementation of programs and activities begins. The better organized the process is the more successful it will turn out to be.

Guidelines to follow to develop a strategic public relations plan and tasking assignments include developing and implementing the following elements:

- *Plan Overview.* The overview should include a brief explanation of the strategic public relations plan and a cursory description of the client or employer it is designed to serve.

- *Mission and Objectives.* The ultimate objective and the individual aims and goals of the plan should be put forth within a working document – the plan-of-action. These missions may include the intent to increase sales and profits, enhance an image, re-position the client or employer in an advantageous manner, resolve a crisis or problem, host an activity or event, *et al.*

- *Tasking Assignments.* Point-persons should be assigned for each task, including for publicity, promotion, print materials, conferences, activities or events, crisis-problem spokesperson responsibility, *et al.* It is the practitioner's job to manage and coordinate the activity and serve as liaison to all involved.

- *Tools, Techniques, Targets.* The tools and techniques developed to fuel the public relations plan should be targeted to reach and influence all appropriate publics of interest, including customers or clients, decision-makers, VIP's, the media, the community, *et al.* And don't forget to keep your client or employer informed.

- *Budget.* The budget must include sufficient funding by the employer to support the practitioner in the implementation of the elements contained within the traditional or strategic public relations plan. The budget must be affordable – not too little and definitely not too much. More on this topic follows in the next segment.

- *Analysis.* The PR practitioner who is managing and/or implementing the plan should prepare a *post mortem* report of the results from preparation to fulfillment for future reference. This will enable the PR practitioner to grow and improve with experience and the employer to prosper. This will uncover successes and failures and prevent duplication of the latter.

14. *The Public Relations Budget*

The most important components of any strategic public relations plan are often the least understood by the management decision-makers and therefore by default are often not properly funded. That makes it imperative for the PR practitioner to educate and persuade the client or employer to invest money in order to make money through viable public relations and marketing action plans.

It is accepted by professionals in the public relations industry that the strategist must not only defend his or her plans of action as being potentially effective and cost-efficient to the funding sources within a company or organization, but must explain in detail why the up-front budgeting commitments are necessary. These difficult tasks are part and parcel to the overall public relations effort.

It is important to promote and advertise in strength as well as in weakness. Rules of thumb range from two-to-four percent or more of the annual gross income, depending on the client/employer goals and market conditions.

For new or expanding ventures where income levels are non-existent and potentials are basically unknown, it is important to make the most educated guesses regarding aims and goals and affordable investment dollars. One technique to arrive at the best-case scenario is through a *retreat* conducted by an outside professional or the practitioner. Participants would include the owner, CEO, president, executive staff, marketing and sales personnel – virtually all concerned. The basic agenda would be to create action plans for the short and long terms by examining sales projections and potentials, existing conditions, competitor evaluations, and estimates of the necessary budgets to attain the stated goals.

Proper PR budgeting is vital to a company or organization in order for it to protect and promote its own self-interest in the marketplace. The value received from a solid effort will be proven valuable in countless ways.

To sell that premise in advance takes common sense, skill, determination and faith in the value of public relations but the practitioner must project in detail what the potential return-on-investment (ROI) can or will be in revenue and profits, and in goodwill and image building to the client or employer.

Fighting for a share of the marketing and advertising dollar is common in the public relations milieu – just ask any successful practitioner how difficult this part of their career can be. The novice PR practitioner must accept this premise and learn how to deal with the inevitable infighting with others who are seeking funding for their own projects. However, the practitioner can use strategic PR tactics to convince and persuade the funding sources to allocate meaningful budget dollars.

Each public relations plan should be viewed as a communications mosaic and each element of the plan should be visualized as an important piece necessary to complete the mosaic. In that way, the relative importance of each individual element – particularly budgeting – will become apparent to the funding source decision-makers.

The public relations budget should include a comparison of outside agency fees and expenses versus the costs to implement the same tasks via an in-house practitioner or agency. When comparing external versus internal costs, a clear picture will emerge of which route is better. In either case, the PR practitioner must project what the potential return-on-investment will be in revenue and profits, as well as in goodwill and image building.

Communications and marketing design and production costs are fixed for such common vehicles as printed materials, including brochures, flyers and newsletters, and promotional items such as special events and activities, plus for photography and graphics and direct mail programs. Advertising through an outside agency includes standard 15 percent markups, sometimes fees and marked up costs for collateral printed materials.

The internal agency can save the 15 percent and sometimes two percent through a pre-pay agreement, as well as some of the cost and mark-up on collateral materials if the affiliated professionals are used regularly and are paid on a timely basis. Discounts will come from professionals who are paid what they are owed on time.

Advertising and direct mail costs can either be funded as part of the PR plan budget or via existing advertising budget. Where any of these items are channeled for funding is unimportant, that they be funded is what counts!

The public relations strategist is usually and should be the point person to determine and recommend final budgeting to support marketing the communications efforts on behalf of a company or organization.

15. Public Relations Definitions

Is there one comprehensive definition of public relations? Is that definition applicable for the PR practitioner who represents a person, company or organization? How about a politician or entrepreneur, a hospital or racetrack, a charitable club or fundraising society?

PR is the science of ideas and communications in action. PR definitions are by nature disparate and ultimately depend on the scenario.

Following are 10 definitions for public relations offered at random, including the one that appears in a major dictionary. Can you discern which is the dictionary definition?

1) Obtaining publicity, promotion and goodwill for a person, company or organization.

2) Enhancing the image of and creating goodwill for a person, firm or institution.

3) Presenting a balanced and positive view of a company or organization to target publics.

4) Advancing an idea, image or reputation to help market a product or service.

5) Utilizing creative techniques to advance marketing goals and management support.

6) Swaying public perception and acceptance of a person, company or organization.

7) A marketing tool to support sales efforts and create awareness of a product or service.

8) Improving the overall public perception of a person, company or organization.

9) Inducing public understanding of and goodwill toward a person, firm or institution.

10) Maximizing positive or minimizing negative views of a person, firm or institution.

The strategic public relations professional will understand and use all of those definitions during the course of his or her career, including the dictionary one: number nine. That definition basically infers that PR is to persuade or influence publics of interest with common demographics to become target audiences, as well as to favor a person, firm or institution beyond the mere value of what is for sale. Simple? No. On-target? Yes.

Credible definitions of PR can be crafted to fit most situations, such as when the practitioner assumes a commanding role in a crisis, or *schmoozes* the media in order to plant a news item, or lobbies a group for support of a political candidate, or promotes a sensitive community relations project, or manages an important employee relations program.

The practitioner can compare his or her regard for public relations profession with that of a lawyer: both are required to protect client confidentiality, both must and should abide by professional standards, and both must act in the best interests of their client or employer, be it a company, organization or individual.

However, while the lawyer generally insists that his client remain mum, the PR practitioner must provide legitimate communications to the media and public in the best possible light without misleading or misinforming anyone.

The tactics of information exchange, persuasion and passionate advocacy are core tools for the public relations strategist but *integrity* is the integral element in defining who she or he is as a careerist and as a person.

16. Substance and Style

The PR practitioner's normal personality should dictate to a large extent his or her style when dealing with clients, the media and the various publics of interest of a client or employer.

If you are naturally very reserved, serious and low-key, then a sudden shift to being outgoing, humorous, and overly friendly would only serve to discredit you to those who know you, to those who eventually discover the real you, and to yourself.

Conversely, if you have a naturally boisterous or aggressive personality, a severe change in demeanor and attitude in the other direction will have the same negative effect.

There are no public relations types anymore. The days of the 'balloons-in-the-air' publicist are all but dead, although certainly there are credible PR gimmicks and outgoing personalities that rely on razzle-dazzle.

The keys are to be your best self, use common sense, do your utmost to create and implement projects and activities that have both substance and style, and keep the client or employer completely in the loop.

In the end, good results are the objective; the manner of obtaining those results is secondary as long as it is professional.

As far as demeanor goes, a PR personality at a racetrack, with its gimmickry and festivity, is likely to be a cigar-chomping extrovert who does a lot of backslapping while a PR person at a hospital is much more likely to be a business oriented man or woman with a low-key persona.

The point is: if the PR professional at the track were handling a hospital account, his or her demeanor would change drastically and vice versa.

That leads to this important premise: *behavior modification* is called for, personality change is not.

The solid public relations practitioner will utilize common sense to size up each situation and then handle it by grasping every legitimate gain in media attention and promotion that is available.

The practitioner who insists on doing things his or her way will be on track as long as the lessons of behavior modification (improvement) are followed and professional standards are observed.

Ethics in public relations should also extend to integrity of personality. Be real. Be yourself. Improve by becoming your best self!

Substance with style also creates synergy and allows the fortunate public relations practitioner who possesses both qualities to hit grand slam home runs for a business or organization. Neither substance nor style is as effective when separated.

How can the novice public relations practitioner develop substance?

Or style?

Substance in PR is being able to understand, create and implement public relations plans and activities by using professional tactics, techniques and tools. All of this can be developed through study, observation and practice. The process can be accelerated through commitment and diligence.

Style is largely dictated by personality, especially in a professional milieu. For the public relations practitioner, style will help to open doors but they will remain open only if he or she demonstrates substance, too.

It is important to understand that it is simple human nature to be attracted to those that who have an appealing personality and style and to turn away from those who do not.

It follows that the public relations practitioner who is pleasant to be around, who has a good sense of humor, who displays a strong sense of self and who tries to do the right thing will get more attention, will be listened to more ardently and will be more effective than someone who is acerbic, defensive, withdrawn or negative.

PR practitioners must grow their skills, learn from their mistakes, stay positive in the face of controversy, remain calm in the eye of the storm and, most importantly, be themselves!

Keys to modifying behavior:
- Temper over-aggressiveness

- Overcome or sublimate lack of confidence

- Trust your instincts and act accordingly but keep an open mind

- Think before speaking or acting

- Don't fake it: if you don't know then find out the answer

- Never say "I can't do that" - retain someone who can

- Accept valid and constructive criticism

- Calmly defend your position when wronged or misunderstood

- Be confident enough to control what you can when appropriate

- Tell only the truth or say nothing

- Be true to yourself

- Set a high minimum standard and never go below it

- Correct and learn from your mistakes

Public relations practitioners who enhance their style and personality through appropriate behavior modification and strengthen their skill sets by thoroughly learning the PR trade can become proactive strategists who are part of the planning and decision-making team instead of followers who merely react to others.

Most public relations strategists rightly view themselves as professionals on a par with lawyers or CPA's but it is their individual styles and skill sets that will dictate how the world views them.

17. Set A High Minimum Standard

There is really no room for arrogance in the public relations strategist's world. You must continuously learn your craft, hone your skills, recover from your mistakes and deal with a variety of type-A personalities emanating from company or organization presidents, CEO's, marketing directors, entrepreneurs, *etc.*

Every practitioner who is in the fray, who deals with difficult clients or employers, a doubting and hard to access media, fellow executives who don't understand or accept the importance of PR to the health and welfare of a company or organization, and who believes in his/her craft should do the following:

Set a high minimum standard for professional behavior and standards and never go below it!

The key is to abide by that standard no matter what, and to do that with the art of persuasion and influence and without losing your cool.

The PR practitioner's job is to persuade, inform and use PR techniques, or whatever it takes, to move others to the point-of-view of your client or employer. These *others* can include the media, the public, buyers of products or services, and your client/employer who must be made to understand the power of public relations.

The effective PR strategist will understand this vital essence in this complex world: the nature of power. To understand the use of power you must develop an instinct that will tell you who possesses it, how he/she uses it, and how you can cope with its misuse by others. The use of power has either positive or negative ramifications, or a mix of both, and it can be observed almost all the time at virtually every level of everyday life.

For example: A waitress has power over her station and the smart waitress uses that power to please diners and gain tips. The restaurant owner has power over employees and the smart owner runs a tight ship to insure good service, build a customer base and prevent losses because of disgruntled and dishonest employees. But it is the customer who has the most power by demanding good food at a fair price or he or she will never return.

In each case positive rather than negative behavior is much more constructive. So it is with the practice of PR.

Another example: A more familiar examination of the proper use of power is that of the motivational decision-maker who opts to influence others through positive techniques, as opposed to the top dog who uses intimidation and threats in order to get his or her way. More often than not, those who use (abuse) their power base end up alone with their wagon circled by disgruntled former associates and employees, and that eventually does them in.

We have all known all types of individuals who occupy seats of power. It became clear to the author during 30 years in public relations that positive reinforcement beats negative tactics hands-down.

It is sometimes true that in the short run negative fear tactics can result in subordinates jumping through hoops for the perpetrator. But it is also clear that the decision-maker who employs such crass tactics will lose in the long run when that wagon is circled and he/she has no where to turn. Nobody enjoys working with this type of employer or client and few will do so for very long.

Negativity from the boss breeds negativity from underlings who are prone to become yes-men and who become afraid to assert themselves and act on their own instincts. This is counter-productive to all concerned.

Here are some basic tips when under fire:

- Stand your ground but do not over-react to intimidation or threats made to you or to others in your presence by a client or employer – first gain your composure and live to fight another day.

- Maintain that composure and confront the client or employer later in private and in a non-adversarial way so as not to make the situation worse.

- That hopefully will positively influence his or her future actions.

- Keep on trying and then either accept your lot or get out of the situation on the best terms you can muster.

- Regardless of the outcome, keep your integrity, confidence and professionalism intact.

18. Moving Up the Ranks

Positioning yourself as a public relations professional is no easy task, especially if you are relatively new to the game. Most practitioners begin as employees of businesses or organizations where they fulfill the PR function, or they start on the bottom rung of an advertising or public relations agency as a junior account rep.

The PR professional who wishes to move up the ranks into the executive level of an agency, advance to a position of responsibility as the PR *strategist* for a large company or organization or become an independent consultant must first pay his or her dues by gaining experience and learning the ropes. It will be worth it.

Starting a consulting business and eventually an agency is possible if the practitioner is willing to pay the price of building resources and establishing a client base that can pay the bills through the lean start-up times.

Here are some basic tips:

- Think as big as you can without fooling anyone, especially yourself.
- Don't wear your lack of knowledge on your sleeve during the learning process.
- Proceed with an inquisitive and professional demeanor and get the job done right.
- Correct any mistakes and forge ahead with confidence and energy – it'll work out most of the time.
- Trust that experience will be your best teacher.

In most cases you cannot realistically be expected to understand fully the products or services of the business or organization that you are pitching. The keys are to learn as much as possible before you submit a proposal and to convince the decision-maker that you are a quick study (assuming you are) and can get up to speed rapidly.

In most cases, management personnel will be happy to share their knowledge and help you do your job because, after all, your success will be their success. And it is the right thing to do. In the end you may become the go-to person in the business or organization in any of the strategic marketing communications and PR challenges and opportunities that arise or that you cause to happen.

19. Muddling Through

It would have been comical if it were not so threatening. We're talking about the many times The Prather Group had to handle a new client without at clue of how to proceed. However, by abiding by our own advice we somehow muddled through and made a positive difference with most of our clients.

Here is an obvious question: How could we reasonably be expected to know much about any of the diverse products and services of the myriad of clients we ended up serving over the past 30 years?

Here is the answer: We didn't know much going in but a combination of research and collaboration with internal and external experts allowed us to serve these diverse clients in such industries as satellite communications, rubber and glass ampoule manufacturing, plastic injection molding, healthcare, the law, environmental consulting, accounting, insurance, Playboy Bunnies (just checking to see if you were paying attention), auto aftercare software, *et al.*

Here are a few of the simple public relations techniques and/or attitudes that will help you to handle virtually any client include:

- Not pretending to know – finding out.
- Reading printed promotional material
- Reviewing technical material.
- Conversing with and asking questions of key management and staff.
- Evaluating the competition to see what they are doing.
- Reviewing publications of interest to the client or employer.

20. Two Niches Unfocused

There are two public relations niches that Jack Prather and The Prather Group have not focused on, partly because of the esoteric nature of the subjects and partly because of a lack of extensive knowledge about or interest in them. Therefore there is little definitive material in this book regarding them.

The primary discipline most foreign to us happens to be one of the most lucrative: financial public relations. Practitioners versed in this are generally in demand and are well paid by corporations and agencies. Another industry in which The Prather Group has recent experience but not longevity is Internet advertising and promotion, mainly because we got a late start in dealing with that industry. Both financial and Internet public relations are niches that PR practitioners are encouraged to pursue, however, and what better place to find the information and instruction that a search on the Internet?

Jack Prather did serve as Director of Public Relations and Marketing for Icas Computer Systems, a manufacturer of software for the auto aftercare market; for Healthlynx.com, a provider of healthcare discount cards to the general public, and for Tellurian Networks, but we still feel rookie-nervous in this milieu.

Question: How did we successfully serve in that capacity for two clients with only limited computer and Internet skills? *Answer:* By following our own advice of reading extensively about the industry and the product lines, asking questions of management and staff, learning incrementally until up to speed, trusting the judgment of experts, and hiring a sales director and reps with industry experience. Somehow this has worked (so far).

Internet Notes: According to the Associated Press of February 6, 2002, more than half of all Americans use the Internet with two million plus going online for the first time every month.

Nine out of 10 school children now have access to computers at home or at school, according to data from the Commerce Department.

Half of America's households have an Internet subscription from home, an increase of 25 percent from 1998.

According to the report, 45 percent of the population uses e-mail, 36 use the Internet to search for products and services and 39 percent are making online purchases.

21. Learn Your Craft

There is no better method to learn the craft of public relations than on the job. If you are lucky an experienced pro will mentor you, your boss will be patient with you and you will turn out to be a quick study.

However, studying the subjects of communications, marketing and journalism (and PR if it is offered) in a college or university will prepare you to go into that PR job with at least the cutting-edge basics.

Writing skills are requisite for the PR practitioner, so if you haven't begun to acquire them in school you will struggle later on the job. So hone those writing skills, learn the myriad techniques and tactics necessary to fulfill missions and become a valued PR professional.

The practitioner should join the Public Relations Society of America (PRSA), read books and articles about the subject, attend seminars and workshops on PR, marketing and advertising, and hone his or her writing skills.

22. *First Do No Harm*

The PR practitioner must measure each action, not only for the potential good it will do for a client or employer but for the possible bad that could result. The PR pro, like a medical professional, must first do no harm.

Dramatic examples of negative PR backlash during 2002 were the Gary Condit and Ken Lay debacles, and the extraordinary accounting and stock option scandals that were still unfolding as this book was being written.

Condit lost his bid to return to the Congress from California, not only because of the cloud of suspicion hanging over him, but also because of his stonewalling and consistently poor public relations tactics.

Enron CEO Lay pleaded his Fifth Amendment right against self-incrimination in testifying about the scandal despite protestations he really wanted to set the record straight. Linda Lay's epistle on national TV about her husband's decency and lack of knowledge about wrongdoing fell flat as she sought sympathy for their own multi-million dollar losses, downplaying the vast remaining Lay fortune. Hubris prevented her from sympathizing with average employee investors who lost everything when company stock prices plummeted. Her appearance was a PR disaster, as are the ongoing public debacles in the corporate and accounting worlds.

The culprits are now well beyond the mitigating influences of public relations: it is simply too late.

Of course, there are many examples of *bad* public relations results that could not have been foreseen among the many that should have been predicted and prevented.

There are some basic principles for public relations professionals to apply when dealing with serious situations for a client or employer. The person on the firing line should:

- Speak the truth or say nothing
- Sympathize with the victims and not themselves
- Accept responsibility within legal parameters
- Maintain a professional but empathic demeanor
- Control emotions and speech
- Work with the media if possible and feasible; don't shoot the messengers
- Set the record straight to all concerned during and after the event

The same basic PR principles would apply at the local level for a businessman facing a hostile reporter or an elected municipal official being charged with wrongdoing as would apply for the Condits and Lays of the world. The main difference is in the scope of media coverage. The situations are just as important to individuals at the local level as they are to nationally known figures.

It is easy to snipe at bad PR performances, more difficult to provide better solutions. Here is what we would have recommended: Condit should have immediately admitted his affair and regret for it, instructed his attorney to be less confrontational and more forthcoming with the media and public, given an immediate statement that expressed empathy and sympathy for the missing victim and her family, instructed his staff to be candid, cooperated more with the police investigation, and not exploited his children in his TV defense. The Lays should have told the truth or remained quiet, rather than dissembling the truth the world to hear.

Chapter Three

Public Relations Case Profiles

Case 1: A Good Week for Political PR

Overview

We have served a state legislator as director of communications and political and public relations adviser since he first ascended to office more than a decade ago, including through four record-setting re-election victories and two congressional primaries where he came within a whisker of knocking off the long-term incumbent. We continue on these separate but equally important fronts as this book is being written.

Mission

The mission now is for the state legislator to win a rugged general election battle in November of 2000 by attracting new supporters and retaining previously expressed support in all geographical areas within the district.

Situation Analysis

The legislator currently represents three rural counties and one urban county. He narrowly lost the previous congressional primary election because voters in the most populous County supported the incumbent. Our man won in the other three counties in the district but that was not enough for victory. It was heartening, however.

As of this writing, formidable challengers in the congressional primary include two other respected members of the legislature plus several lesser-known candidates. However, the campaign staff is undeterred by the field of challengers and is focused on overcoming any monetary disadvantages that could limit advertising through extra hard work and intense campaigning.

Our candidate's strong showings in the past despite enormous obstacles have made him the current odds-on favorite to win the primary and the congressional seat, according to the media and early polling.

A Special Week

The centerpieces of an especially satisfying PR week in mid-January of 2002 included a by-lined piece by the legislator in a major newspaper, three television interviews, positive print media coverage, strong polling results and a positive reaction to a speech delivered to an influential organization.

The Prather Group was active in assisting in all of the following activities that special week:

- Authoring the first draft of the by-lined article about his newly enacted legislation and placing it in the most influential newspaper in the district.

- Arranging a Comcast Cable-TV interview with him on its Newsmakers program about the legislation.

- Arranging an interview on the state cable-TV channel, owned by the largest newspaper in the state.

- Capitalizing in the media on a report on a political website that reported polling results that showed him with a double-digit lead over his closest rival but with about half of the respondents undecided.

- Arranging a speech to a Rotary Club in the heart of the populous town previously referenced.

The PR Role in the Events

Things don't happen in the world of public relations unless you make them happen, so the activities will continue on a daily basis through November. The focus during that incredible week was on his legislative accomplishments with no mention of his campaign for congress, and properly so, but the heavy exposure no doubt elevated his credibility within the electorate which will translate into votes.

Following are the strategies that went into that single successful week that also serves as a microcosm of activity undertaken on his behalf over an the decade-plus of representing him both legislatively and politically:

- *The by-lined article.*

  First we discussed with the legislator the topic for the article and wrote the first draft.

  Next we pitched the editorial-page editor by telephone and followed-up with a detailed e-mail. He agreed to review the article and then accepted it. Of course, we obtained the standards for publication such as length and deadline prior to writing the draft version for review and revision by the candidate.

  Then we serviced the final article by e-mail to the editor.

  The results: The article gained prominent placement in the Sunday editorial section, that being the best day for publication in any daily newspaper. The piece was well received, according to feedback in letters-to-the-editor and telephone calls from readers.

- *An appearance on 'The Newsmakers' television program (multiple airings).*

  Previously we had established a bond and mutual-trust with the producers and on-air personalities at the TV station and that made our pitch for the legislator to appear to discuss his new legislation that much easier.

  The results: important exposure to a vital audience of constituents and voters.

- *The appearance on the state channel. Multiple airings.*

  We reached out with a telephone and e-mail follow-up pitch to the producer and our man was booked on this popular morning news show to discuss the new law. The show was repeated four times.

  The results: important exposure to a vital audience of constituents and voters.

- *Newspaper/Internet coverage of poll results that showed our candidate in the lead by double-digits.*

  The campaign manager had serviced the poll results to the newspapers and scored a big hit in the main local county daily and on the political site on the Internet. The PR role was that we had worked long and hard to convince the editors, reporters and columnists about the legislator's enhanced credibility and that opened the door to other entities within the campaign to request and gain coverage.

The results: This coverage memorialized the front-runner status bestowed on him by the major media.

- *The speech to the Rotary Club.*

    We arranged for the legislator to address about 60 members of one of the largest clubs in its district, home of the former incumbent and vital to his campaign for that seat in the Congress, about the new law.

    The results: the legislator's remarks and answers to questions were well received and earned positive feedback from the Rotarians in attendance.

Post Mortem

Our congressional candidate from New Jersey handily won the June 2002 primary against two arch rivals and, as of this writing (August 2002), is the favorite to win a seat in the House of Representatives in the November general election.

Getting Involved

Public relations practitioners or students who are interested in pursuing the political and/or legislative arenas can learn the ropes and get involved in many different ways, including by:

- Serving as an unpaid intern in a legislative or congressional office
- Serving as a paid intern in a legislative or congressional office (college or high school students)
- Assisting as a volunteer in a grassroots campaign
- Becoming a paid assistant in a campaign
- Establishing connections with elected officials and party leaders via a letter and resume
- Volunteering at political special events such as fundraisers or rallies
- Studying to become a lobbyist and applying for a position at a lobbying firm
- Running for elected office

Remember, an elected official or candidate needs attention and handling with aplomb and tact. The public relations practitioner needs to know and understand what he or she stands for and what their mission is, and then serve accordingly.

Public Relations Tip: *Good PR not only promotes, it protects.*

Case 2: Microwaves and Crisis-Problem Management

Mission

A satellite microwave communications company wished to construct three or more satellite dishes of up to 40 feet in diameter in a small town where approximately currently 12 existed, three at the site and nine at competing company sites nearby.

Situation Analysis

The project was stalled because of enormous public pressure from a citizens group and ongoing negative publicity and talk. The leaders of the anti-satellite dish program were well organized and extremely difficult for the firm's0 management to deal with from their corporate headquarters, and none of the on-site employees had any strategic public relations or crisis-management experience.

The local 'antis' (they are ubiquitous in any development project) maintained without evidence that the existing satellite dishes had radiated harmful microwaves over the past two decades that had already harmed the area population, especially children.

The move to ban the project by the citizens group included inflammatory newsletters and advertisements in the local media.

The most aggressive tactics were a grass-roots citizens group campaign that sent members door-to-door and to shopping malls with scare tactics, such as stopping expectant mothers and warning them that microwaves from the proposed expansion would harm their babies. One member of the citizens group went so far as to tap a pregnant woman on the tummy and insensitively say, "Your baby might be deformed from microwaves."

Ouch.

Solutions

Spearheading the expansion project were an experienced and capable attorney from a prestigious law firm and the company President and CEO, an intelligent and soft-spoken advocate for his cause.

After a careful vetting process, they reached out to The Prather Group to help them bridge the education gap in the community that blurred reality and fiction regarding microwaves, and to get the expansion proposal solidly back on track.

After studying the situation we determined to our own satisfaction that the charges leveled by the citizens group were false and the product of mass hysteria. (*Note:* If we did not believe microwaves to be safe we would *not* have taken on the assignment.)

The Action Plan included:

- Retaining an expert from a major laboratory to provide complete factual information re microwaves.

- Preparing a booklet asking and answering all of the pertinent health questions regarding microwaves.

- Arranging discussion seminars with business groups.

- Booking speeches for the president at civic organizations.

- Pitching and arranging print and broadcast interviews with the president.

- Submitting photographs and a feature article to local media re the company's positive history.

- Speaking with and providing information to the mayor, council members and VIPs in the town

- Hosting tours of the site of satellite dishes

- Doing follow-up PR in the community to pave the way for future expansions.

The Results

The Action Plan was extremely successful: the company's position was understood and accepted by almost all concerned, and in an inordinately short time frame.

Two more expansions followed over the next three years.

The company had agreed to monitor the dish sites with high-tech devices and conduct annual studies of health problems in the surrounding areas. There was no harm to anyone in the town or surrounding areas ever discerned that was caused by microwaves from satellite dishes.

Post Mortem

There were several lessons learned during the years spent with the satellite communications company and the good citizens of its host town, but none as worthwhile as this: most people have an open mind and will listen to facts and reason and admit they are wrong or misled if they are approached in the right manner at the right time by the right person - *but not everyone!*

That realization crystallized during the strategic public relations campaign in the town. When it came down to votes, the town council and the planning board approved the expansion unanimously but the Zoning Board of Adjustment had one holdout who voted no.

We asked her if she had read the compilation of material from the federal and state agencies that deal with health issues and the environment, and from credible independent science investigators, who all agreed that directed microwaves from satellite dishes are not harmful to people.

She said she had read and understood it all.

When asked if she had any information counter to the accepted position she said she did not.

When asked there could be any evidence that would convince her to change her position she said no.

When asked why she replied: "Because I don't want to take a chance."

This conversation made us remember our favorite saying and stop fighting a losing battle (with her):

"Give me the strength to change the things I can, the serenity to accept the things I can't, and the wisdom to know the difference."

Case 3: Creating A Foundation, Building an Image

The next three case profiles are drawn from 10 dynamic and enjoyable years of representing PlayboyClubs Inc.

Mission

The ultimate mission was to position the new Playboy Resort and Country Club at Great Gorge as a family and convention resort in order to bolster its image and reputation and thereby make it an acceptable site for gaming once New Jersey voters approved upcoming referendums. Playboy Inc. needed the public to distinguish between the image shaped by Playboy Magazine and that of the family resort if it was to succeed in the mission.

Objective

If the referendums passed, gambling would become the major draw to the $50 million resort.

The Plan

A comprehensive plan to not only soften the Playboy image but to aggressively publicize it as pro-family was formulated with this centerpiece: The Sussex County Playboy Foundation. Jack Prather served as The Foundation Executive Director for five years, overseeing board members from the clergy, the educational community, elected office, a business and a non-profit organization.

The Foundation donated $1000 scholarships annually to graduating seniors at 10 area high schools who were going on to study hotel management or culinary arts in college. The scholarships were presented to the seniors at a Scholarship Dinner attended by the parents and school principals. The Foundation also sponsored Bunny charity softball games versus such major news organizations as WCBS-TV and local radio stations, police and fire departments, gave away overnight packages for raffles, hosted events and meetings for non-profit organizations, and sponsored charity celebrity golf and tennis events.

In all, The Foundation raised or donated a total in cash or services of more than $1 million in five years or operation to communities within a 20 mile range of the resort (40-mile width).

The Results

The Foundation and therefore the resort received consistent print and broadcast media coverage for its good works. It also was publicized in the Foundation newsletter mailed quarterly to 50,000 area residents.

These Foundation activities resulted in a legitimate family image that helped to euphemize the traditional Playboy Bunny image. This was reflected in vastly improved attitudes toward Playboy from residents in the area who used the facilities for special events and fundraising gifts, and generally felt part of the scene.

Personal Note: It was during the Playboy years that The Prather Group learned the essences of community relations and their relative value to an employer or client: that those who give to the community are fulfilling a responsibility that should never be taken lightly. Since then each client has been advised that the main reasons to give cash, goods, services or time to the community are twofold: it is simply the right thing to do and the return on investment in community relations will be enhanced image and reputation, increased networking opportunities and greater acceptance of the giver and his products or services.

Case 4: Nixing a Potential Playboy Problem

Mission

To hold a media conference with all of the major networks to establish credibility for Playboy Inc. and its new resort by demonstrating and defining the good character of its executives, essential to get the backing of New Jersey elected officials, community leaders, the media and the voting public.   Otherwise, Playboy would not gain necessary approvals and therefore would not share in the high-profit gaming casino industry being proposed for the Garden State in general and Sussex County, in particular.   Playboy Club Inc.'s ultimate objective was to host gambling casinos in Atlantic City and at the Great Gorge resort.

This is a story best told by employing the famed 5-W's of journalism:

Who?   Hugh Hefner, his top executives and entourage, the on-air talent from major networks and your author.

What?   A Playboy Clubs Inc. hosted media conference.

When?   Three months prior to the scheduled referendum on gaming in New Jersey.

Where? In The Hefner Suite of Playboy's Great Gorge Resort & Country Club in New Jersey.

Why?   To help publicize and position Great Gorge as a family resort worthy of hosting a gaming Mecca.

How? As the resort's Director of Public Relations, we studied gaming in Great Britain and subsequently lectured and gave media and broadcast interviews about the subject. The role: to host the press conference and direct questions from the media to the proper Playboy representative: Hef, his girlfriend at the time, entertainer Barbi Benton, plus high-level executives from various segments of the Bunny Empire.

The Problem: It was more than disconcerting when the Playboy entourage arrived because in its midst was a man alleged to be an international swindler (who will remain anonymous here for obvious legal reasons - see libel section).

The Solution: We delicately managed to keep the inappropriate visitor under wraps until after the media conference was completed - whew!

The Results: The media conference was a major success and became one small piece of the PR mosaic that led voters to approve gaming in Atlantic City where Playboy eventually opened a casino. However, the voters denied gaming elsewhere in New Jersey, a costly setback for the Bunny Empire.

Post Mortem: The media conference went off without a hitch and without exposure of the alleged swindler thanks to a little diplomacy and a lot of tact that kept him out of view until the press departed. And it was a good lesson in advance planning for who will be at a media conference and, more importantly, who should not, including for the master, Hef.

Note: The lack of understanding by Playboy executives and Mr. Hefner of the potential impact that this notorious guest could have had on the credibility of the company in its quest for a gaming license was surprising, to say the least. The reporters from the networks that attended the media conference did not find out about the individual, nor did other reporters who frequented the resort in those golden days of Playboy. Whew!

Case 5: A Bunny Brainstorm

A Personal Reminiscence • • •

Playboy Enterprises Inc. had invited executives and consultants from around the nation and world to a meeting in the Hefner Suite at the Great Gorge Resort in New Jersey in the early 1970's to discuss potential ventures for the company to consider so it could expand its business base.

To my utter dismay the meeting agenda, request for ideas and invitation to participate from Lee Gottlieb, my PR client-boss in Chicago, had been lost in transit, unbeknownst to either of us. I was the director of public relations at Great Gorge on a consulting basis and he expected me to offer a viable idea, according to the lost and unread missive (that arrived a day later).

Lee showed up unexpectedly in my office at 9 a.m. and told me I was expected to contribute an idea at 11 a.m. He explained that *every* Playboy executive and consultant was involved in the search to identify potential spin-off business ventures in which the company could potentially compete.

I had less than two hours to come up with an idea or bite my tongue and mumble "pass" when it came my turn to contribute. Instead I decided to drop back six yards and punt.

I pondered business ventures that could be successful within the Bunny Empire, feeling intimidated in advance by no doubt well-prepared fellow executives and consultants. I was certain all of them would offer great ideas. Embarrassment loomed.

What to do?

Should I remain mum? Toss out a half-baked idea? Jump off the roof?

The answer hit me while I begrudgingly trudged to the eighth floor luxury suite: *cable television!* It seemed viable and hopefully I would not be interrogated about it. Luckily I had recently read a comprehensive business article on the subject but that was hardly an exercise in deep research. Unless someone beat me to the punch, I would offer that idea when my turn came.

I did.

They told me later that I spoke enthusiastically and knowledgeably for five minutes about the potentials of the relatively new cable television industry; I don't remember, I was in a fog and was winging it.

Hef's right-hand man and the meeting facilitator, Vice President Bob Preuss, said he would look into it.

Cable-TV became the only venture to be acted upon and matriculated into an integral part of the Playboy Empire.

-Jack Prather

PR Tip: It is important to be prepared. If you don't know what you are talking about, don't talk. I was lucky that my contribution turned out all right in the above case.

Case 6: 'Goliath' - A Star is Born at Space Farms Zoo

Space Farms Zoo and Museums was founded in Sussex County, N.J. in 1927 and continues to be successful to this day under the management of the third generation of the Space family. This is part of their PR story.

When we took over the public relations and advertising function for Space Farms for about eight years through the early 1980's, it was being co-managed by founder Ralph Space and his son, Fred, we immediately inquired what was special about the park. This case profile begins there.

It was a natural question that was designed to isolate features that could be used to promote ticket sales to the park, the obvious foremost mission.

We discovered during an extensive tour that the zoo was home to the world's largest bear ever, Goliath, a Kodiak who stood 12 feet tall and weighed more than 2000 pounds. We were ecstatic and a star was born!

Goliath was promoted as the featured attraction and he lived up to his billing for more than a decade by attracting many thousands of new visitors annually to the 100-acre park.

We hit two publicity grand slam home runs thanks to Goliath: first when his photograph and description was featured in "Ripley's Believe It Or Not" and later when a layout on the gigantic Kodiak bear appeared in the Guinness Book of World Records.

By chance, the Ripley's layout was published in thousands of newspapers on opening day of a new season! The Guinness exposure was equally important, much to the glee of our public relations Associate Rick Bolger, who had made the submission.

Over the years, Goliath was featured in television ads, brochures and feature articles – the public could never get enough of the gargantuan Kodiak.

He was a PR man's dream.

When Goliath eventually passed away, it was like a member of the family had been lost. The Spaces had Goliath stuffed and mounted on a pedestal in the lobby of the entrance and cafeteria and to this day kids of all ages continue to marvel at his height and girth.

The extensive wildlife knowledge of each of the members of the Space family has made them famous in their own right and has been an important and natural part of the overall public relations efforts.

Promoting that fame and knowledge appropriately was one of the imperatives during the years The Prather Group handled this client. It was easy: from placing a Space family member on television with a bear cub, to having one appear at a mall with baby tigers, to having one write an op-ed piece for the local newspaper, it was successful tour and great fun, too.

The Spaces have been invited to be members and most often officials of virtually every meaningful wildlife organization. Strong in public service, they lecture at schools, host countless school groups, provide information to owners about pet injuries or illnesses, are experts on snakebites, and write and speak extensively about many important matters involving animals. All of this contributes to the overall Space family image and has positioned them as experts who are called upon repeatedly by the media for quotes and information.

Case 7: Crisis Averted, Baldrige Award Won

A personal remembrance to set the tone . . .

Onstage just 10 rows away, three men with arms-entwined smiled widely for the television networks.

I physically pinched myself to see if I would wake up.

It hurt: I was not dreaming!

At stage right was Ames Rubber Corporation President Joel Marvil.

At stage left was Commerce Secretary Ron Brown (who later was killed in a tragic plane crash).

And in the center was President of the United States Bill Clinton.

It was 2:45 p.m. on December 14, 1993 and President Clinton was handing President Marvil, *my client,* the Malcolm Baldrige National Total Quality Award, the top honor in the business world.

Watching the ceremony live in historic Mellon Auditorium in Washington D.C. were 50 members of the Ames team and an audience of 2500 while closed-circuit TV beamed it back to the Ames plant in New Jersey so 500 employees could also share in the momentous occasion.

The nation also watched as the major TV networks covered the event live and for their evening news programs.

It doesn't – can't – get any better than that.

A Long Journey

The Ames journey toward winning the top business award in the world had begun with an enormous effort that earned a site visit from the Baldrige Award qualifying judges two years before.

It is not commonly known but preparation to simply qualify for the award is expensive and time-consuming, and actually getting a Baldrige site visit is considered a victory in and of itself.

However, the president and executive team of the manufacturing company that makes rubber products for the copy and automobile industries, lured by its potential to win the grand prize, decided to invest the time, effort and money necessary to viably compete for the award a second time.

This time Ames was determined to claim the award named for the late Commerce Secretary in the Reagan Administration, Malcolm Baldrige, who had been tragically killed in a fall from his horse.

The Ames team put enormous effort into further assuring product quality, decreasing the rate of defects, enhancing customer service, establishing better training programs, making a host of internal improvements – whatever it could do to pave the way to fulfill the Baldrige standards and win the award.

It worked!

Public Relations Contributions

Prather Group public relations contributions to the Ames team effort included:

- Consulting in crisis-problem management
- Greatly expanding and improving the corporate newsletter, the Ames *Echo*
- Generating good media exposure
- Offsetting negative publicity
- Gaining favorable editorial comment
- Cultivating community and civic leaders and elected officials

By far the most important strategic PR contribution was in coordinating and implementing the crisis communications action plan designed to overcome mostly bogus charges that the company was an environmental polluter.

No company that is or perceived to be a polluter could hope to win the national total quality award. Nor could it hope to flourish with existing or new customers while coping with regular reports (attacks) by the major daily in the area that questioned the company's environmental standards and integrity.

The action plan had the following elements:

- The lead attorney for the company and The Prather Group analyzed information that determined the company was essentially caught in a Catch-22 situation caused by Department of Environmental rules that failed to spell out certain specific standards that therefore were impossible to follow.
- The company settled with the state and that problem was resolved.
- We prepared a fact sheet and chronology outlining the history of the alleged problem and its satisfactory resolution.
- We invited key members of the daily newspaper to meet with the company's top environmental engineer and other involved executives to examine the situation from the company viewpoint, ask questions and then correct the record.

The Results

After an intense four-hour meeting, the newspaper showed enormous integrity by admitting it had been unintentionally erroneous and misleading in its reporting and agreed to run a comprehensive article correcting the record. A week later an editorial appeared that congratulated the company for being "a good neighbor".

To prevent further problems and upon our request, the newspaper tacked copies of the explanatory article and editorial of support to all newsroom and morgue file on the matter so future reporting would be on the mark.

We gave the editorial legs by distributing it to Ames Rubber customers, employees and vendors, inserting it into the media company's information kits and reprinting it with permission in the company newsletter.

It took a mosaic of many pieces to win the Baldrige and to be one tiny piece of it was a dream come true.

Case 8: Community Relations Might Have Saved the Theme Park

The client was Warner Bros. Jungle Habitat, a major theme park on the East Coast, and it had a problem: if it did not expand it would die in the face of increasing competition.

The PR consultant had a problem too: convincing management that it finally time to cultivate and pay attention to the local folk who could either help or hinder expansion.

Previously all of the park's efforts and activities were directed toward the major metropolitan markets with the singular objective of attracting large numbers of visitors to the park. That made sense for most of the initial thrust when the park opened.

However, with this new mission – to expand - local fences needed to built or mended. The management team needed access to and acceptance by the mayor and council, civic and social organizations, education groups and local residents who had never been made to feel they had a stake in or were part of the park.

We thought a solid community relations program may have bridged that disconnect and saved the park but management simply did not embrace the idea and the 'locals' never did identify with the park even though it was located virtually in their backyards.

The program to soften the image and promote acceptance by all local publics of interest included:

- Inviting local decision-makers to meet the management at a luncheon and tour
- Providing discount tickets to students and senior citizens
- Creating a special day or weekend for the local residents to visit free or at half rate
- Hosting local uniformed personnel and their families during a day in their honor
- Offering discount programs for as fundraisers for charities
- Hosting media day with prizes for best articles and photography

The purpose was not to buy favors but to cement relationships so that all of the local publics of interest would become favorably disposed toward the park and its management, and by extension its problems and needs. After all, more than 1,000 jobs and a healthy tax contribution were emanating from the park each year and its closing would have had disastrous effects locally, we reasoned.

But upper management did not agree and refused to implement the grass roots PR program designed to bring the locals into the fold actually and psychologically.

Because the locals were missing from the equation, a troubled national economy and highly aggressive competition, the park fell on hard times.

To survive, expansion had become necessary. To expand, local ordinances had to be amended. To amend local ordinances the governing body - resident decision-makers - had to agree. That is the way it is in small towns.

But the bridge that was not built could not be crossed and locals refused to let the park expand. The failed expansion plan put the park at a competitive disadvantage and it soon closed, and 1,000 jobs and all that tax money was lost to the community. Everyone lost this battle.

Case 9: Synergy from a Shared Client Event

This case profile explains how we merged a current client, Sunrise House Alcohol and Drug Rehabilitation Center and a former client, the Karen Ann Quinlan Center of Hope Hospice in a mutually beneficial project.

The Hospice

Two of the nicest and most well meaning people we have ever represented are Julia Quinlan and her late husband, Joe, who started the Center of Hope that for more than two decades has provided invaluable services to the terminally ill and their families.

The devoted couple began the Hospice with revenues from their book about their daughter, Karen Ann, whose history is familiar to most Americans.

When we served the Hospice as director of development and public relations for three years during the early 1990's, we launched a fundraising program titled *Let Us Light the Way*. We selected that name to capture the warmth and comfort generated by hospice as it serves those who are dying and their families.

Sunrise House Honors Dinner

Two more of the finest and most well meaning people we have ever represented (and still do) are CEO Dr. Philip Horowitz and COO George Dominguez of Sunrise House. They are dedicated, talented and funny, which makes our job all the more enjoyable. It was especially gratifying when they bought into and ran with our idea that Sunrise House host an Honors Dinner to recognize individuals for outstanding service in their cause and other worthwhile community endeavors while raising much-needed funds in the process.

The debut dinner served as a vehicle to publicize and promote the Center's Halfway House and new inpatient and outpatient adolescent programs.

It also raised $26,000 for the Halfway House, greatly enhancing its ability fulfill its mission of housing and helping indigent pregnant women with children in their care.

The Second Dinner

In 2002 for the second Honors Dinner, we were especially pleased to legitimately combine the interests of both Sunrise House and the Center of Hope as Julia Quinlan was selected as an honoree for her remarkable community service to the terminally ill for more than 20 years. Two other honorees were a former Congresswoman who had supported the Sunrise House cause and a substance abuse prevention professional.

Synergy resulted from this shared event: in goodwill, in media exposure and in funds raised. The event proved to be beneficial to both service agencies and to everyone associated with them. And it was great fun.

The PR Role

The ongoing public relations role was to work with the Honors Dinner Committee in selecting the honorees, promoting and publicizing the event, providing contacts for ticket sales and ensuring that each entity was properly represented.

Case 10: Growing A Software Designer/Manufacturer

Mission

The mission was to increase sales of a computer systems software company by 20 percent in year one and incrementally by at least 10 percent each year beyond that through a national strategic sales and marketing program headed by Jack Prather/The Prather Group on a consulting basis.

Situation Analysis

It was 1982 and the company had reorganized from its formation as one of the original designers and manufacturers of software for the automobile aftercare markets.

The software had been designed specifically for auto parts stores to track their sales, provide automatic inventory counts and electronic reordering.

At that time, the company had only one fulltime salesman and one sales rep in the field to reach out to potential customers in the industry.

Solutions

The Marketing and PR Action Plan called for:

- Hiring of a fulltime national sales director
- Hiring on commission a network of sales reps
- Sales training for all involved
- Tripling of existing advertising and promotion budgets
- Targeting advertising and promotions for key U.S. cities
- Increasing publicity efforts re personnel, product and service
- Expanding participation in industry
- Holding special promotions such as contests

Results

The Action Plan we prepared was accepted and funded virtually as submitted by the CEO/President and majority owner.

We searched for a hired the national sales director and jointly we hired and trained a national sales rep force that would operate on a commission basis.

Initially the sales goals were filled but internal problems and loss of personnel slowed things down the next year. (*Personal note:* Prather chose not to renew his contract when an opportunity with another choice client arose and the demands precluded continuation with Icas.)

Case 11: A United Sprint Survey Project

The Mission

United Telephone was preparing for the acquisition and merger with Sprint in the new fiber-optic world of communications and needed an assessment of how the various users in New Jersey regarded the service and equipment to help guide decision-making. It was making the same requests in all states within the system.

The Solution

The Prather Group was retained to direct a management Task Force and create and manage survey of six publics of interest: residents, small businesses, large businesses, educators, elected/appointed officials and employees. The deadline for completion was established at six months from initiation.

The consulting agency and the Task Force developed six specific questionnaires, five that could be done through telephone calls and one for employees that would be accomplished internally via handouts. Prather retained a project manager and jointly they hired and trained 23 telephone surveyors to make the calls at convenient evening hours.   A computer expert was also retained to tabulate the information and create graphs and charts that would tell the story along with written explanations, as well as a final two-page matrix summary.

The Results

After numerous meetings and much analysis and detail work, the final 181-page report was presented within deadline to the Task Force leaders, Steve Ellis and Glenn Lewis. It became the national standard from among the company-wide survey teams.

12: Partnerships Make Progress

The Mission

Jack Prather was retained for two years as director of a county Economic Development Commission, a task that took half of his time but was both interesting and challenging, with a mission to help stimulate relocation, retention and expansion of businesses through traditional venues of publicity, promotion and advertising.

The Solution

Traditional marketing techniques were employed but an element was added to the equation: partnering the public and private sectors. The EDC and the county Chamber of Commerce, with a grant from county government, combined to produce a four-color magazine to promote the area. A major exposition was designed and was held in a prime local hotel, drawing local businesses and professionals.

The Results

Business retention and expansion were particularly improved and the synergy created by that initial partnership of the public and private sectors is still thriving today, a nice legacy for The Prather Group.

13. *Promoting Funeral Home Owners*

Mission

Two young entrepreneurial brothers were partners in a century-old funeral home and were about to purchase another, owned a monument company and planned to open an antiques center. They naturally wanted to improve their position in the death-care industry, but also to improve their public awareness and image. Recognizing that they needed professional public relations help to accomplish their goals, they retained The Prather Group.

Solution

The main recommendation was to use publicity as the primary vehicle to enhance the brothers' images. News or feature releases were prepared for the media, particularly the local daily newspaper, on a regular basis.

The promotional content ranged from participation by the brothers in legitimate community involvements such as serving on organization Boards or sponsorships of charitable and civic activities, to seminars conducted by the clients, to teaching stints at colleges and high schools.

The older brother (by two years) was publicized for his notable work in a foreign country for training technicians to remove healthy eyes from the deceased for transplant in a living human and for hosting students from that country, as well as for working closely with such local groups as Hospice. We also placed him on a television interview show to discuss his many involvements.

We publicized the other brother for being elected as an officer in the state and regional funeral associations and for a local Rotary Club, among other activities.

The public relations efforts continue through 2002.

Results

The media coverage of the brothers, coupled with their personal on-air advertising spots on an area radio station, helped to increase their funeral and monument business beyond the original goals set for each of three consecutive years.

In year two, The Prather Group nominated the elder brother for the County Chamber of Commerce 'Humanitarian of the Year' for his good works and he was so honored at the annual awards dinner, perhaps the biggest PR triumph of the relationship, at least thus far.

Post Mortem

Currently, the brothers are putting the finishing touches on a new business venture in a nearby small town that looks extremely promising for all concerned.

PR Thought: Publicity is inherently more believable than advertising.

14. Promoting an Environmental Consulting Firm

Mission

One of the largest environmental consulting firms in the state retained Jack Prather to stimulate connections with decision-makers from municipalities, businesses and industries based out of a regional office that covered a significant portion of the state.

Situation Analysis

The firm had many top-notch environmental engineers on staff but was undermanned in the public relations and marketing departments that were focusing on a potential merger and a proposed plan to diversify services. The company therefore had only a modest reputation and limited exposure within the area that had been designated for growth.

The staff in the regional office was amenable to boosting business, of course, and would assist the PR plans in an appropriate and enthusiastic manner – a boon to any PR pro.

Solutions

The main ingredient to the PR and Marketing Plan was setting up meetings with potential clients by exhausting the many contacts and acquaintances in appropriate venues that we had built up over the years. We provided the access but it was up to the firm to make its presentations and close the deals.

The solutions included producing and placing media articles and items in area newspapers such as:

- Successes with clients
- Educational advancements by engineers
- By-lined articles on important environmental issues
- Quotes in articles by engineers positioned as 'environmental experts'

The solutions also included community relations activities such as:

- Sponsorships of civic activities
- Presentations re the environment to business organizations
- Speeches re the environment at appropriate business forums
- Classroom talks to college students about jobs in the industry
- Seminars about environmental services for local municipalities
- Attendance at important local events and activities

Results

The firm worked closely with the public relations consultant for three years and acquired many leads and a fair amount of business before the potentials were tapped out.

15. *Promoting a Law Firm*

Mission

The law firm of Zachary, Michael, Camryn, Ryan and Nicholas* wanted to establish itself as the leading legal entity in the area, increase its client list and publicize its new corporate building and location.

Situation Analysis

The firm was solidly entrenched in the communities it served and was highly respected. Two of the original partners, still youthful, were still on board, another had recently accepted a judgeship, a third had recently been named and a fourth was waiting in the wings to be named. In total, there were eight attorneys and 16 support staff on board. Competition for clients, of course, was stiff.

Solutions

After a careful interview and proposal presentation at a management retreat, the firm retained The Prather Group to help fulfill its marketing and public relations objectives.

• The initial effort was to create an in-house marketing team consisting of a partner, another lawyer and a member of the support staff and this worked efficiently.

• Next, we presented a seminar on public relations to the entire legal and support staff at which time we informed them of the plans, motivate them about the firm and gain their support and participation. We also conducted a seminar for the younger lawyers on image and reputation building, dealing with such sensitive topics as demeanor, dress and persona.

• Two of the partners were pitched as experts to newspapers and were regularly quoted on legal issues and matters and in prestigious law journals.

• Publicity, advertising and direct mail programs were designed and implemented to promote the newest partner. We helped write and placed his by-lined article in the Star-Ledger, NJ's largest daily newspaper.

• Ongoing media activity included writing and placement of appropriate articles and items about the firm's client successes, educational advancements, career enhancement activities on boards and in organizations, *etc.*

• A feature article and photo of the partners in front of their new corporate center was pitched, then serviced to the largest local daily newspaper. The picture also served as cover for newly designed printed materials.

• Increased activity in the community included sponsorships of charitable events and participation in civic and business events such as local expositions and shows.

• Educational connections were made with the two local colleges and at high school career days.

The Results

The firm did well.

(*This real firm is lovingly re-named after five of my grandchildren.)

16. Promoting a Ski Area

Mission

The Unnamed Ski Area retained The Prather Group to help increase its annual ski pass membership, increase corporate and family ski outings, and generally improve the reputation and image of management with all publics of interest.

Situation Analysis

The short winter season in New Jersey is always a serious problem for ski areas but winter had been made even shorter by mild weather for two consecutive years, cutting into revenues and leading to losses and serious cash flows. This in turn created a situation where vendors, the independent restaurant operator and even some employees were not paid except with small installments or not at all. To make matters worse, area printers and media advertising venues that had been stuck with unpaid bills refused to provide services or materials without advance payment.

Solutions

The initial phase was to support the group sales department by designing a kit of new materials with dynamic theme, colors and style, to replace the dated ones currently in use.

Then we made a concerted effort to attract corporate and family business by pairing with the sales director to create exciting new functions on the slopes, in the lodge and at the quaint ski village across the street. These attractions included an October-fest, an antique ski and apparel show, a giant discount sale week for modern equipment and apparel, and special ski fun events for families, executives and members of the media. Non-skiers were made to be judges and to handle other fun assignments connected with the event so no one was excluded.

We retained a noted female skier to be a spokesperson for the ski area in print and on radio and television areas in the metropolitan area, as well as at ski shows and conventions.

Numerous feature articles were produced and placed in ski magazines and newspapers about such varied subjects as professional instructors, disabled and elderly skiers, and accomplished amateurs who trained at the slopes. The traditional media placements about condition of the slopes, events and activities, *etc.,* kept the name of the area in front of the skiing or potentially interested in skiing public.

The vendors and others who were unhappy with past due bills were partially satisfied with a promise to pay (in increments) and generous free or heavily discounted use of the slopes and restaurants, and deep discounts in the company-owned shops in the village.

The Results

The ski area did have a much better run the next two seasons with all skiing publics, owing to the new strategic public relations and marketing initiatives and, even more importantly, the colder weather that allowed steady snowmaking and increased snowfall. The reputation and image of the resort was also under repair, a process that would be ongoing for many years until it is now flourishing under new ownership.

Chapter Four

PR Action Plans and Proposals

Following are samples of Action Plans and Proposals that can serve as unique templates or guidelines for public relations practitioners and strategists. They have been edited for length but are otherwise representative of PR activity by The Prather Group.

Each of the examples was custom-crafted for a client or potential client based upon situation analysis, available budget dollars, unofficial or professional research, brainstorming and common sense paired, plus *creativity*.

Another purpose for publishing these samples is to provide insights into the public relations strategies employed by Prather for a myriad of clients with diverse financial backgrounds and varying histories of successes and failures.

Their needs ranged from increasing sales to crisis-problem management to getting elected to boosting image and credibility to – well – you get the picture.

PR professionals should remember to build plans and proposals to fit the specific need (mission) of their client or employer by using an appropriate mix of tools, techniques, tactics and methods along with a healthy dose of creative and dynamic vision. That is what can and will set you apart from your public relations competitors, be they consultants or agency employees.

The samples presented are from actual Prather Group files *sans* much of the deep research, forecasts of results and graphics basically of interest only to the client that accompanied each of the plans and proposals.

There is no single formula to construct an Action Plan to fulfill a specific or general mission. You can employ all the esoteric terms, clever jargon and convincing presentations you wish but the proof of the pudding is in the results.

Proposals too can vary depending on the type of client, the mission, the budget and the marketing and sales team that is in place or not.

If you are a sole practitioner or operator of a boutique agency, stay within the limitations of resources available to you. Add resources to your public relations arsenal as you need them to be cost-effective.

Be creative, dynamic, forthright and smart in presenting your material to the client or employer and don't try to match presentations with the big boys.

A good sell to a client or employer is that he or she will get you personally and not a junior account executive representing top-management from the agency that pitched the account. Explain why that is a good choice.

The company or organization names on the plans and proposals have been euphemized to protect the client involved. The results are also not included, although we can state unequivocally that the sample clients all did very well through efforts from The Prather Strategic Public Relations and Marketing Group.

1. for a Plastics Technology Corporation

Strategic Public Relations and Integrated Marketing Communications Plan
for
Unnamed Technology Corporation

Plan Table Of Contents

Company Overview

Unnamed Technology Corporation, a 15-year-old custom and stock plastic injection molding and finishing-services company, has 85 employees based in a modern 44,000-square-foot plant with state-of-the art and upgraded equipment in Custom Junction, N.J. The manufacturer currently registers approximately $14 million in packaging industry gross sales in the pharmaceutical, personal care, household chemical and food/beverage markets to customers headquartered primarily in the Northeast region of the country.

Company Mission

The company's mission and that of this plan is to continually improve its position as a recognized manufacturer of packaging components to the consumer products and pharmaceutical markets through its high quality, value-added and deadline-conscious products and 'single source service'. The Prather Group will help UTC to increase gross sales in the expanding markets listed above, including the burgeoning pet care market, at a projected annual rate of 10 percent.

Sales Situation Analysis

The sales pattern at UTC reflects consistent annual growth, featuring steady increases in 13 or the 15 years of operation, sandwiched around the major surge of more than $3 million in 1997 resulting from two major new customer in the cosmetics industry.

The stair step growth in each of the first 10 years of operation resulted in $9 million in annual gross sales by 1996, the jump to more than $12 million in 1997, and then a resumption of steady growth the past three years to its current $14 million.

Unnamed Technology Corporation has accomplished its impressive growth in revenues through internal improvements of the facilities, capabilities, processes and personnel. These include expansion of the physical plant, upgrading and/or installation of state-of-the-art machinery, addition of trained personnel, expansion of the sales team and investment in a more comprehensive marketing program.

Sales Goals

The primary goals of the marketing communications plan are to:

- Increase sales by 10 percent in 2001 and by 30 percent or more over the next three years that would propel UTC into a stronger competitive position with its competitors (see addendum).

- Create a strong marketing base from which the company can seek to increase its sales to as much as $20 million or more by the year 2005.

Marketing Objectives

Unnamed Technology's current marketing techniques are typical of most small businesses in that immediate objectives are usually met but without the benefit of cohesive short and long-range planning. Developing and implementing such plans will maximize sales potentials and provide substantial return-on-investment (ROI) from marketing programs.

These objectives include:

- Establishing a Unique Selling Proposition (USP) stating what makes the company compelling to potential customers and different from the competition.

- Creating an image, style and acceptance level for the company through unified and enhanced use of power marketing tools and techniques.

- Creating an in-house marketing committee to brainstorm, share ideas and information and provide marketing research from the field.

- Developing a synergistic sales team effort to add customers from traditional markets, retain and grow current customers, and explore new markets by geography and industry targets.

- Enhancing the goodwill of the company in the community, state, region and nation.

- Stimulating employee involvement through an internal relations program.

- Implementing a plan that is cost-efficient and that provides maximum return-on-investment will lead to the development of a flexible longer-range plan in three years.

Target Audiences

The effectiveness of any communications and marketing program hinges on the targets reached and influenced for Unnamed Technology Corporation.

Reaching and influencing all of the appropriate publics with this dynamic plan will contribute to the ultimate overall success for Unnamed Technology which is deemed very solid in three of the four important: P's - Product, Price and Place. The Prather Group intends to buttress the dual fourth P: Publicity/Promotion. That will complete the mosaic needed for UTC to accomplish its optimistic goals.

The company's universe that will be dealt with extends to:

- Current customers
- Potential customers from regional traditional target markets
- Potential customers from new geographic target markets
- Potential customers from new vertical target markets
- Industry associations - leaders/spokespersons
- Editors and writers of industry publications/magazines/newspapers
- Community/county/state leaders
- Employee teammates
- Vendors and suppliers

56

Marketing Team Building

The existing sales force at UTC must and should concentrate on what the primary mission is: to sell! This, of course, must continue to be strongly supported by customer service and satisfaction, quality assurance and continued modernization of resources.

The goal to increase sales and revenues must be a team effort between management, sales staff and marketing consultant, with everybody on the same page!

Under this new scenario, Jack Prather and The Prather Group have become part of the company's marketing team. The plan will eventually be implemented with less, not more, time requirements from sales and management. This more efficient use of internal time and talent will translate into an ROI that will more than fund the marketing program in the long run.

Following is a review of the various (optional) elements of the marketing program.

Marketing Program Overview

This marketing communications program provides a road map of recommended messages, strategies and tactics to be launched in 2001 and continued through 2004. The program is integrated to provide flexible options so that each part helps the whole and creates synergy.

The plan is a powerful tool that effectively and cost-efficiently tells the Unnamed Technology story to the customer, the industry, the community and the employee teammate.

The marketing plan is in harmony with business and financial objectives as UCT aims to broaden its universe, increase sales and profits, and improve its bottom line. It is generally accepted that a prospect requires nine impressions to inquire about a product or service from a mix of sales calls, advertising, public relations, direct mail, print materials, *etc.*

This Prather Group plan blends methods of attracting interest in and sales for the company by providing:

- Creative imaging and positioning
- Publicity and promotion
- Advertising
- Printed materials
- Video presentation
- Shows and expositions
- Community relations
- Internal relations
- Marketing team building
- Planning
- Market research and analysis
- *Post Mortem* Analysis
- Crisis Problem Management

57

Understanding and evaluating the customer base and the competition are vitally important to the ultimate success of this PR/marketing plan. One approach is to consider entire industries as potential markets. Another is to isolate and try to compete favorably within specific geographical and target markets. Either way, an integral key to successfully competing in the marketplace of choice is to fully understand the company's position and reputation and that will be done.

Knowing the attitudes and concerns of current and past customers is paramount. The Prather Group will assess customer feelings about product or service rendered, relationships with personnel, customer service and satisfaction of the buying experience through a survey.

Potential new customers should also be surveyed, but as step two in research. Niche marketing requires analysis and planning so that limited funds are invested wisely.

Identification of all decision-makers for participation in the plan is extremely important. Whether it is the engineer, the general manager, the owner, the purchasing agent or another combination of important people in the company, the survey will identify and help to cultivate all those who should be in the marketing loop.

Obtaining necessary information can be inexpensive and effective by utilizing existing resources rather than employing a market research company at high cost. The results will be less scientific but in-house analysis will give a strong common-sense result that will be useful for the first phase of the new marketing plan.

The Procedure

An *ad hoc* research team from the sales department, including field reps and customer relations personnel, will be asked to help the marketing activities. The Prather Group will craft esoteric survey questions and cull current and former customer lists for appropriate targets.

The tabulation and analysis of the returned surveys will be a joint effort of the marketing team.

Recipients will receive the following in the mail:

- A carefully crafted survey questionnaire
- A postage-paid return envelope or card
- A cover letter signed by an appropriate UTC executive
- A gift of appreciation from UTC

The mailing will be designed to acquire valuable information and amplify the customer-relations attitudes of UCT's current and former customers subliminally but effectively.

Note: A telephone survey runs with it the risk of skewed answers and an appearance of ulterior motive and is not recommended except in certain instances.

Building a mailing list for regular contact through newsletters, postcards, surveys, *etc.* is important. It will consist of current customers, select past customers, potentially strong new customers, *et al*.

The survey will be step one in building or expanding the communications bridge for UCT to its future customers while helping to retain current ones and maybe even attracting former customers.

Overview

Unnamed Technology stresses quality products, full service, dependability, problem-solving, timeliness and personal contact with customers. A proposed new formation of alliances with customers and suppliers and a vision to seek out innovative product designs are other aggressive management intentions. They should be custom-marketed.

The combination of UTC strengths are what sets the company apart from its competition, and that difference will be reflected in appropriate communications resulting from the flexible short and long-range marketing plans.

The company's customer-friendly corporate style is in contrast with the hard-sell advertising and sales style rampant in the highly-competitive packaging industry. *Viva la difference!*

The UTC story can be effectively told through a variety of messages about product, service and customer testimonials. The unified but mixed messaging will enhance the corporate image and influence relationships with customers, and that will result in increased sales.

Motto and Theme

This motto describes Unnamed Technology's products with a soothing problem-solving message that positions the company in a customer-friendly manner:

"Relax, We've Got You Covered"

The premise that UTC is a customer-relations oriented company with responsive people is further reflected in this ongoing theme designed to pamper the customer.

Following are recommended incentive programs that can be used in advertising, direct mail and personal contact with existing and potential customers:

Red Carpet Service

- Tour our plant and meet our people
  An individual tour or open-house event

- Receive our gift packet with any quote
  The UTC date-book/keychain/desk ornament)

- Receive our 'One-*Top* Shopping' kit
  A kit of sales promotion materials

- Join us at Our President's Golf Outing
  18 holes of golf, dinner and lodging

Publicity

The theme of Red Carpet Service described above, besides being promoted in ads and printed materials, will be the subject of a news release for all appropriate print media titled:

> "Unnamed Technology Rolls Out 'Red Carpet Service' Program"

The company's new messaging - "Relax, We've Got You Covered", "Red Carpet Service" and "One-Top Shopping" all conjure up positive imaging that lend themselves to publicity and promotion, as well as to creative graphics and communications uses.

Other publicity opportunities that will be explored include:

- Management and sales personnel news
  Promotions/programs/achievements

- Product/process news
  Non-proprietary items

- By-lined articles by UTC management
  Co-authored with Prather Group assistance

- Expansions/upgrading
  Physical plant/equipment upgrades

- Employee news items
  Local/state/national

- Feature articles
  UTC history/president's success story, *etc.*

- Case histories
  Appropriate customer success stories

Notes: Articles and features will be co-written or written and edited by The Prather Group, with final approvals from management before material is serviced to a select publication or to the general media. The lists are currently being formulated. Accompanying photography will be arranged in a cost-efficient manner. A UTC media kit with appropriate materials - history/bios/photos/fact sheets/cover story, etc. - will be developed for select use,

Information from UTC will be forwarded to The Prather Group through its standard fact sheet form (printed or typed) or through interviews in-person or by telephone or fax.

Publications will be examined for policies in accepting articles and features, news notes and blurbs, etc. Relationships will be established with the trade media and local-state media on behalf of Unnamed Technology. Publication calendars will be examined to target material to themed issues.

Advertising is a major component of any marketing program. Creativity in theme, messaging and graphics can infuse life into the pitches for otherwise colorless products. The goods and services such as those offered by UTC provide solid material for an effective ad campaign – see attached samples - that have been designed with the following elements:

- Themes that are clear and compelling
- Messages that are succinct and interesting
- Graphics that are sharp and attractive

The ad schedule submitted includes publications that are both suitable and effective to the mission of increasing sales and sales leads.

Advertising thusly will influence the reader to:

- Recognize UTC's product or service
- Understand their benefits and value
- Accept the company's credibility

And this advertising will increase sales productivity by influencing prospects to shop UTC!

Ad Studies

The recent Advertising Research Foundation and Association of Business Publishers (ARF/ABP) recently supported the generally-accepted theories that advertising:

- Increases sales
- Creates more sales leads
- Has a lengthy residual effect
- Helps build a network of reps

The study added two conclusions

1) Color in advertising dramatically increases sales, and

2) The heavier the ad schedule the more cost-effective the result, resulting in lower advertising expenditures. The initial ad schedule will be according to budget and future allocations will be based on an analysis of results.

Cahners Publishing Company stated in a recent study:

When ad size increases readership and inquiries increase, smaller but more frequent ads will generate inquiries at less cost per inquiry, ads draw most inquiries within one month but some benefits accrue for months.

Advertising Factors

The Prather Group considered the amount of investment that should be made for advertising and the outlets to use by considering the following factors:

- Is UTC known in the industries it wishes to serve and if so, how well?

- How extensive is primary competition advertising and who are they?

- Are marketing programs for UTC's growth goals-and-expectations sufficiently funded?

- Is the company seeking expanded vertical markets and/or larger geographic markets?

Advertising Outlets

Trade Publications

Trade Publications evaluated for advertising (some) and publicity (all) include the following. These and other appropriate publications will be considered for the final placement schedules.

- Food & Drug Packaging
- Published by Advanstar Communications, this monthly is edited for packaging decision-makers involved with chemicals, cosmetics, sterile medical disposables, beverages, *etc*. Circ. 83,000+

- Drug & Cosmetic Industry
- Monthly directed at marketers and manufacturers of cosmetics, toiletries, personal care products and OTC pharmaceuticals. Primarily goes to manufacturers in the Mid-Atlantic region. Circ. 13,000.

- Packaging
- Leading publication in packaging, broad-based and expensive. Supported by massive Cahners Publications database.

- Medical Product Manufacturing News

- Closures & Containers (new)

    A sample of other publications includes -

For Packaging	For Personal Products
Canadian Packaging	Cosmetics & Toiletries
Contract Packaging	Drug & Cosmetic Industry
Good Packaging	Soap/Cosmetics/Chemical Specialties
Packaging Digest	Packaging Technology

An analysis will be forthcoming of publications for the household, chemical, food/beverage and pet care industries

Direct Mail

As the UTC marketing communications program takes effect, the direct mail campaign will harvest the leads and inquiries and generate qualified sales calls.

Additional target mailings have been optimized by carefully selecting:

- The lists
- The messages
- The products or services being touted

The program will include:

- Postcard series
- Sales letter
- Kit of UTC materials

Business Directories/Catalogs

Trade journals and association publications often publish directories and catalogs of key players in the industries they cover. UTC will be included where appropriate. The company should also consider a small ad and bold listings in the Thomas Register.

Trade Shows

A display for trade mini-shows and expositions will be prepared, leading to a larger display for larger opportunities. Only shows advantageous to UTC will be selected – see recommendations attached.

Benefits include:

- Company exposure
- Feedback from visitors
- Building rep forces and utilization
- Establishing rapport with prospects
- Possible sales closings on the spot
- Qualification of leads
- Invitations to current and potential customers to the display
- Free publicity surrounding the show

Video Presentation

A video has been designed in draft and storyboard form (see attached) with the following elements:

- A corporate profile
- A capabilities review
- Schedule for use as a tool for sales

Sales Promotion

The attached final drafts of sales promotional materials are the cornerstone of the marketing communications effort as they most clearly and concisely tell the manufacturing story in words and pictures. They have been designed in a unified fashion and comprise the primary components of the sakes kit for salesmen, reps, customer service personnel and management.

Theme

The brochures and flyers, direct mail postcards and letters, and advertisements all carry the motto of the marketing communications program previously discussed: "Relax, We've Got You Covered" and the theme: "Red Carpet Service".

The term "excellence" will also accent the product and service description.

Printed Materials Review

1) Main Marketing Piece - 12-Page Full-Color Brochure.

This piece has been designed for select audiences. It leads the reader through UTC's history and growth in pictures, words and appropriate graphs/charts and creates a 'graphic identity'. It encompasses capabilities, equipment, quality assurance program and commitment to customer satisfaction. It highlights the current successful company status, enormous potentials and the unveiling of the Red Carpet programs. Testimonials are featured throughout the capabilities brochure and it concludes with statements by key executives emphasizing the UTC mission and value system.

This primary printed piece would be sent to important current and former customers, prospects and vendors, and be utilized for sales calls and selectively at trade shows. The press run for the first printing is suggested at 5,000 pieces.

2) Universal Use Piece - Tri-Fold Full-Color Brochure

This traditional brochure is a condensed version of the main piece. It features fewer photos/words/charts but it also effectively relates the overall UTC strengths. It is the universal brochure for sales and marketing use, including for direct mail programs. It folds to fit into a # 10 envelope.

This attractive and readable brochure has been designed in the same style as the main piece. The initial press run is suggested at 10,000 pieces.

Designed to hold all UTC promotional materials in its pockets, this attractive standard 9x12-inch folder will be used selectively to build sales kits targeted at key customers and prospects.

Gold foil stamping on a rich burgundy stock has been coordinated with the print pieces in style and color for a consistent look through all of the materials.

The initial production is suggested at 1,000 pieces.

4) Spec Sheets

Separate sheets for each primary product or service offered by the company will be used selectively for appropriate customers and prospects.

An example is the stock closure spec sheet that contains measurements of each type of closure, typical applications, benefits, types of liners available, decorating options, etc. We will also give the buyer an understandable guide to available resins.

UTC will also benefit from the spec sheets for stock closures, custom closures, packaging and custom injection molding work. All sheets carry some version of the theme.

The initial production is suggested at 1,000 per spec sheet.

5) Direct Mail / Postcard Series

The 'postcard series' will complement other direct mail options, including the mini-brochure, spec sheets and letters.

The postcards are designed to go to specific target mailing lists on a regular basis over a period of time. They will serve as 'ticklers' to inform or reminding customers of UTC products, services and programs.

Sample messages in the drafts attached include:

- Need Dispensing Closures? We'll fill your needs.
- Need Custom Closures? For quality and excellence call UTC.
- Have Packaging Problems? Relax, We've Got You Covered.

The initial production is suggested at 1,000 each for a series of six postcards.

Ad Production

Production of four-color, two-color and one-color fractional ads has been accomplished and awaits final approvals. Full page ads will be designed and stand ready for production when and if the advertising budget allows their placement.

Internal Relations

Management and staff of UTC will function to their fullest potentials as teammates in the eyes of employees by joining with the The Prather Group in implementing the Internal Relations Program. The key to developing company pride is through this ongoing commitment that recognizes effort, empowers teammates to share ideas and sponsors them in community and company activities. The relatively inexpensive Internal Relations Program has the following elements:

Employee of the Month:
- $100 prize per monthly winner
- Special parking space for the month
- Photo displayed on bulletin board for month
- Article with photo to local newspapers
- Framed certificate or plaque from UTC

Employee of the Year:
- $500 prize for yearly winner
- Day off
- Plaque from UTC
- Name on internal plaque with all annual winners
- President's Awards Dinner with all monthly winners
- Article in area newspapers and appropriate trade pubs
- Article in company newsletter

UTC Newsletter
- Format 4-page, 8 1/2xl I ", 2-colors
- Production quarterly
- Content: personnel, product, service news; features, profiles, items
- Editorial commentary by president/key executives
- Photography
- Distribution to teammates and select external mailing

Company Events
- Annual Picnic
- Christmas Party
- Thanksgiving turkey gifting
- Departmental-wide monthly birthday cakes

Company Rewards and Recognition
- Certificates of achievement
- Best idea contest – suggestion box
- Bonuses for efforts 'above and beyond!
- 'Atta-Boy' or 'Atta Girl' recognitions

Community Relations

This plan for UTC teammate participation in community organizations plus a small charitable contributions program will create pride in teammates and enhance the corporate image and visibility to the general public, business leaders, elected officials and the media.

An ongoing and increasing annual budget will be established for corporate contributions, sponsorships and participation that has balance and is monitored with an eye to spending each dollar wisely. The Prather Group will closely monitor the participation to ensure the contributions are spent wisely.

UNNAMED TECHNOLOGY CORP. MARKETING PLAN RATINGS

Marketing Method	Rating Overall	Rating For Leads	Rating For Sales	Rating For Image
Ads` Trades	V	V	E	E
Features/ Trades	E	M	M	V
Publicity/ Trades	E	M	M	E
Printed Materials	V	V	V	V
Creative Imaging	V	E	E	V
Video Presentation	M	M	M	M
Trade Shows/ Expositions	E	E	M	M
Community Relations	M	M	M	M
Internal Relations	M	M	M	M
Research/ Analysis	E	M	M	M

(Key: V-very effective. E - effective. M - moderately effective.)

Explanation: This chart indicates the relative importance of key elements of the plan for Unnamed TechnologyCorporation and provides the guidance led to budget allocations for the elements within the plan.

The Budget

Marketing Communications Management Fee – monthly   <u>$</u>
- Program management and development
- Concepts and planning time
- Meeting/telephone time
- Publicity writing/editing
- Media relations/placement
- Client communications/reports

Program Development Fee - one-time charge   <u>$</u>

Sales Promotional Materials - total   <u>$</u>

Main Marketing Piece: $_____
- 12-pages
- four color
- design/layout/typesetting/copywriting
- photography
- 2,500 copies first printing

Universal Marketing Piece: $_____
- tri-fold to # 10 size
- full color
- design/layout/typesetting/copywriting
- photography from main piece
- 5,000 copies first printing

Pocket Folder: $_____
- custom gold foil
- deep burgundy on rich stock
- 1,000 folders first printing

Four Spec Sheets: $_____
- four separately designed sheets
- two color
- design/layout/typesetting
- editing
- 1,000 each = 4,000 total first printing

Postcard Series: $_____
- six separate postcards
- design/layout/typesetting/copywriting
- 1,000 each = 6,000

Ad Production and Design   <u>$</u>
- four color (2-color deduct $700/1-color deduct $1,000)
- island half-page design
- design/layout/typesetting/copywriting

continued . . .

Trade Show Display $\underline{\$}$
- table-top materials/set-up for standing display (see estimate)
- fee schedule for shows/expenses (see attached)

Video Presentation $\underline{\$}$
- *writing/direction*
- *sound/graphics*
- *5-to-7 minute format based on best bid*

Internal Relations – at cost plus 15 % $\underline{\$}$
- quarterly newsletter
- 4-pages
- two-color
- design/layout/copywriting/typesetting
- photography
- 1000 copies each edition
- other IR programs at cost plus 15%

Community Relations – monthly $\underline{\$}$
- corporate giving management
- sponsorship determinations
- event participation management

Advertising – payment schedule attached $\underline{\$}$
- flexible program
- placement schedule attached

Expenses – monthly tbd
- telephone
- fax transmissions
- postage
- copying (normal quantities)
- mileage
- approved extraordinary charges at cost

Payment Schedules - invoices attached

- Management fee payable monthly in advance.

- Program development fee due.

- Advertising costs payable monthly in advance.

- Promotional materials due in three progress payments of initial design, final draft approval, delivery.

- Expense reimbursements payable monthly.

2. for a Tableware Manufacturer/Distributor

Strategic Marketing and Communications Plan
for
Customware Inc.

Overview

Customware Inc. has a strong opportunity to corner significant shares of desirable target markets thanks to its artistic and delightful line of tableware and the vigorous and professional sales effort currently being designed.

The Prather Group is enthused about the opportunity if being part of the introduction of the CI lines in the northeast tri-state region of New York, New Jersey and Connecticut and helping to establish the line to buyers, retailers and the general public, *ad infinitum.* This Strategic Marketing and Communications Plan will help the company grow and prosper.

The integrated marketing communications program of publicity and promotion, supported by printed materials and advertising fueled by creativity, will effectively accomplish the CI goals and objectives (see addendum).

The Prather Group will provide comprehensive and cost-effective public relations services by employing our existing resources as needed and by working closely with other consultants or agencies according to their expertise when appropriate. This method frees sales executives to do what they do best: sell!

The outline of the plan that is now subject to final approvals and budgeting follows:

Goals and Objectives

The initial marketing communications goal is to create and implement a program that will help the marketing efforts by persuading 100 or more substantial retail outlets in the tri-state area to carry Customware tableware in 2002 and to gain maximum exposure in the mid-to-upscale tableware markets to grow the geographic sales base and number of outlets to 250 within three years.

The funding parameters required for fulfillment of these goals are attached in a separate addendum.

Philosophy

The essences of Customware as a unique and eclectic tableware line will be communicated through creative and innovative messages delivered to target markets through publicity, promotion, supportive advertising and printed materials.

The program will be geared to positively influence the identified decision-makers as quickly as possible for a maximum return-on-investment (ROI) of public relations dollars.

Product Review

CI tableware is distinctive, never boring, and each plate or cup emerges as a conversation piece. Besides providing table decorators with unique mix-and-match choices, the line is attractive, utile and durable. It should also appeal to buyers and retail outlet managers or owners for its sales and profit potentials.

Results will be forthcoming re the product review undertaken by The Prather Group research expert, John Allen.

Product Positioning

Customware will be positioned to retailers as artistically unique tableware that is elegant yet great fun; a product that will appeal to the creativity of the purchaser, and that will generate profitable sales from a large universe of commercial and consumer buyers.

Target Markets

The sales and profit potentials for CI tableware will appeal to retailers and their buyers. The enormous retail market includes homemakers, party/wedding planners, restaurateurs and caterers, gift-givers - virtually everyone who has an appetite for food, fun and good taste in combination.

Market Areas

CI Customware tableware will eventually be marketed to target publics throughout America. However, the initial introduction and marketing concentration will be focused toward retailers, buyers and consumers in the cosmopolitan tri-state area of New York, New Jersey and Connecticut.

Marketing Methods

A unique blend of publicity, promotion, support advertising, direct mail and brochure messaging for Customware should be targeted to specific buyers and retail owners and managers, and to an eclectic consumer audience that can comprehend the unique value of the product.

Point-of-purchase displays and presentations at exhibits or shows, or in malls or stores, will show the product line to a wider universe of buyers, who can see, feel and meditate about the purchase first-hand.

A full list of publications aimed at target markets, including trade and association journals, magazines and newspapers, will be compiled and evaluated.

Article and photo placement in appropriate outlets will focus on product line introductions and news. Additional coverage will be generated about participation in exhibitions or shows, business or financial activity and executive news. Feature articles about the CI decal artists and their work will be crafted and placed.

Methods employed in attaining success in the expanded national and international markets will be evaluated and integrated into the final marketing communications program.

Final in-depth plans will be developed in each of the specific areas of public relations according to budget.

Publications Review

Target Areas: Most print outlets pertinent to CI in its initial publicity and supportive advertising campaign are regional. However, many national publications are also listed for current and future reference.

Publicity Target Markets

The selected target markets include those involved with and interested in mid-to-upscale home decor, entertaining, dining, collectibles, *etc.*

Goals and Objectives

The main goals and objectives are to create interest from buyers and managers/owners to purchase and promote Customware within key department stores, malls, or specialty shops, and to generate consumer awareness and interest in purchasing the product line.

Select Media

Viable media in which interest from buyers would result from publicity or advertising are included in the following list. There are only a few publications that influence this market but there are comer and marginal publications that will also be evaluated for ad and publicity placement.

Select Media to Influence Buyers	**Media Description**
CHINA, GLASS & TABLEWARE	An industry-specific magazine with 3,000 copies published monthly. Editorial copy is directed at executives, purchasers and managers of department stores and individual retail outlets. The only trade magazine in this field also publishes annual 'Red Book'.
BETTER HOMES & GARDENS	National publication.
ELLE DECOR	National publication.
GIFTS & TABLEWARE	Canadian publication.

Buyers will also be motivated through a carefully-crafted and targeted direct mail campaign.

Select Media to Influence Executives	
HFD	A weekly newspaper-style publication with a circulation of 30,000. Centers on the home products industry and edited for executives involved with volume retailers/distributers. Publishes a daily edition during the annual Housewares Show in January. This is the main pub to retail household products trade.

continued . . .

INTERIOR DESIGN	A monthly publication of 18,000-plus copies edited for professionals involved in residential interior design. Includes coverage of upper end furnishing with limited table top material. This is the leading publication to the industry.
STORES	Info forthcoming.
HAUT DECOR	Published in Florida - future use.

Select Media to Influence Hoteliers

RESTAURANT/HOTEL DESIGN INT.	Aimed at national and international hotel executives. Total circulation each month is 36,000. Editorial matter directed at all aspects of the design function, including for tableware - including restaurants. Aimed at mid-to-upscale hospitality market.

CLUB DIRECTORY
HOTEL & MOTEL MANAGEMENT
HOTEL & RESORT INDUSTRY
HOTELIER (Canadian)

Select Media to Influence Specialty Market

GOURMET RETAILER GOURMET NEWS	Both publications are directed at the specialty store markets, particularly those that carry food and food preparation products. Upscale, discerning readers.
(More forthcoming)	

Select Media to Influence Mid-to-Upscale Consumer Market

WOMEN'S WEAR DAILY	The leading authority on fashion trends influences buyers and purchasers from major retailers in mid-to-upscale markets.
ELLE BRIDE MODERN BRIDE BRIDE & GROOM BRIDE'S & YOUR NEW HOME ELEGANT BRIDE	These outlets reach brides re purchases and gifts from the home.

continued . . .

Select Business Media in Tri-State Region

CRAIN'S NEW YORK
LONG ISLAND BUSINESS
WESTCHESTER COUNTY BUSINESS
LONG ISLAND BUSINESS NEWS

CONNECTICUT BUSINESS
BUSINESS TIMES (CONN.)
BRIDGEPORT BUSINESS REVIEW (CONN.)

NEW JERSEY BUSINESS
NEW JERSEY MONTHLY
BUSINESS JOURNAL OF NEW JERSEY

FOCUS (Pa.)
PHILADELPHIA BUSINESS MAGAZINE
PHILADELPHIA BUSINESS JOURNAL

Publication Review

All pertinent regional and national publications will be listed and evaluated. The publications judged important to the mission(s) of Customware Inc. will include the following information:

- Evaluation of editorial placement opportunities

- Editorial calendars

- Issue Themes

- Advertising recommendations and rates

- Direct mail support recommendations

- Exhibitions/trade show recommendations

- Subscriber mailing lists (pertinent)

Creative Input and Ideas

The creative process will remain flexible until ideas and input from all sources have been evaluated and factored in to the final plan of action.

Before final recommendations can be offered about themes and slogans, *etc.*, it is necessary to understand parent company protocols, guidelines, restrictions and past successes and failures.

It is recommended that Customware retain a strong modern flair in its programs to reach American buyers, retailers and consumers.

The following ideas are offered for evaluation and discussion, with the final selections for each of the elements to be agreed-upon according to the timeline submitted last week.

Slogans

"Gift Wrap Your Meals".
Explanation: speaking to the decorative nature of CI tableware.
Strength: clever play on words, nice feel.

"Customware - the Fashion Plate".
Explanation: well-dressed women in America are often called 'fashion plates'.
Strength: clever appeal to upscale fashion-minded women.

Promotions

"Spokes Model Contest."
A $5,000 prize and 1-year contract to represent Customware Inc.

Explanation: an appealing and cultured young woman would be selected to represent CI at exhibits and trade shows, to appear in select advertising and printed materials, as well as to assist the sales effort generally.

Strength: the contest would generate good media coverage in the metropolitan area and the Spokes model would provide good public relations throughout the year. Contract renewal with the model will depend on the success of the program.

"Introductory Events."
Planned events to introduce the CI tableware lines in interesting venues.

Explanation:
CU would hold promotions at dynamic sites such as Tavern on the Green, The Plaza Hotel, the Meadowlands Sports Complex, large shopping malls, *etc.*

Strength: Unique hands-on promotions to be determined would generate media coverage and attract important guests from the various publics CI wishes to influence.

(Plan Notes: budget recommendations, advertising and materials copy-design drafts, additional research graph and other support materials in separate attachments. Timeline decisions requested within seven days please.)

3. for a Marketing Communications Company

Strategic Public Relations Plan
for
The Unnamed Communications Group

Mission

This Strategic Public Relations Plan is designed to initiate the process of publicizing, promoting and memorializing the many assets of The Unnamed Communications Group to its existing, former and potential customers and to the general public in order to increase sales.

The focus of The Prather Group Plan is to generate awareness and acceptance of client UCG through a variety of public relations and support activities.

The main goal is to stimulate business for UCG both in the short and long runs. This will set the stage for ever-increasing returns-on-investment as the Action Plan is finalized and matures.

An evaluation of current and past corporate efforts shows that potentials exist (see attachment A). Appropriate successful and proven past activities and programs have been factored into this final Action Plan that in reality is a marketing map for UCG to follow well into the 21st century.

Jack Prather of The Prather Group will immediately begin to implement the Action Plan and get the ball rolling for the UCG team upon final agreement to proceed and receipt of the first month's payment for materials and fees (see budget attachment).

Aims and Goals

Fulfillment of the first stage of the Action Plan during the next quarter will launch for UCG the processes necessary to move forward throughout the year and beyond in the highly competitive search for clients who will avail themselves of the UCG expertise.

These plans include:

- Establishing a dynamic and modern image

- Increasing awareness within its various markets

- Increasing acceptance with existing/past/potential customers

- Helping to establish its rightful market positions

- Helping to increase sales and profits

- Maximizing the potential return-on investment of marketing dollars

- Managing the public relations and writing projects for UCG

Themes and Slogans

UCG will celebrate its 40th birthday in 2000!

This extraordinary longevity can be effectively employed as a unique corporate theme, with commensurate publicity, promotional print material activity, through the entire anniversary year – with planning now.

This theme speaks directly to the experience, credibility and pride that four decades in business implies. Properly touting these attributes can help separate UCG from much of its competition.

Suggestions of ways to promote the 40th anniversary, besides the publicity that can be generated, include the following tasks:

- Producing a '40-Year Report' similar to an annual report,

- Creating a periodic newsletter, comprehensively covering each specialty,

- Devising a clarifying slogan for appropriate use during 2000, example -

   "Our 40th Year and Counting".

Examples of a slogan or motto that could accompany the UCG logo where appropriate have been fashioned through conversations with the executive staff. The Prather Group will develop a 'standards manual' that will outline the correct use of the logo and slogans.

Examples of possible slogans for use by UCG are:

- We Deliver Your Message
- Communications is Our Middle Name
- Substance, Style, Technology
- Experience, Credibility, Pride

Methods and Techniques

A program to capitalize on the 40th year of UCG includes employing all of the traditional PR methods and techniques in varying degrees. The various elements include:

Publicity

Exclusive or general placements will be created and serviced to the media segments attached:

- Targeted industry magazines and journals
- Business magazines
- Newspapers
- Radio and cable television broadcast outlets

Media Relations

To deal with all appropriate print media, The Prather Group will initiate and implement the "Three P's":

- 'Pitch' feature and article ideas to appropriate outlets

- 'Produce' the material, in cooperation with UCG

- 'Place' the feature, news article or item in the appropriate publication(s)

- and cultivate the media – editors, reporters, broadcasters

Publicity Content

The Prather Group will create and/or implement *newsworthy* and *interesting* media opportunities that will help tell the whole UCG story, including writing and servicing the following:

- Feature stories
- General news articles
- Executive interviews
- Items about events and activities
- Photos and captions

Examples of features, articles and items will include:

- The history of UCG from 1964-2002
- The UCG President and industry changes
- Modern technology used at UCG
- Current status and future predictions for direct mail
- Items about events and activities

Promotion

A series of internal and external 40th Anniversary special events and activities will include:

- An open house and reception for potential clients
- A VIP reception for key customers/VIP's at a local restaurant
- A special sales incentive program
- A unique direct mail campaign with a gift for select customers
- A job-seminar for college and high school groups
- A new 'Red-Carpet Service Program'

Community Relations

UCG is solicited for donations and other contributions by every non-profit and civic organization and cause known to man, as are almost all viable businesses. Obviously, 'pet causes' and other meaningful charitable organizations and events that are regularly supported by the company will continue to receive UCG support while new ones will be considered within an established community relations budget.

The list of recommended community relations involvements are attached recommendations. Each can help generate positive goodwill and exposure for UCG.

UCG can also escalate its community relations image by one or more of the following techniques recommended for consideration in the plan.

They include:

- Becoming a primary sponsor of a specific organization such as the American Cancer Society, the local hospice organization or a youth athletic league
- Hosting and sponsoring an activity like a charity golf or tennis tournament
- Encouraging and sponsoring key employees into civic organizations
- Joining and being active in business organizations like the County Chamber of Commerce or the State Business League
- Creating and servicing a newsletter – *The UCG Times* - to existing, former and potential new clients. A sample masthead, format, list of articles, publication schedule and budget are attached.

Support Services

In addition to the public relations and strategic communications Action Plan elements described above, The Prather Group will provide support services as needed in one of three ways: through companies or individuals currently and satisfactorily used by UCG, through Prather Group affiliated professionals or through the more traditional bid, screening and recommendation process.

The services above and beyond the strategic public relations and marketing communications consultation documented here will include but not be limited to:

- Graphic design
- Printing
- Direct Mail
- Research
- New logo design and placement

Advertising

The Prather Group will consult with the management and marketing teams at UCG to develop creative, effective and affordable advertising plans for the 40th Anniversary. The ads would be carefully-conceived and produced and placement would be targeted to the most effective outlets according to the company goals.

Following are the categories of support for UCG by Prather:

Elements of Advertising

- The ads would be within the standards of UCG and the industry involved

- Placement of ads would be strategically timed for maximum exposure and effect

- Outlets would be carefully selected to reach specific market segments

- Ad copy and artwork would reflect the desired UCG image

- The ads would be designed in unison with the firm's printed materials for synergy

- The ad budget recommendations would be within allowable budget limits (see recommendations)

Advertising Strategies

The advertising would be designed for select print and broadcast media with a mix of techniques. It would be implemented in conjunction with direct mail and publicity campaigns to create maximum synergy. The ad campaign would include the following through 2001:

- A regular by-lined column* by a UCG executive

- A paid ad designed to look like an editorial column

- Institutional and traditional ads designed to promote the new logo, slogan and look

- Public Service Announcements to promote special UCG causes and involvements

- Sales promotional ads with incentives

- Direct mail and publicity support

- Question-and-Answer Ad+

Notes: *The column masthead would include the author's by-line and photograph, authorship would be rotated among the president and key executives, the copy would reflect the 40th anniversary and be of general interest, a series of four different columns presented in select publications, the columns would be edited or co-written by The Prather Group. +-The ad series produced in the form of questions-and-answers about specific UICG specialties, establishing the firm as 'the answer-man',

The Internet

The Internet is one small piece of the strategic marketing mosaic but an important one. But it should be viewed as a major resource and not as a panacea or the ultimate problem-solver. The UCG site must be made more clear, informative, attractive and conducive to short and long-term results.

Per request, a review of the current UCG Internet site was undertaken by sources available to The Prather Group. A cursory review reveals that the site would benefit from a full redesign to reflect clear and compelling information about the company, its executives and its specific services.

Following the redesign, a vigorous promotion of the site is essential in order for it to be effective in return-on investment of time, effort and money.

We recommend that the UCG site be redesigned and updated to present the following information:

- More comprehensive biographies of key executives
- A history of the company
- The product and service lines
- Listings and graphics showing award-winning direct mail and promotion pieces and ad campaigns
- More information with professional photos about the president and key executives, to breed familiarity
- A photo or rendering of the exterior of the facilities to create an impression of size and power
- An appropriate client list (with permission) and testimonials
- A history of the company as it celebrates its 40th year
- Promotional incentives to utilize the various UCG services
- Links with other resources important to the overall UCG effort.

We also recommend that UCG eliminate the spacey spinning balls and globes - they are too vague, too glitzy for the image being portrayed and dated.

NOTE: The Prather Group will further develop the requirements for the UCG site with the UCG programmer (web expert) and the management and marketing teams.

Client Consultation

Jack Prather/The Prather Group would consult with UCG on its existing or potential clients in an appropriate fashion in joint efforts to 'grow' existing business and/or to attract new business. The attached list of standards will apply to The Prather Group and UCG.

Remuneration

Remuneration to The Prather Group for consultation or for additional work-for-hire for UCG will be according to the rate sheet attached from The Prather Group or through an agreed-upon rate for each specific project or activity. Confidentiality and exclusivity are guaranteed from The Prather Group to The Unnamed Communications Group for its existing or potential clients.

Budget

The attached budget recommendation spells out the exact amounts for monthly fee and monies approved for advertising, printing or other out-of-pocket expenses that are payable in advance to Prather by UCG, and in regular monthly increments following that.

The fee includes public relations and strategic communications consultation by The Prather Group for The Unnamed Communications Group according to the spirit and intent of the Action Plan submitted this date.

The fee portion of the agreement includes but is not necessarily limited to fulfillment of the following tasks by Jack Prather and The Prather Group:

- Media research and relations
- Publicity writing, editing and placement
- Newsletter or special materials concepts, writing, editing
- Promotional and special event concepts and management
- Community Relations management
- Internet consultation with CCG webmaster
- Crisis-problem consultation

Fee. The monthly fee of $_____ is payable monthly in advance and monthly thereafter.

Additional Budget Items - Payable as expenses are incurred.

- Advertising concepts, design and placement: 15% Standard Agency Commission
- Consultation with existing UCG clients and potential clients or proposals to 'grow' existing clients: tbd.
- Approved and justified miscellaneous expenses out-of-pocket: at documented cost

4. for a Tool Manufacturer/Distributor

Advertising and Public Relations Proposal
for
XYZ Tool Manufacturer

Overview

This Action Plan Proposal is designed to acquaint the Unnamed Tool Company executive team with The Prather Group's perception of the company's marketing and promotion needs for its varied tool product lines, our initial recommendations on how you can achieve greater market penetration in your trading area, and our general ability to handle the XYZ Tool Company account.

Recommended are ideas that we believe can make an important contribution to the overall effectiveness of your advertising and public relations programs. Detailed sub-program proposals will be forthcoming upon request.

Product Category - Audiences

Due to the variety of products offered by XYZ Tool Company, we have divided the Company into two categories, with subdivisions for appropriate market audiences:

> 1. HOMEOWNER TOOL PRODUCTS
>   A.   CONSUMERS
>   B.   DISTRIBUTORS/SELLERS
>
> 2.   COMMERCIAL TOOL PRODUCTS
>   A. MANUFACTURERS/BUILDERS
>   B. DISTRIBUTORS/SELLERS

The product categories should be approached individually and budgeted appropriately. Advertising materials, publicity, appeals, concepts, *etc.* will be developed by the consulting agency for each product category.

By breaking down the marketing needs into two categories, we will be able to:

> 1. Plan and develop each in a distinct manner.
>
> 2. Evaluate advertising and publicity efforts more efficiently.
>
> 3. Maintain tighter control of budgets for each segment.
>
> 4. Compare the two categories.

The Creative Approach

XYZ Tool Company commitment to quality tool products must be stressed in all advertising or public relations efforts. To maximize effectiveness of advertising and promotion, the agency will establish a strong and consistent visual format. This will particularly relate to header and sign-off areas, borders (or other visual elements), typeface selection, logo standardization, and other graphic aspects of the ads and promotional materials.

Each product line will have its own requirements, but each advertisement and sales promotion effort will reflect the company as a whole. In essence, we want to project the XYZ image uniformly in order to achieve optimum mileage from the budget.

Advertising, Publicity Promotion

The objective of this phase of the plan is to increase consumer market penetration within the present trading area. The agency feels this can best be accomplished by establishing a well-balanced advertising effort between the XYZ Company and its distribution chain.

Each retail outlet represents a direct means of promoting XYZ products in that geographical area. Consider the dealership as a company sales representative with a specific geographic sales territory. Providing him with the incentive to promote XYZ products will help develop consumer demand in his trading area. Our recommendations on this subject are outlined in more detail further on in this preliminary plan.

For Consumer Products -

Consumer Advertising

Newspaper Advertising - It is important to increase promotion through retail outlets. Advertisements should continue to promote company image and quality of products, but will be used in a supplementary capacity to dealer advertising, rather than as the main consumer message.

Magazine Advertising - We recommend a consistent ad program in a group of appropriate trade publications, with a program based on fractional (e.g. one-page) ads, with a second color for impact and increased visibility. Ads will be simple, straightforward, and geared for dealer response and would have a call to action to generate live leads for XYZ salesmen.

Radio Advertising - A portion of the budget should be in radio advertising, since there are a number of effective metro/suburban stations available.

Direct Mail - The development of promotional flyers and/or advertising tabloids to be mailed in appropriate areas. Since the immediate metropolitan area represents a large portion of the sales volume, it is here we might test a direct mail program.

Cable-TV - Defining the market audience as primarily male, we will consider sponsoring sporting events such as Rangers hockey and Knicks basketball, *etc*. These media buys would be timed for late winter/early spring when, depending on the fortunes of the metro area hockey and basketball teams, viewer interest is at its peak.

Consumer Magazines – The agency will evaluate advertising in regional editions of homeowner and related periodicals. Fractional page ads would be used.

Point-of-Purchase - We also recommend a strong dealer-support program consisting of advertising materials, in-store promotional material, publicity material, XYZ dealer newsletters, *etc.*

Co-op Advertising – As the consumer associates a product with a retail outlet, greater consumer penetration will require greater effort on behalf of the dealer to promote XYZ Tool products.

The cooperative (co-op) advertising programs with dealers can establish the all-important "availability factor," answering the consumer question of "Where can I buy XYZ products?" Lacking the big budget dollars to establish the company as a household name, co-op newspaper advertising will help promote local availability.

XYZ is one of many tool companies most dealers represent. The product chosen to advertise is influenced by the financial participation offered by the manufacturer. The product line which offers non-cooperative participation is often left' to promote itself.

The sales force of local newspapers has a direct influence on the retailer's advertising habits and co-op is a strong selling tool within every newspaper's advertising presentations.

Consumer Publicity

Themes - Should be linked to the XYZ dealer, and towards developing public awareness and local availability of XYZ products. Avenues of publicity we can take advantage of include:

Open Front News Releases – For distribution to dealerships for insertion in local publications. Types of releases would be the appointment of a new authorized dealership, new products, homeowner tool-related articles and tips in a weekly column.

New Services - As capabilities are added to the roster, appropriate new product releases will be distributed.

Personnel Releases - New sales personnel, executive promotions, *etc.*

New Literature Releases - The facilities/capabilities brochure, direct mail units, and other brochures developed as the program progresses.

Promotions

Informational Seminars - Manufacturer or distributor representative would appear at XYZ dealerships to host question and answer sessions on tool application and proper use for homeowners. The "event" would be tied into a sale on XYZ tools.

Distributor/Seller Promotion - Promotional efforts will be geared to the dealer's ability to recognize a saleable, profitable product. Point-of-purchase materials will stress product quality, market demand, quick product turnover, high ROI, increased sales volume, etc.

Direct Mail - The agency recommends a moderate direct mail program. This will ensure a consistent flow of leads for XYZ' salespersons. In addition, it will add support to the concurrent ad and publicity placements.

Distribution Areas

Existing Prospect Lists - Even if these prospects have already received company information, mailings will add impact and reinforcement to an already established prospect.

New Inquiries - As the ad/publicity program draws inquiries, these prospects should be scheduled for a follow-up mailing shortly after their inquiry.

Present Customers - Serves as a reminder of the XYZ products and may open up additional areas of business from these established customers.

Acquired Lists - Key dealers in prime marketing areas not presently handling the XYZ product line.

Dealer Newsletter - As the foremost direct mail vehicle, we recommend a periodic XYZ external newsletter. The newsletter will have a dual purpose of strengthening dealer support and as a sales promotional tool for new dealer prospects. Subject matter would include marketing and promotional tips for the dealers, general company news, how to use tools, sales success stories with XYZ products, Dealer of the Month, *etc.*

For Commercial Tool Products -

Direct Mail - We recommend a steady, concentrated direct mail program. Since we are now appealing to a professional market, materials should also reflect professionalism. Printed material should be full color. Photographs should represent a wide variety of industrial and commercial tool uses, emphasizing the quality, practicality and efficiency of XYZ products.

Promotional Material - Prospects should be scheduled for an immediate mailing of promotional materials once lists of key firms in all markets are acquired. Existing prospect mailings will help to enforce the XYZ image and familiarity, and present customers should be reminded of products and services.

Magazine Advertising - The intended advertising program will add additional impact to the previously outlined publicity program since the placement of ads directly affects the placement of publicity. The agency recommends a moderate but consistent ad program in a group of appropriate tool trade publications. The ad program should be based on fractional ads, utilizing a second color or full-color for impact. The advertisements directed towards the manufacturer/builder will be simple, straightforward and geared for response.

Publicity - Although the two markets differ, the nature of the publicity program is essentially the same for both. Releases would focus on new products, new literature, new services and new authorized distributors.

Case History Articles - Particularly well-suited for either market, case histories might show how a particular construction project utilized various XYZ tools, or how a particular XYZ tool was 'creatively' used. As these articles appear in appropriate magazines, reprints will be produced as an additional sales tool in all direct mailing efforts.

Technical Bulletins – The technical bulletin is particularly well suited for the tool marketing effort. Such bulletins would be drafted by qualified XYZ personnel, edited by the agency and sent to appropriate trade magazines and users. This type of publicity would be effective in presenting XYZ as knowledgeable and as a spokesman in the field. It will also appeal to the user's quest for technical knowledge regarding the products.

Sales Promotional Material - A Facilities/Capabilities Brochure will play an important factor in "image building" and in presenting XYZ as a big business with quality products. The material will be used as a general sales promotion tool, applicable to all product categories. This full-color brochure will have emphasis on products-in-use photos. The copy will delineate the scope of products offered by XYZ. Since this brochure will be used in a variety of ways, it will incorporate a postpaid reply card to act as a call to purchase and simplify the prospect's response.

Individual Brochures - The agency recommends that an additional portion of the budget be dedicated to supplementing the Facilities/Capabilities Brochure with individual brochures on each major segment of the company's products. These additional brochures will enable each segment to be covered in greater detail, as well as serving as an effective follow-up once a prospect's interest has been defined.

Flyers, Envelope Stuffers, Postcards - Various promotional materials such as flyers, envelope stuffers and postcard ads for all products will be developed as required. Such materials will be used in appropriate direct mail efforts and as leave-behinds for XYZ salesmen.

Working With XYZ Tool

The Prather Group will serve as your advertising and marketing support department. We will prepare and administer the advertising and public relations budget, make promotional recommendations and even tend to such nitty-gritty functions as providing media with the company catalog, making trade show arrangements, preparing all printed materials and other functions heretofore carried out by your staff.

As part of the budget management process, we will prepare recommendations for each of the programs addressed in this report. Each program phase, be it preparation of sales literature, handling direct mailings, media production and placement, *etc.*, will be pre-estimated and XYZ Tool will know in advance what each specific project will cost.

Our proximity to XYZ home offices assures the kind of close working relationship your company's marketing efforts require. In addition to regularly-scheduled advertising and marketing meetings with designated XYZ personnel, Prather Group representatives will spend the time necessary to the job at the site.

We look forward to working with you.

5. for a Long-Shot Political Candidate

Strategic Public Relations Plan
For
Freeholder Candidate

Overview

Following are the recommendations to promote Freeholder Candidate Joe Klampett (pseudonym) in his quest to become elected to the Board of Freeholders in and Unnamed County in New Jersey.

The Timeline

Announcement of his candidacy in the June primary in four months will be made within two weeks. The general election is in six months and ongoing PR will be implemented through then.

Situation Analysis

The County Party for 22 years had been without a member on the three-person freeholder board and it has been stagnating in its role of minority party.

Entering the campaign, the candidate's chances for victory appear slim. However, with proper budgeting, planning and teamwork, The Prather Group believes he can and will win.

Informal and low-budget monthly polling will enable us to determine how the campaign is faring and dictate which areas should be shored up.

The first meeting regarding this invigorated plan of action should be set immediately upon agreement to proceed between the candidate, his campaign staff and The Prather Group.

Action Plan

The Prather Group recommends an action plan that includes the formation of a public relations team to consist of the candidate, the party chairperson, the campaign chairperson and a key volunteer.

Recommendations include:

- Candidate attendance at all public meetings in the area
- Formation of coffee-klatch clubs hosted by party members throughout the county to promote the candidate

- Formation of a club called "Klampett Kids" to carry banners and signs and attend rallies.

- Regular media releases about the candidate's stance and platform on issues of substance

- Candidate availability for media interviews and for regular calls for comments

- Production of position papers on key issues in the campaign for widespread handout

- Challenge to debates with the opposition

- Advertisements espousing the candidate's views and accomplishments

- Door-to-door campaigning at convenient hours in select districts

- Brochure and position paper handouts by campaign workers at events and activities in the various key municipalities in the county.

The tenor of the campaign:

Choices have to be made on the tenor of the campaign so it will be consistent. This campaign should and must quickly establish the highest integrity and ethical stance possible. Therefore we recommend:

- No negative personal campaigning about the opposition.

- No dirty tricks.

- Campaigning only on the issues

- Positive personal campaigning by and for our candidate

- Maximizing personal appearances

- Positive campaign printed materials

- Negative campaign materials only on issues

- Cultivating solid media relations

- Servicing newsworthy releases to area media

- Agreeing to do interviews

- Participating in debates and other public forums

Note: Previous campaigns have been marred by excessive and over-zealous personal attacks and mudslinging. A Prather Group poll indicates that the voting public is very turned off because of this type of campaigning.

Advertising

A budget for all media has established to span the time from the announcement that Joe Klampett is entering the primary election right through the general election. The ad schedule will be light at first and escalate as the primary approaches.

The same time format will be followed through the general election.

Print and broadcast outlets and direct mail each receive 40 percent of the advertising revenue, and billboards and other signing received the remaining 20 percent.

The print ads include a photograph of the candidate and his family with an appeal for votes, positions on the issues, campaign pledges, endorsements and past record.

The broadcast radio and cable-TV advertisements will be recorded by the candidate, who has an excellent persona and speaking voice, and by several key endorsers from the political, business and civic arenas.

Special Materials

The campaign theme and slogan, modern typestyle and dynamic design are consistently portrayed within the ads and printed materials. The color choices of red, white and blue and a patriotic motif will portray the candidate in a positive light.

Materials include:

- A brochure on the candidate featuring a family photograph, personal and professional resumes, political resume, statements of positions on campaign issues and key endorsements.

- Position papers for the candidate on vital issues on white 8"" x 11" stock for handouts during speeches, personal appearances, to the media, *etc.*

- Photographs for media use, including an 8" x 10" black-and-white head-shot and a family portrait with wife, four children and the family dog.

- Buttons with the campaign slogan and candidate's captions photo for handout at the County Fair and at personal appearances.

- Souvenirs of pens and matches for handout

- Endorsements listed in a flyer, including from civic and business leaders, union officials, certain opposition party members, veteran's leaders, firefighters, *etc.*

- A media kit that includes all of the above and other material such as articles and copies of advertisements.

Personal Appearances

The candidate will make personal appearances and speeches at a carefully organized variety of events, including for civic, social, religious, union, senior citizen and veterans' groups, *et al.*

At each appearance a copy of the speech or a release pertaining to the remarks and prepared and submitted by a credible person was sent or given to the media in standard form.

The Results

That plan was followed and Joe Klampett, our candidate, won by 112 votes out of 30,000 total votes cast in the county-wide election.

Post Mortem

Personal Notes: We can still remember the first meeting with the candidate at a local restaurant. It almost seemed surreptitious as the atmosphere was filled with whispers, ideas being tossed around and suggested methods for the democrat to unseat the all-powerful two-term incumbent from the opposition party who was highly favored by any measure. (Of course, all of the elements of that meeting were perfectly legitimate and really quite common.)

We had originally misjudged the candidate, thinking him a hayseed that should remain on the local council and not yearn for a place in the seat of county power. Could this be the Peter Principal at work in local politics?

Boy, how wrong we were! The candidate who seemed hopelessly drifting amid a sea of members of the majority party turned out to be extremely bright, an innovative and hard-working campaigner who rapidly grew to be immensely popular. He was a grassroots politician of the first magnitude!

More importantly: he was the right person, in the right place, at the right time and knew it!

We quickly jumped on the express train that day and the team – and history - carried our candidate through a rugged campaign where he claimed victory easily in the primary and by 112 votes out of almost 30,000 cast in the general election.

That initial victory was narrow and by itself had no real bearing on a second term: only a successful three-year stint as freeholder could accomplish that as the opposition party still outnumbered Klampett's party by 3-to-1, and now he would be incumbent and fair game for a challenge in the next election cycle.

He had to serve well and then run again well. He did, serving two more terms on the Freeholder Board.

Our team did it the right way: positively, persuasively and honestly.

We were all proud of that, and of him.

PR Advisory: *In politics as in all public relations ventures, establish a minimum standard and never go below it.*

6. *for a Resort and Conference Center*

Public Relations Proposal
For
Unnamed Conference and Meetings Resort

Overview

The purpose of this proposal is to begin the process of creating a viable public relations and advertising plan that will enhance the immediate and long-range bookings potential of the Unnamed Conference and Meetings Resort by improving its image and restoring its reputation to all publics of interest.

The attached analysis examines (1) the efforts of competing resorts and hotels and (2) past successes and failures of the resort's marketing programs.

The objective is to attract new and former convention and general public guests to the revitalized and attractive Unnamed Resort.

Situation Analysis

The Negatives:

In the almost 20 years of operation of the resort, several factors contributed to its negative image in the industry and in the community, including:

- Eight changes in Managing Directors and recurring manager firings in critical areas like sales and F&B.

- An employee turnover of more than 7,000 in 20 years.

- Continually changing resort policies as to community use of the facilities.

- Internal operational problems re telephone operator response time, 800 number failure, training.

- Poor condition of meeting and some guest rooms.

- Poor cleanliness of hotel (low maid pay is a factor).

- Inconsistent advertising re special events, holidays, drive-in business, restaurants.

- Poor payment record with vendors.

The resort's commitment to changing each one of these problems for the better provides a solid base for a vigorous marketing and public relations program.

The Positives:

The positive side of the ledger for the resort includes the following:

- Commitment to community, regional and statewide charity, civic and social involvement.

- Seeming stability in the Managing Director's office.

- Naming of a Sales Director with experience and a commitment to the community.

- Massive investment in redecoration and restoration programs.

- Adding facilities such as Nautilus equipment and an ice skating rink.

- Budgeting for major activities and entertainment.

- Budgeting for an aggressive advertising campaign.

Any promotional program or publicity release undertaken for the resort has to rely on factual back-up; we can't rave about the new menus unless they are tried and tested and ready to be fully implemented; we can't do features on the new facilities until the contracts have been signed and target dates make the action a reality; we can't talk about renovation until it is certain.

When the many parts of the new program are in place, like the new menus and specialty cuisine, new facilities, renovations and new holiday packages, then the program can be promoted within a universal theme.

The story must be told in complimentary terms so that the hotel is appealing to all publics of interest.

Recommendations

The Prather Group makes the following recommendations based on intensive discussions with the managing director and the new sales director:

- Form a Marketing Committee to be headed by the public relations consultant and the managing director to provide input and support for an increased effort in advertising, promotion and publicity and to work more closely with the agency of record. The committee should include the director of sales and other key department heads who can contribute.

- Select a new advertising and public relations agency by inviting up to five pre-qualified agencies to give proposal presentations. The resort would benefit from a medium-sized agency where it is one of the stars rather than with the current giant agency where it is an also-ran in total billings.

- Budget enough dollars for an ad campaign that can realize more than a million-dollars in new package bookings over the ensuing three months from conventions as well as attracting families and the general public.

- Prepare holiday packages for the next 12 months with name entertainment and expanded activities and authorize a budget that can advertise and publicize each one according to its potential (see attached examples).

- Trade potentially empty rooms and a limited number of packages for advertising on radio and television stations, as well as to specialty publications such as TV guidebooks, chamber of commerce journals and business journals for print ad space.

- Host civic, charitable and business organizations at discount rates at slow times to build local traffic in the restaurants and entertainment rooms.

- Cross-promote the resort with regional attractions such as Meadowlands Racetrack, Great Adventure and Broadway Shows.

- Host sports promotions involving members of the Knicks, Nets, Rangers, Devils, Giants and Jets to generate publicity and public interest.

- Host local promotions such as antique shows, art shows, talent contests and wine-tasting.

- Hold tennis, golf, boxing and swimming events at the resort.

Theme

Following is a general theme that has many parts that revolve around the core public relations programs for the Unnamed Resort.

The suggested theme is: Unnamed Resort - *OUR 20TH SPRING*

A "20th Spring Package" will be created with emphasis on the newness in decor, facilities, menu, *etc.* This will be advertised and publicized in all media, newspapers, radio, cable-TV, brochures, flyers and direct mail to potential customers.

Promotional Ideas

- Devise radio and cable-TV trade promotions where possible, awarding free 20th anniversary packages as prizes to listeners and/or to the station management team in return for airtime and other promotional consideration.

- Distribute flyers and brochures to cooperating shopping centers offering prizes of resort packages to those submitting winning entries and offer a discount to those not winning a prize. Man a display booth where suitable.

- Promote to convention group booking agents by offering groups a special 20th Spring cocktail party as a free bonus plus other incentives such as return trips at half-price, *etc.*

- Host a giant spring ball for hotel guests and area.

- Do cross-promotions with area attractions.

Publicity Ideas

- Generate feature stories on the '20th Spring' theme to all outlets.

- Release articles on the renovations and expansion to appropriate outlets.

- Release items on the new holiday packages, special menu items, *etc.*

- Place a '20th-Spring' feature article highlighting major improvements and efforts.

- Publicize the new managing director and sales director to the trade publications.

- Host a Spring media/VIP party to launch the program, generate media exposure and promote positive word-of-mouth advertising.

Sample Promotional Material

Charity Donation Letter

To: Chairman Todd Branigan
United Charities

From: Unnamed Resort
Public Relations Office

Dear Chairperson Branigan:

The Unnamed Resort is happy to donate a double room for two good for two weeknights as space permits to be raffled off by your organization, United Charities. The winner of your contest should immediately contact the Reservations Department at 212-555-1212 to arrange for the room according to our room availability. The code number for this prize is X87426Y.

The winner should provide the name of your organization, the code number in this letter, and the winner's name, address and telephone number. Confirmation will be granted on the telephone and by mail. This offer is valid for one year from the date on this letter.

Please forward to my office any copies of publicity connected with this donation, which has an approximate value of $450.00. Good luck to your organization.

(Signature)

Post Mortem

The resort had a great grand reopening celebration, a first-year boost in occupancy of 20 percent, a second year increase of 10 percent and a break-even third year. The resort did not grow again until initiating a new plan five years later. It is important for resorts and hotels to keep facilities up to par or improved and to invest in dynamic new entertainment, food and activities programs, and to let the world know about them!

Public Relations Action Plan
for
Unnamed Stardom Theatre

Mission

The purpose of the Public Relations Action Plan for the Unnamed Stardom Theatre is to help establish the theatre as a major entertainment and performing artist center for the Metropolitan area and region.

The creative marketing, advertising and publicity plans are the product of thorough market research and analysis and are designed to reach all publics of interest in an efficient and cost-effective manner to maximize the return-on-investment.

Methods

Among the methods that will be employed to promote and publicize the theatre are:

- The creation and distribution of promotional materials including brochures, flyers, road signs, incentive pieces, bumper stickers, decals, playbills and other collateral material produced with an eye to theme, color and logo. (See examples attached.)

- Print and broadcast media relations will be multi-faceted with an eye to building and maintaining bridges with all entertainment editors, writers, reviewers and media liaisons.

- Community relations will include establishing rapport with all governing bodies and officials, all businesses, and local residents through service to the area, goodwill involvement with hospitals and charities, and youth.

- Image and reputation building will be dynamic through the use of a high-tech logo and appropriate slogan.

- Direct mail programs will reach out to all potential individuals and groups for one-time or seasonal ticket purchases. This will be coordinated with the Group Sales Department.

- Publicity will include writing and placing pre-opening articles with photos, arranging interviews, suggesting coverage by the media, planting items with columnists, working with the agents of the stars, and lining up television and radio show appearances for the stars.

- A gala grand opening of major proportions will be planned for the week of the grand opening.

- A complete first-class media kit will be prepared in advance of the opening and updated regularly.

- Creative programs such as talent shows will identify Stardom Theatre as a major showcase for new talent.

PRE-OPENING PROGRAM:

Announcement - Initial Major Exposure

Hold a pre-grand-opening media and VIP party at the Holiday Resorts Hotel, followed by a theatre tour.

Book a major star booked for a future show to be general host or hostess of the festivities.

Present a pair of tickets for opening night to qualified media and invited VIPs.

Distribute press kit with articles about the theatre and its upcoming schedule of stars.

Service news release(s) and media kit to all media not in attendance (simultaneous).

Present photos from reconstruction through the upcoming grand-re-opening.

Promote the laser-light show, the amateur comedy competition and other creative endeavors.

Release series of articles and photos on upcoming shows and activities at the theatre.

Build a media kit with appropriate articles, fact sheets, photos and schedules.

Building Bridges

Contact media to learn the best method of obtaining publicity from each writer, columnist, editor, reporter, interviewer, *etc.* See attached list.

Contact stars to remind them to mention the new theatre on any television, radio or newspaper interviews they do.

Contact program directors and talent coordinators to book stars or theatre management to discuss the exciting new entertainment venue.

Invite area elected officials and civic leaders to a pre-opening tour and luncheon at the theatre.

Collateral Material

Bumper stickers, decals, flyers and posters will be delivered in two days.

Brochures, playbills and directional maps are in storeroom.

Sales kit for Group Sales Department is on hand in quantity.

Artwork for billboards approved and ready for production and mounting (14 boards).

The Public Relations Team

Overseeing of the Public Relations office will be by Jack Prather with Pamela Ludlam serving as the PR assistant based at the theatre.

Janene Kurtzow, the on-site secretary, will be responsible for arranging appointments and tours, print distribution production and general office work.

The schedules of all concerned will be worked so someone is in the PR office during standard business hours Monday-Friday and from 10 a.m. through show times on weekends.

A photographer is on retainer and available for assignments from the PR office, including for publicity shots upon media request, to cover the openings, and to supply artwork for advertising and printed material.

Community Relations

The Prather Group is posting signs and placing flyers within area restaurants and retail businesses in return for tickets or discounts.

The PG is distributing tickets to charitable and civic organizations for joint promotions.

The PG is working with Group Sales to provide deep discounts to school and senior groups.

The PG is discussing scholarship donations to performing arts students at area colleges and universities.

Creative Programming

A "New Talent Series" of shows has been approved by Stardom Theatre management team and will begin three months after grand-opening week. It has been designed to create and sustain the Stardom Theatre as a new force in entertainment on the East Coast.

It features a weekly show at Stardom Theatre on (available) Monday nights, including four new acts. The four shows would each be up to 45 minutes in length beginning at 7 p.m. and on the hour through 11 p.m.

Payment for each act would be at the union minimum and each act would need its own lighting, sound and staging technicians under the direction of the theatre manager.

The ticket charge for each show is $20 with no discounts or group rates. One dollar from each ticket sale will go into a general scholarship fund for performing artists.

Certain shows will be competitions and ballots will be provided to spectators. The winning act of the night will be rebooked at union minimum as an opening act for a headliner and will be the subject of a news release and photo to area media.

Stardom Theatrical Museum

Hundreds of known performing artists have been invited to place their memorabilia and old/new photos and posters in the theatrical museum at Stardom Theatre currently under construction in the lower level. Once finished, this will be highly publicized and promoted and will be a great value to the theatre's draw and reputation.

The museum will display or feature:

- Newspaper and magazine reviews from noted performances of yesteryear, currently being acquired from appropriate publications for framing and mounting

- Old show bills are being acquired from venues in New York, Las Vegas and other major areas for framing and mounting

- Show-business memorabilia collectors are being invited to contribute materials-with credit

- Reviews of Stardom Theatre shows will be framed and hung as they are received (at the entrance to the museum)

- Puppet and magic shows for school groups and families

- Star photograph signings

- Private fundraising parties for civic and charitable groups

- Space for school group seminars and talks with professional staff

The First-Quarter Budget:

Media - $80,000
Includes print and broadcast outlets

Signing - $20,000
Includes road signs and on-site signs

Billboards - $25,000
Includes highway signs and bus stop sign

Collateral Materials - $75,000
Includes brochures, flyers, buttons, playbills

TOTAL FIRST-QUARTER BUDGET: $200,000   (Detailed budgets attached.)

8. for a Community Hospital

Strategic Public Relations Action Plan
for
Unnamed Memorial Hospital

Overview

This Preliminary Strategic Public Relations Action plan requested by Unnamed Memorial Hospital is designed to publicize and promote the hospital and its Foundation, Outreach Centers, and medical and professional staffs to all publics of interest in the greater Northwestern New Jersey marketplace.

These publics will include potential and past patients, the media, civic and political leaders, and those boards, organizations and personnel that have a stake in the welfare of the hospital.

Implementation

The Prather Strategic Public Relations Group will partner with the designated executives and support personnel at the hospital and its various entities as needed to fulfill the missions.

As the professional public relations arm of the hospital, The Prather Group will provide executive account management services through its offices in Newton and Sparta and at the hospital for important activities. Prather will also place and manage a qualified public relations representative approved by the hospital on-site for a minimum of 20 hours per week.

Prather will provide easy to-follow forms for information collection, and will report on all activities on a regular basis to the designated representatives of the hospital.

Mission

The Prather Group public relations team will provide ongoing consultation and management support assistance to the hospital to fulfill missions that will include but not be limited to:

- Obtaining positive and extensive print and broadcast media coverage.

- Cultivating and maintaining a strong media relations program.

- Assisting in community activities and programs.

- Providing creative input and support for new and existing activities and programs.

- Providing crisis-problem communications management and developing a rapid-response plan of action.

- Developing and implementing short and long-term PR plans for specific projects and events.

- Providing writing assistance for newsletters, speeches and other communications.

- Developing an active hospital 'Speakers Bureau'.

- Positioning the hospital appropriately at healthcare industry seminars and exhibitions.

- Associating the hospital with the educational community, including state and community colleges, universities and secondary schools in the coverage area.

Publicity

Prather will write, re-write or edit and attempt to place media releases in full cooperation with the hospital marketing and public relations internal teams.

All materials that are disseminated to the media, as well as other public relations printed materials, will be approved in advance by the hospital prior to release.

Media publicity program will include but not be limited to:

- **Standard News Articles and Items.**

    These articles and news blurbs will report news and information about the hospital executives and management staff, resources and facilities, special events and activities, etc.

- **Feature Articles and Case Histories.**

    This material would be include human-interest articles about noteworthy accomplishments by and for the hospital staff of professionals, its involvement in the community, new technology and resources, events and activities, etc. Prather would work with the media to write the article or craft and submit it to the appropriate outlet, and arrange for the photos and other artwork to accompany the submission.

- **By-Lined Articles.**

    Key hospital professionals would be selected to author appropriate by-lined articles of importance of interest to target markets in concert with The Prather Group. Prather would first pitch and then submit the articles and appropriate artwork (photo) for publication to the appropriate magazine or newspaper. The pieces would be informational within the expertise of the authors. They could be formatted as opinion or op-ed pieces about notable topics within the healthcare industry.

- **Interviews and Commentaries**

    Key hospital executives or medical professionals will be presented ('pitched') to select media editors, reporters and on-air broadcasters as ideal spokespersons (experts) on healthcare or medical industry topics. The objective is for the media to contact the hospital through Prather for interviews, information and quotes on specific healthcare or medical topic whenever opportunities arise. This will include the submission of cover letters, resumes and photos of spokespersons to the media.

- **Placement**

  Prather will attempt to place materials with all daily and weekly newspapers, appropriate magazines, and radio and cable television outlets within the target market area, and selectively to healthcare industry publications that are important to the hospital and its professionals. Placement will include an advance pitch or query, followed by submissions with deadlines and standards set by the media outlets.

  Note: Clips and reports of media successes will be submitted periodically to the hospital.

Projects and Events

The Prather Group recommends that UMH become involved or continue to be involved with the following area projects and events during the coming year.

Prather will provide specific public relations support, including media releases and mini-plans, as requested for the events that include but are not limited to:

- County Hospital Week
- The Annual New Jersey State Fair
- The Annual Economic Development Day
- Community education/benefit programs
- Various Municipal Days in the coverage area
- Outreach Centers activities or promotions
- Special events and activities
- Seminars and exhibits
- The Annual County College Health Fair
- Internal employee events
- Hospital Board events
- Foundation Board events

Procedures

Upon signing the attached agreement and scope-of-services memorandum, a series of internal meetings and/or a retreat to determine the final goals and detailed budgets for implementation of the public relations programs will be conducted. The final strategic plan will be meshed within the overall marketing plan to create synergy and to maximize the return-on-investment (ROI).

Attached are the specific budget recommendations, lists of media outlets to pursue for advertising and publicity, and the company resume.

9. for a Financial Counseling Group.

Preliminary Public Relations Proposal
for
Unnamed Private Client Group

Overview

This Preliminary Public Relations Proposal is designed to precede an action plan that will enhance the exposure, credibility and acceptance of the Unnamed Private Client Group to its potential clients of interest within target markets, as well as to generally promote the executives of UPCG

Objectives

The goals and objectives are to position the firm as the leading financial resource in the area and thereby increase its customer base and firm up the retention and expansion of existing clients in a cost-effective manner.

Plans

The final public relations plan will be designed to:

- Publicize each member of the executive team individually
- Increase the client base through newspaper and radio advertising
- Enhance retention and growth of clients through seminars and promotions
- Build goodwill in the communities of service through civic participation by firm members
- Establish the executive team as good citizens through college sponsorships
- Promote each new financial product with a news release and ads

Target Markets

The final plan will be designed to reach potential, past and current clients, including business owners and wealthy individual within the target markets of Sussex County and appropriate portions of Pike and Orange Counties in Pennsylvania and New York, respectively.

Procedures

All publicity, advertising or written/verbal communications on behalf of the Private Client Group will be accomplished in a highly professional, dignified and confidential manner.

Advance approval of all activities on the firm's behalf and subsequent reporting of results will be standard operating procedure.

The final action plan will be reviewed and approved by the executive team prior to implementation.

Techniques

Techniques for positioning the company and its key executives as stakeholders in the community and the leading consultants in the area will include:

1. Recommending and helping to fulfill personal affiliations for executives in key civic and business organizations, such as Rotary, local chambers of commerce, key not-for-profits.

2. Recommending participation, sponsorships or contributions for certain important events, such as exhibitions, shows, seminars, the County Farm and Horse Show, *etc.*

3. Recommending and cultivating educational connections, such as with Sussex County Community College and the high school Vocational Center.

4. Writing, re-writing and servicing news items, feature stores and by-lined opinion pieces to The New Jersey Herald, the Independent Group, the Star Ledger and the Daily Record.

5. "Pitching" an interview with the appropriate executive about cutting-edge financial investment issues on the Sussex County Lines cable television show on Channel 8, on WMBC and on Comcast Cable-TV.

6. Writing a personalized monthly company newsletter insert or bulletin for targeted direct mail, hand-out at seminars and shows, and for existing and potential clients.

7. Recommending an advertising theme and placement schedule for area media.

8. Crisis-problem management and counsel.

9. General public relations consulting.

10. Communications.

Note: The Prather Group will also consult with UPCG on developing appropriate contacts from among its roster of clients in a *quid quo pro* arrangement.

The Budget

Development of this proposal into a final action plan will begin upon agreement to proceed between The Prather Group and the Unnamed Private Client Group. Recommendations attached.

10. for a Pet Care Company

Preliminary and Flexible Public Relations Plan
for
Unnamed Pet Care Company

Overview

This preliminary and flexible public relations plan for Unnamed Pet Care Company will be followed by a detailed and comprehensive final plan upon agreement to proceed aimed at fulfilling the mission of boosting awareness and therefore sales of the myriad products and services offered by the company.

The Objectives

Twin elements of the plan are to launch an ongoing publicity campaign and to introduce a dynamic themed promotional campaign with mutual goals of increasing sales by 20 percent or more in year one and by that or more in subsequent years.

The Targets

The main thrust will be to create, develop and implement programs that will reach that will reach:

- Pet owners (consumers)
- Veterinarians
- Pet-care professionals
- Vendors of products and services
- Shelters
- Veterinary Schools
- Animal Welfare Organizations
- Health Officials
- Game Wardens

Publicity

The publicity and promotion efforts will be designed to inform and influence all concerned to the

"Comprehensive Membership Savings Program"

Publicity will be prepared and serviced to media outlets and industry journals that effectively reach and are read by important publics, including: veterinarians, animal hospital administrators and owners, chain or large pet shops, pet food and product suppliers, kennel owners, animal trainers, pet groomers, dog walkers, pet sitters, pet photographers, *etc.*

Factual articles will be prepared and regularly serviced about the company and its various products, services and personnel.

Feature articles will be developed about the company history and innovations, and by-lined articles about pet safety and care.

Other editorial matter will be Op-Ed pieces and letters-to-the-editors that will provide the company view in response to published articles re key issues of concern to pet owners and providers.

Publicity will also be gained through relatively cost-free Public Service Announcements (PSA's) on radio or cable television regarding pet safety and care.

Media Relations

A Media Kit will provide all appropriate media members with information about the company, its personnel, its products and services. It will be mailed to the media when completed and handed out at company events or activities.

Pitches will be made to editors and each publication's guidelines and deadlines will be observed.

Special Promotion Idea

A major new promotional campaign has been designed for consideration. It centers on the suggested new *Spokesdog'* – PAL.

An artist's rendition of PAL, a Labrador retriever, and several suggested advertising, promotional and brochure uses of PAL are attached.

The mascot would promote a dynamic new corporate identity in a variety of creative ways and enliven the overall image.

The Labrador is a breed of dog that is universally loved and, because of its size and general public acceptance also represents protection and care.

Marketing Strategies for PAL

PAL would be designed as a lifelike cartoon character with appealing eyes and an expressive and sympathetic face, in other words "child friendly".

PAL's image would be crafted into a mascot costume that could be comfortably transported for models to wear at appropriate pet shows, trade shows, and school events, *etc.*

PAL would be the model for a hand-puppet, or stuffed animal to be given away or sold at pet stores or veterinary offices, *etc.*

PAL would be utilized as the centerpiece of promotional campaigns

PAL's image would be added where appropriate to advertising and printed materials

PAL would serve as the *spokesdog* when and where appropriate

NOTE: see artist's preliminary rendering of PAL.

Reputation and image enhancement of PAL will be garnered through participation in various industry trade shows and exhibitions, involvement at pet shows and events, cooperative promotional campaigns with other product and services companies, and sponsorship of contests such as 'cute pet photos' or essays, *etc.*

Newsletter

A newsletter will be created (see sample attached) to provide comprehensive news and views about the company, the pet industries, *etc.* It will be serviced to all major publics of interest.

Budgets

Preliminary budgets for public relations fees, advertising projections, printed materials are attached.

Also attached are the development fees for PAL, the *spokesdog,* including for final artist's renderings and costume design and production. Additional costs would be for the human inside the mascot costume.

PR Thought: *Proactive PR is creating, reactive is implementing.*

Section Two

Chapter One

Publicity and Journalism

1. Publicity: The Cornerstone of PR

The cornerstone of any public relations program is publicity - that relatively free *entree* into newspapers and trade publications or onto radio and television shows. It is imperative that PR practitioners understand the many opportunities presented via publicity and maintain high standards as they ply their trade in that highly competitive world. This section first discusses publicity in general and then product publicity.

Across-the-board publicity guidelines include the following tasks for the practitioner:

1) Generating and submitting publicity material that is newsworthy and timely.

2) Producing and placing feature material that is interesting and publishable.

3) Following high journalistic standards of accuracy and integrity.

4) Respecting the publishing guidelines of each publication or broadcast outlet.

5) Protecting the proprietary interests and confidentiality of the client or employer.

Publicity can be attained for an event or activity in any of four ways:

1) Servicing an approved article and artwork in a timely manner to appropriate editors via mail, e-mail, fax or PR wire service.

2) Writing a detailed pitch letter to an appropriate editor suggesting why the outlet should consider interviewing or quoting a key executive, covering an event or activity, or accepting an enclosed news or feature article.

3) Writing a query letter that proposes an article to an editor and then following the guidelines if successful.

4) Conducting a media conference to make an announcement about personnel or new product, service, program or activity with scripted remarks from a spokesperson, a question-and-answer session, and a media kit handout containing a news or feature article, artwork, fact sheet, bios and contact information.

The media retains three options regarding publicity regardless of the delivery system: acceptance, consideration or rejection. The better the PR practitioner's media relations skills, the better chance there is of gaining a positive response from a usually busy and almost always cynical print editor or broadcast director.

Only rarely should the PR practitioner call a media conference to dramatically 'get the story out'. If the mission of the conference is solely to promote a positive development, then there are few down sides to consider. However, if the conference is called to deal with a crisis or problem, then it can become a double-edged sword unless all involved are thoroughly prepped to deal with potentially tough questions.

The objective of PR is always to position the client or employer in the best possible light without misleading or misinforming anyone at anytime about anything - especially the media! (Note: it is better to leave a question unanswered than to tell an untruth! "We'll get back to you" is an acceptable response to tough questions, but then the practitioner must do exactly that.)

Important to the process is the review of the publishing guidelines and editorial calendars that are provided free upon request by all legitimate outlets. Publicity releases can then be targeted for *themed* editions of publications or for specific broadcast programs. The material must be crafted with journalism's famed Five W's: Who? What? Where? When? Why? and sometimes How?

It is usually wise to give all interested media outlets an equal opportunity for coverage so they won't be scooped. However, serving an *exclusive* to one important media outlet is also appropriate. The key to success is to understand and select the best option.

Publicity is the voice of the client or employer – it should be expressed wisely.

2. Journalism and Public Relations

In the dark ages, public relations practitioners primarily emerged from a pool of reporters and editors who were mainly interested in earning more money. These men and women had honed their skills at writing, editing and reporting in journalism school and on the job, bringing those valuable assets into the world of PR.

In the last quarter of the 20th century, public relations evolved into a disciplined and respected profession with many facets, with publicity remaining as one of its cornerstones.

In this the 21st century, many colleges and university offer a public relations major and graduates are commonly hired directly into PR positions without first earning their journalism spurs with a newspaper, magazine or local radio station.

PR practitioners who have been taught the basics of public relations but who lack internal media experience must apply special efforts to learn the culture of the newsroom and editorial boards. They must study textbooks and review publications to learn how the pros do it. They must understand that their mission is to create and place articles and briefs, request coverage in a newsworthy and professional fashion, suggest valid column and editorial ideas to writers and editors, conduct meaningful media conferences and more, all to gain positive ink or broadcast exposure for their company or organization. Understanding the relentless demands of reporting, writing and editing that journalists face will help the PR practitioner immensely.

Any PR practitioner can learn how to produce a news or feature release in format and then service it to the media. What is more difficult is writing a *newsworthy* piece in *pyramid style* of importance using the previously discussed and essential *five-w's:* who, what, when, where and why, and sometimes how?

The PR *strategist* will cultivate relationships with reporters and editors by being reliable and trustworthy.

The practitioner can earn coveted *access* by following specific predicates: learning in advance what types of articles or story ideas editors or broadcasters want, providing only newsworthy material, following publication or broadcast standards, adhering to deadlines, not becoming a pest and over-reaching, correcting the record in a courteous and professional manner whenever incorrect information is printed or aired, remaining accessible to the media, and bonding in friendship with media members within professional limits.

Practitioners can also cultivate members of the media by visiting a newsroom by appointment to learn about coverage policies and editors by category, or by inviting a key editor or broadcaster to lunch. (Don't worry, to avoid conflicts of interest, most journalists will insist on lunch being Dutch Treat if they accept the invitation.)

Certainly there is much more to the science of public relations that will benefit a business or organization than simply gaining publicity and solidifying media relations. It is equally important for the public relations strategist to help develop communications that will reach and influence all publics or interest, provide common sense solutions to difficult problems and crises, devise dynamic methods to improve a reputation or image, provide a creative boost to sales and retention, lend support to marketing and advertising programs, participate on the management team and share in decision-making.

In evaluating the public relations practitioner, all concerned will view her or his knowledge of communications and journalism as major assets.

3. Media Relations

The importance of developing good media relations to the public relations professional, and by extension to his or her client or employer, cannot be overstated!

Where do you begin and how do you get there? The PR practitioner must first understand the standards and constraints inherent to the media relations process before attempting to cultivate and bond with inherently cynical members of the Fourth Estate (journalism to the unitiated).

The initial proactive effort with the media should be to establish *trust and credibility*, the benchmarks of any successful business relationship. From that solid base will come *access*, and that will vastly increase opportunities for the publicity to find 'legs'.

Appropriate media relations activities should include these elements:

1. Each submission, pitch or query letter should be made in a professional manner to the appropriate print editor or broadcast news or assignment director,

2. There are no guarantees - nor should there be - for the publishing or airing of an article based on a professional relationship, personal friendship or any factor but news or feature worthiness as decided by the media,

3. The PR practitioner should rely on the value of the material to earn its way into print or onto the radio or television airwaves,

4. Material can be serviced either through a carefully considered exclusive with an appropriate and significant outlet or en masse to all outlets of interest,

5. The public relations practitioner should always avoid becoming a pest who besieges print editors or broadcast directors with often counter-productive and repetitive calls, faxes, mail or third-party pressure,

6. The practitioner should request and follow the publishing or broadcasting guidelines provided by all legitimate media outlets, the list of themes for specific newspaper or magazine issues, the list of editors or directors by title, and the advertising kit,

7. It is important to maintain records of successes and failures of publicity attempts with the media, and then to figure out what went right and what went wrong so the efforts can be improved in the future,

8. Asking broadcast directors, or print editors, reporters and columnists, in advance what types of material they consider suitable for airing or publication and then following their leads can bolster Media relationships,

9. The practitioner can establish a client or employer as 'the expert' for the media to contact for quotes or analysis on a particular issue or industry matter through a cover letter that states the case and a review of qualifications, plus contact information,

10. The most important result of a good media relations effort is for the practitioner to earn access to editors and directors who are in a position to render positive editorial judgment on a submission or request, vastly increasing his or her chances for success.

4. Planning Publicity

The Publicity Planning Calendar can serve as an effective tool to record the wide variety of information and ideas that can be turned into articles, feature stories, case histories or news blurbs by the public relations practitioner on behalf of his or her employer or client.

Creativity and journalistic skills are the keys to producing a meaningful piece, public relations savvy is the key to 'pitching' the material and getting it published, and diligence is the key to getting the material in the hands of the editors at the publications of interest.

The public relations practitioner can maximize the quest for and success of a publicity campaign by following the guidelines, learning from each effort, and establishing solid relationships (bonding) with the media. After the various opportunities are discerned and the methods are fully understood, the PR practitioner will begin to develop an intuitive sense about conceiving, developing and placing publicity of all types. And once the relationships with the media are cemented and the PR practitioner is viewed as a source for publishable material, editors will gladly listen to a pitch and/or evaluate the material.

Publicity serves a multitude of purposes, but ultimately the goal is to increase volume of sales and profits and to stimulate both short and long-term return-on-investment (ROI) of PR marketing dollars. An effective and cost-effective publicity program can play an important role in implementing or furthering the goals of a company or organization.

The simple exercise of compiling pertinent information will help shape the program and lead to the creation and placement of a variety of publicity material. The successful publicity program will create a valuable world of exposure within target markets and beyond.

The publicity can take the form of a news release or item submitted to various industry trade journals or consumer publications, a full-length illustrated feature article or case history targeted to an specific important trade publication, a management opinion column for the op-ed pages of a daily newspaper, a news 'blurb' . . . the possibilities are great.

Publicity can fall within many news or feature categories such as:
1. Company or organization policy, methodology, changes,
2. Personnel promotions, additions, continuing education,
3. New products, services, programs,
4. Events and activities,
5. Board and shareholder news,
6. Sales and revenue reports,
7. Management news and opinion.
8. Feature articles

The news, feature material or brief, should be serviced to all appropriate venues of traditional print and broadcast media. The media list should also include specialty publications for the industry or organization of interest, local business publications, *et al.* Publicity opportunities can be implemented through teamwork and solid communications between the business or organization and the PR practitioner. (Read in depth about publicity in the Basic PR Section.)

5. *The Query Letter*

The best method to get an article published is through a carefully crafted query letter from the PR practitioner to the appropriate editor of a specific publication that demonstrates its potential feature and news value to readers.

The query will request that the editor consider an article the practitioner will craft and submit within the editorial standards and deadlines of the publication.

The letter must highlight the proposed article's main news or feature 'peg', provide substantive credibility to the person(s) to be quoted in the article, and outline the salient points that will make it interesting and worthy of consideration. It should be concise, no more than one page.

This is a strong forum to *sell* the idea of an article; then it is up to the practitioner to execute an acceptable-plus news, feature or case history article.

The submission would of course be an exclusive, and this makes it even more attractive than an unsolicited submission that may be going to competitors.

Remember, most editors are cracks shot when it comes to pitching unsolicited material – queries or articles – into the round file, so do your work well on both scores.

Following is a sample query letter. It was directed to a daily newspaper, proposing acceptance of an article about a new adolescent drug and alcohol treatment program at Sunrise House, a Prather Group client. It worked and the article was accepted and published.

Sample Query Letter:

(on letterhead)

April 12, 2002

Dave Brown
Managing Editor
The New Jersey Herald

Dear Dave:

Do New Jersey Herald readers know that tranquil and rural Sussex County has a serious and escalating drug and alcohol problem among its teenage population?

The enclosed statistics compiled by the Sussex County Council on Drug and Alcohol Abuse (SCADA) and the State of New Jersey prove that this dangerous situation exists.

A major response and solution to the problem has been the new Sunrise House Alcohol and Drug Rehabilitation Center in Lafayette adolescent inpatient program that began operations in 2000. Sunrise House began a successful outpatient program the year before.

The management and professional staff have created a scenario that can help save our youth from the ravages or alcohol and drug abuse.

Please consider accepting an article about the first year of the inpatient program. It would outline the problem of adolescent alcohol and drug abuse, quote key involved professionals and outline the solutions offered through Sunrise House programs.

Sunrise House will also make available 'graduates' of the program who volunteer to go public with their hart-rending and uplifting stories.

This article would provide valuable information and be interesting to your readers of any age.

As a former journalist, I am prepared to write this article and submit it exclusively to you for publication in The Herald, along with appropriate photographs. Or, I will be happy to assist your reporter and photographer in developing an appropriate piece.

Of course, I will follow your editorial standards and deadlines in either case.

You will be invited to the media conference scheduled at the one-year anniversary celebration next month.

I will contact you regarding your acceptance of the article later this week, or call me.

Sincerely,

Jack Prather
for Sunrise House Foundation

(Note: The coverage turned out to be extensive.)

6. *The Pitch Letter*

A concise and appealing pitch letter can get a newspaper or magazine editor to assign a reporter or columnist to do a story or interview of your client or employer, or convince a broadcast outlet to place him/her on an interview or discussion show or to at least arrange an audition.

Positioning your client or employer as an expert with all of its potential exposure and goodwill can be Herculean task. Not a lot of work, just difficult to accomplish.

The pitch scenario would include providing background information and arranging photos, if requested, about an executive who would then serve as an expert analyst or commentator to a publication. He/she would be available for commentary, information and analysis on a business, product or service specialty when called upon by an editor, reporter or columnist.

For television or radio the public relations practitioner would school the executive on how to prepare for an on-air appearance including demeanor, tone and dress.

Next, they would need to drill him or her with potential questions and help research the facts for the answers.

Good quotes and information to a media outlet will cement the niche and provide excellent exposure, even in negative situations as long as the truth is well told by the executive.

The PR practitioner should encourage the client or executive to take a proactive role and call the publication or broadcast outlet when appropriate to stimulate the relationship and demonstrate accessibility. The returns in exposure and goodwill for the client or employer will be worth it.

Sample Pitch Letter:

(usual letterhead and address/date info)

Dear

James Alexander Corporation, a leading producer of plastic ampoules for the health industry, has made a major breakthrough in the industry – crushable and safe glass dispensers that will revolutionize the medicine delivery systems available to consumers in America and abroad.

The president and developer of this innovative glass ampoule product (sample enclosed) to be announced next month at a media conference during the packaging exhibition in Atlantic City is highly active in women's business organizations and community service within New Jersey.

As your magazines are the leading publications for medical and pharmaceutical over-the-counter products, we would like to invite you or an appropriate reporter to visit James Alexander for a tour of the facility, an interview with our key engineer, and a demonstration of our product line.

Photography is permissible, of course, but we have an assortment of professionally produced photographs and slides on disc or hard copy that you may opt to select.

This visit would prepare your magazines for an exclusive in-depth analysis of the product that will be unveiled at the media conference. This would enable you to prepare it for immediate publication along with material that will be jointly released to all media at the product-launch conference. We would be happy to arrange for your transportation and overnight accommodations upon your request.

I will call you to schedule an appointment or further discuss the new glass products from JAC.

(sign off)

7. Understanding Libel

Public relations practitioners must and should abide by industry and journalistic standards when they write, speak or print words on behalf of a person, company or organization. This adherence to standards not only provides legal and ethical protection, it is the right thing to do.

PR generalists and strategists consistently generate statements for others through publicity, printed materials, electronic messaging, speeches, advertising, material for broadcast interviews or discussion shows, *et al*. This creates vulnerability to civil action for any mistakes or statements that are deemed to have malicious intent.

The bottom line is: the reckless misuse of words can prove costly and damaging in civil court.

The law guarantees free speech and a free press but there are caveats. PR practitioners must understand the limitations imposed by libel law in order to avoid legal action by a defamed party.

By definition, libel is: "A written or oral defamatory statement or representation that conveys an unjustly unfavorable impression."

Libel can be contained in words, photographs, illustrations or cartoons that expose a person to ill will or opinion, shame, disgrace or financial loss.

The single defense to a civil action for libel is provable truth.

Privilege provides two other defenses: absolute, which is contained in judicial, legislative and official public proceedings and in most public records and qualified, which pertains to the media handling of material.   Journalists must understand these defenses in depth.

A newsperson can lose privilege if the reporting is in error, or if malice on the part of the media outlet can be proven.   The protection for journalists, however, is fairly substantial providing the material printed is fair and accurate.

There is no protection for those who repeat or reprint a libelous statement or article even though the quote(s) are verbatim and are attributed to a published source.

Fair comment and critique are inherent rights of journalists and, it follows, for pieces submitted by public relations professionals but it is important to remember that maliciousness can be considered libelous in commentary and the key elements that should shape any writing are honesty, fairness and accuracy.

8. Two Guiding Documents

Public relations practitioners who correctly view their discipline as a profession like a lawyer or CPA will take the time to read and understand two previously discussed documents that are essential to conducting business in this highly litigious society. We refer to them again because of their importance to PR professionals as they place publicity, news and feature articles.

They are:

1) The Public Relations Society of America's "Declaration of Principles and Code of Professional Standards for the Practice of Public Relations"
   and
2) The American Society of Newspaper Editors' "A Statement of Principles".

Both of these documents appear at the end of this book in their entirety.

As stated earlier, public relations practitioners would be wise to read, analyze and digest the many components of each of these two guiding lights in the world of PR and communications.

9. Sample Release

Media releases can be serviced in a variety of methods, including mail, fax, modem or wire service, making it relatively simple to get appropriate material in front of the right editors. However, the format, style and content of the release must be up to standards as follows:

- The document should be labeled as a news or feature release and have proper formatting, including one-inch margins and double-spacing.

- It should be produced on an appropriate masthead or letterhead with the name, title and telephone number of the sender.

- The suggested headline should capture the essence of the article.

- The lead paragraph(s) should contain the five W's of who, what, when, where and why and sometimes the often forgot how?

- A concluding symbol of -30- or -end- should be centered at the bottom of the material.

Following is a sample news release:

The Unnamed Public Relations Company

News Release: **Further Information:**

For Immediate Publication   John J. Jones, PRC Director

Mailed February 15, 2002   212-555-1212

(The release is on the next page.)

Local Executive Smarth Wins Environmental Leadership Award

(who)
Birchwood, N.Y. – President and CEO Jonathon B. Smarth of the Berman

Industrial Waste Disposal Corporation located in Birchwood, N.Y. was presented
(what)   *(why)*
the first annual Environmental Leadership Award for his efforts to clean-up toxic
waste water in New York State by the United States Private Industry Association
(where)   *(when)*
in Washington, D.C. on Tuesday night.

(how)   *(quote)*

"I accept this recognition on behalf of our 550 Berman employees," Smart said in

accepting the silver chalice, the award given by Association President Anthony Sharp.

(etc.)

-end-

10. The Case History Article

An effective method for the PR professional to gain exposure and credibility for a client or employer is to produce a case history article that will appear in an important magazine, trade publication or newspaper.

The case history article would chronicle methods used by that client or employer to successfully solve a problem or fill a need for an important customer.

The proposed case history article and appropriate artwork must first be pitched to the appropriate editor of an important outlet through a telephone call and/or brief outline. Upon acceptance of the article in advance by the editor, the final presentation and submission of the article and artwork by the PR pro must be according to the standards and deadlines set by the publication.

The public relations practitioner will generally follow these guidelines in writing a case history article that will demonstrate in detail how he or she solved a problem or filled a need for a customer or client:

1) Chronicle the initial problem/need of the customer.

2) Report the solutions that were designed to solve the problem or fill the need.

3) Define the results that were attained by the client/employer for the customer.

The article should include quotes from both the PR pro's client or employer *and* the customer whose problem was solved or need was met, as well as accurate and meaningful statistics and/or charts. All involved must provide access to information and accurate material to the PR pro. organization, and will help to position it as an industry leader within its marketplace.

This type of publicity exposure will enhance the reputation and image of the company. To proceed with a case history, the company or organization need only complete the confidential Case History Information form included in this kit. Additional information and quotes will then be obtained from appropriate sources within the executive and management networks. High quality photographs or illustrations appropriate to the article will also be produced.

The PR consultant or employee will submit a draft of the article for approval from all concerned *prior* to servicing the final article to the media of choice according to agreed-upon deadlines, After the article is published, it can then be reprinted for insertion into sales portfolios and media kits, be included in target mailings to existing and potential clients and posted for all to see.

Note: The information must remain confidential until all concerned approve the final draft and it is published.

11. *Local Radio and Cable TV*

Local radio and cable television stations feature news, discussion and interview programs that are ideal for key representatives of businesses and organizations to tout their community involvements, expertise and opinions.

Companies, organizations and entrepreneurs have a duty to serve the community in charitable and civic causes. That is the right thing to do and brings goodwill and positive imaging in return. Broadcast outlets that service those areas with commercial programs have a responsibility to open the airwaves to help promote legitimate causes and to air the views of decision-makers.

The PR practitioner has the responsibility to get the employer or client on the radio or cable television program. When this happens, virtually everyone benefits: the guest from a business or organization, the broadcast outlet and the PR practitioner who caused it to happen.

It is important for PR practitioners to get to know the names of the assignment editors, hosts and decision-makers at each broadcast media outlet, and then to get to know them individually.

The public relations practitioner should learn the ropes of how to gain airtime for their employers or clients and how to place public service announcements - PSA's - that will effectively promote a non-profit organization or activity. The first steps are to determine who should receive the information and how it can best be presented. Second is to learn the programming schedules and available air times and third is to pursue airtime with valid materials and/or ideas to station directors of public or community services who can help in the process.

For broadcast news and features, PR practitioners should follow these 15 guidelines:

1. Supply copy to the Program Director in advance and on deadline for consideration.

2. Write copy more informally than for a newspaper - an example, use *let's* instead of *let us*.

3. Accept broadcast jargon rewrites of submitted graciously.

4. Insert organization name, address, telephone, e-mail and contact name at top of copy.

5. Triple-space on 8 ½-11-" white paper, 1-side, ample margins, beginning 1/3 from top.

6. Provide concise, clear and correct news and information.

7. Provide background info and phonetic name pronunciation of the guest to the host.

8. Escort the guest to the appearance in ample time for a secure comfort level.

9. For PSA's, allow about 20 spoken words for 10 seconds, 40 words for 20 seconds and approximately 125 words for 60 seconds, slightly more for radio, less for TV.

10. Request PSA's only for appropriate non-commercial purposes.

11. Cooperate with directors and technical staff at all times but help control the content.

12. For TV, insure that written copy is appropriate to visual aids – slides, video or film.

13. Provide one or two slides for a 10-second TV spot, up to three for a 20 and so on.

14. On-TV clothing should be dark or pastel; avoid contrasting patterns and color.

15. Record the appearance and provide dupes to the employer or client.

12. Media Resources

Public Relations practitioners need to plug into media resources that will help them deal with newspaper, magazine and broadcast outlets by supplying names, addresses, telephone and fax numbers and e-mail addresses of editors, columnists and news editors or directors; organizations that will service the media for you for a fee, and clipping services that track the success of your efforts.

These media resources will enable the practitioner to service a news or feature release and to contact the proper media person and will track where and when the press release appeared in print or on the radio or television airwaves. The first portion – the contact information – is inexpensive, merely the purchasing of a book or disc. Clips are provided for a monthly fee plus a cost-per-clip. Wire services are effective but can be expensive.

The practitioner who services a news or feature article, arranges for an interview or quotes, or calls a media conference has invested in money, time and effort on behalf of a client or employer who ultimately ends up with the bill. It is important to see the results of that media investment and to learn if it all worked, both for the PR practitioner who has to justify his or her existence _and_ for the client or employer who will require proof of good results before funding further public relations media programs.

It is penny wise and pound foolish to try to scour the media by buying all of the publications or attempting to track the airwaves during the media push unless the program is of limited scope and easily tracked. There are many more resources than are listed here and you can tap in to them by checking the appropriate directories. There are also many local, state and regional resources for the PR consultant.

Clipping Services and Directories

Allen's Press Clipping Bureau
Tel. 415-392-2353 Fax 415-362-6208
E-mail: jmcc102706@aol.com

Bacon's Information Inc.
Tel. 800-PR-MEDIA Fax 312-922-3126
E-mail: info@bacons.com
Website: www.bacons.com

Burrelle's Information Services
Tel. 800-631-1160 Fax 973-992-7675
E-mail: solutions@burrelles.com
Website: www.burrelles.com

CompetitivEdge
(electronic clipping)
Tel. 860-726-1047 Fax 860-726-1052
E-mail: info@clipresearch.com

eWatch
Tel. 800-482-4220 Fax 800-856-4514
E-mail: ewatchsales@prnewswire.com
Website: www.ewatch.com

inkbd.com
Tel. 866-346-3246
E-mail: info@inkdb.com
Website: www.inkdb.com

Luce Online Inc.
Tel. 800-518-0088 Fax 480-922-3174
E-mail: info@luceonline.com
Website: www.luceonline.com

Luce Press Clippings
Tel. 800-528-8226 Fax 480-834-4884
E-mail: clip@lucepress.com
Website: www.lucepress.com

multivisioninc
Tel. 800-560-0111 Fax 800-966-0280
E-mail: info@multivision.com
Website: www.multivision.com

PR Fulfillment Services

Bacon's Information Inc.
Tel. 800-PR-MEDIA Fax. 312-922-3126
E-mail: info@bacons.com
Website: www.bacons.com

Media Distribution Service
800-MDS-3282 Fax 212-714-9092
In NYC Tel. 212-279-4800
E-mail: services@mdsconnect.com
Website: www.mdsconnect.com

PIMS
866-GET-PIMS Fax 212-244-9603
E-mail: information@pimsinc.com
Website: www.pimsinc.com

Medialink
Tel. 800-843-0677 Fax 212-682-5260
In NYC Tel. 212-682-8300
E-mail: info@medialink.com
Website: www.medialink.com

Orbis Broadcast Group
Tel. 312-942-1199
E-mail: Randy.Seffren@orbisnews.com
www.orbisbroadcastgroup.com

PR Newswire
Tel. 888-776-0942 Fax 800-959-5934
E-mail: information@prnewswire.com
Website: www.prnewswire.com

DWJ Television
Tel. 201-445-1711 Fax 201-445-8352
E-mail: dwjinfo@dfwjtv.com
Website: www.dwjtv.com

Network Broadcast Network
Tel. 800-840-6397 Fax 800-920-6397
Website: www.newsbroadcastnetwork.com

NAPS
Tel. 212-867-9000 Fax 212-867-9010
Website: www.napsinfo.com

Business Wire
(NY)Tel. 800-221-2462
(SF)Tel. 800-227-0845

Feature Photo Service
Tel. 212-944-1060 Fax 212-944-7801
E-mail: editor@featurephoto.com
Website: www.featurephoto.com

Metro Editorial Services
Tel. 212-947-5100 Fax 212-714-9139
E-mail: mes@metrocreativegraphics.com

Note: Public Relations TACTICS of February 2002 announced that U.S.-based public relations practitioners can obtain one free Pocket Media Guide that lists names, addresses and telephone numbers for approximately 700 major United States print and broadcast media from MDS. For complete information on the 36-page palm-size guide: www.mdsconnect.com.

13. *Good Writing A Must!*

Every journalist and every professional public relations practitioner recognizes the value of good writing. It's a good thing because so do editors.

The most important portion of a news or feature release is the lead, that key first paragraph that captures the editor's eye and, hopefully, that of readers.

Next in importance is observance of the legendary 5-W's of who, what, when, where and why, and sometimes how. They should all appear in the lead or first two paragraphs and capsulated in the suggested hed (headline).

News releases must not carry editorial comment *except* when it is attributed to an appropriate subject. The structure of an article is usually by the following standards:

The lead:

All of the key 5-W ingredients should be in, or near, the lead paragraph of a news story. Feature stories have their own 'unique' techniques and literary license extends to format and style. But capturing the reader with important news reporting or vibrant feature article writing is important and will work best with a strong lead.

Sample news article lead:

A first-place trophy and $15,000 prize were presented to Executive Chef Bart Collins of The Carriage House Restaurant of Brighton for his innovative recipes by Blanton Digby, president of the Chef's Association International, at a banquet in the Atlantic City Convention Center last night.

Bert Collier of The Palate Restaurant in New York City, last year's winner, tipped his chef's hat and said of Collins, "Chefs everywhere salute you for your achievements." (Continued . . .)

The breakdown shows all six key elements contained in the two lead paragraphs of the article, including the 'how' question:

What	$15,000 prize and trophy
Who	Executive Chef Bart Collins of The Carriage House Restaurant
When	last night
Where	Convention Center in Atlantic City
Why	for innovative recipes
How	at a Chef's Association Banquet

Quote attribution is important, and it was properly applied for both the comment "Chef's everywhere salute your achievements", with a description: tipped his chef's hat.
The stature of the person being quoted usually dictates where the quote will appear. In the following example, the name obviously would come first:

> President George W. Bush declared "We will never negotiate with terrorists" at a White House media dinner at the Plaza Hotel in New York City last night.

In most cases, the opening paragraph should deal with the person central to an event and not the person who is simply making the announcement. Unfortunately, the latter is the customary practice of PR writers for corporate decision-makers. They consider it good PR to stroke the boss. It may be but it isn't good journalism.

Example of a weak lead:

> Maximilian Mulldowny, supervisor of the Brighton Water Advisory Council, today announced that Robert Teagarden, assistant supervisor for 37 years, has been appointed to head a task force to study pollution in the town reservoir.

Example of a more effective lead:

> Robert Teagarden, supervisor of the Brighton Water Advisory Council for 37 years, will head a task force to study pollution in the town reservoir, Supervisor Maximilian Mulldowny said today.

Example of a better lead:

> Pollution in the town reservoir will be dealt with through a Task Force headed by Robert Teagarden, assistant supervisor of the Brighton Water Advisory Council for 37 years, Supervisor Maximilian Mulldowny said today.

The opening reference to the most important element of the story – the pollution study - makes that lead better focused and structurally superior.

Adjectives can be overused:

There is no better way to lose credibility when you are talking or writing than to overuse adjectives.

Here is an example of an overdone and editorialized lead paragraph that detracts from a good subject for an article:

> An interesting and exciting new way to communicate via radio airwaves is being tried by WRMZ Radio through its new cutting-edge CAV-RX3 Monitor that catches laser beams from the Empire State building and hurtles them into the void of space, then patiently awaits their return three minutes later.

> An innovative method to communicate via radio airwaves is being tested by WRMZ Radio through a new CAV-RX3 Monitor that catches laser beams from the Empire State building, hurtles them into space and awaits their return three minutes later.

Note the use here of the phrase 'innovative method' instead of interesting and exciting (opinion).

Samples of writing:

Economic (tight) writing for releases, feature articles or other types of manuscripts is preferable.

For example:

Poor: The members of the Elks Club attended their annual meeting in Brockton last night.
Better: Elks Club members attended their annual meeting in Brockton last night.
Best: The Brockton Elks Club held its annual meeting last night.

Poor: He decided to keep half of the $1000 prize money he won & donated the rest to charity.
Better: He kept half of the $1000 prize money and donated the rest to charity.
Best: He kept half of the $1,000 prize and donated half to charity.

Poor: The group is scheduled to hold a meeting this evening.
Better: The group is scheduled to meet tonight.
Best: The group will meet tonight.

Poor: Both buses involved in the accident were totally wrecked.
Better: Both buses were totally wrecked in the accident.
Best: Both buses in the accident were totaled.

Poor: The Board of Directors will hold their meeting on Friday night.
Better: The Board of Directors will meet on Friday night.
Best: The Board of Directors will meet Friday night.

Poor: The site of the dedication ceremony is in the park on the corner of Elm and Vine Streets.
Better: The dedication ceremony will be held in the park located at Elm and Vine Streets.
Best: The dedication is scheduled in the park at Hollywood and Vine Streets.

Poor: The awards ceremony lasted for a period of two hours.
Better: The awards ceremony lasted for two hours.
Best: The awards ceremony lasted two hours.

Poor: "Past experience taught me the correct procedure," he said.
Better: "Experience taught me the correct procedure," he said.
Best: "Experience was my teacher," he said.

Poor: The principal was listened to attentively by his students.
Better: The students listened attentively to their principal.
Best: The students listened to their principal.

Poor:	The strike involved only a limited number of workers.
Better:	The strike was limited in the number of workers.
Best:	A limited number of workers went on strike.

Poor:	Busy as bees in heat.
Better:	Busy as bees.
Best:	Busy.

Poor:	"I take great pride in my accomplishment."
Better:	"I'm very proud of my accomplishment."
Best:	"I'm proud of my accomplishment."

Poor:	He is very well qualified to do the job.
Better:	He is qualified to carry out the job.
Best:	He is qualified to do the job.

Tip: Keep your writing simple, concise, lucid and as professional as possible. A good way to practice is to rewrite your leads until you get the knack. Read local and daily newspapers.

A sample news release:

For Immediate Release
Mailed December 12, 2001

For Further Information:
Chief Information Officer
J. J. Perry (800)555-1212

CANCER RESEARCH DELAYS LUDICROUS, SAYS NOBEL PRIZE RESEARCHER

Birch, N.C. - "Delays in cancer research in this country are ludicrous," said Dr. Angus W. Cooper, Nobel Prize winning researcher, to 2,000 American Cancer Society volunteers Friday night in the Forbes University Arena here.

The host Birch ACS Chapter polled the audience and received unanimous support for Dr. Cooper's assessment, Melvin Perlman, executive director of the North Carolina ACS, reported.

Dr. Cooper received standing ovations five times during his 45-minute speech as he documented the rising incidences of cancer of the throat and pancreas in the region and country, and compared it to the rising abuse of tobacco and alcohol. He said, "We must stop abusing our bodies as well as starting to find ways to cure disease." (The rest of the article follows.)

021202   -000-

14. 10 Guidelines For News Releases

1. Prepare the release on the letterhead of the agency or organization that contains the mailing address and telephone number.

2. At the left margin is the information on when the release can be used, immediately or anytime, and the date it was mailed to the media or a select outlet.

3. At the right margin is the name, title, and telephone number of the person preparing the release, or who to contact for additional information.

4. Leave ample margins (at least one inch) on either side and at top and bottom of the release and double-space on 8 1/2" x 11" white paper.

5. In the sample release, an advantageous headline is suggested; an alternative is to leave that space blank so the release copy begins about one-third of the way down the page and the editor has space to write his own headline, if he or she prefers.

6. Begin with the name of the town of origin of the story, as indicated.   Double-space.

7. Make your lead count!   In the preceding sample news release, the lead includes who-what-when-where-why-and-how, all of the basic ingredients, and is readable. It is almost too long but still works. A catchy alternative: "The stalling of cancer research in this country is ludicrous." The next paragraph could explain that startling comment thusly: So said Dr. Angus Cooper, Nobel Prize winning researcher, to 550, _etc._ Leads should be interesting, informative and concise!

8. Credit to the host Birch group, the special interest of J.J. Perry who submitted the story, is gained in the second paragraph, in deference to the lead mention of Dr. Cooper and the statewide volunteers. The story continues in interesting fashion, relying on Dr. Cooper's comments.

9. The release concludes with the Journalists' -30- that means "the end." You can also use -endit-, or ###, or your initials (in this case, JJP). Do not use the words "The End", as some ambitious typesetter or errant scanner is sure to set them into type. Also, the date of preparation is printed to the left of the sign-off (in this case 021202, meaning February 12, 2002).

10. If you have a multi-page release, "slug" the top of each page with a key word and its number in the upper left-hand corner (in this case it would be Nobel Prize-2, Nobel Prize 3, and so on).

Two Bonus Tips:

- Do not break a sentence fragment to the next page regardless of the amount of space involved, and

- At the bottom-center of each page to be continued insert the word 'more'.

15. 10 Publicity Reminders

1. Service via fax, e-mail or mail an edited news or feature release to the appropriate editors or news directors that you have pitched, plus others you think will consider your material.

2. Use standard 81" x 11" sheets of paper, double-spaced with one-inch margins for copy editing convenience by the recipient.

3. Provide source(s) for additional information, including the name and title, address, telephone and fax number, and e-mail address.

4. Send a follow-up release with any corrections or changes clearly indicated when and if necessary and ask that the original release be returned or destroyed.

5. Avoid superlatives, keep the release as brief as possible, with the most important information first - except for exceptions in certain feature stories.

6. Check all facts about the subject and have background material on hand in case an editor or reporter calls. Include a copy of literature with the release, if appropriate.

7. Know and respect the deadlines of weekly newspapers and keep your mailing list up to date. Send your releases addressed to the appropriate editor or reporter.

8. Check published versions against the original release. (This provides a guide to the acceptability of your material and helps train you for future submissions.)

9. Properly identify all persons referred to in the story as to title or status.

10. Properly identify artwork and photos and attach brief captions.

16. 10 Publicity No-No's

1. Do not mislead the media by presenting dated material as news; be 'newsworthy'.

2. Do not overload your release with irrelevant material; stick to the facts.

3. Do not be angry when your material does not get published; ask why.

4. Do not send multiple copies of the same release to the same outlet; once will do.

5. Do not over-promote your organization or business; use only solid material.

6. Do not send carbon copies or use onionskin paper for releases; use plain white paper.

7. Do not ask the media for tear sheets or clips; buy the publication or use a service.

8. Do not use highly technical language unless for a technical publication, write plainly.

9. Do not send material too far in advance of the release date but brief editors it's coming.

10. Do not try to pass something off as an "exclusive" if it isn't; be honest with the media.

Bonus Tip: *Advance and follow-up calls, faxes or e-mail contacts to editors and broadcasters should not conflict with deadlines. Learn the correct timing for every outlet you deal with.*

17. Sample Release for Radio

A news release to radio stations will hopefully be aired as is, so it must be in format – all caps and short paragraphs. The news director may rewrite it but a well-written submission just might be aired as is.

Following is a sample:

LETTERHEAD OF THE ORGANIZATION

FOR IMMEDIATE AIRING   Further Information: Josie Beck 800-555-1212
Prepared February 20, 2002   Bellvale Women's Club

Bellvale Women's Club Wins Speech Contest

THE BELVALLE WOMEN'S CLUB HAS WON THE $1500 FIRST PRIZE IN THE "WOMEN AGAINST POVERTY" SPEECH CONTEST SPONSORED BY THE CALIFORNIA HUMAN RESOURCE COUNCIL IN LOS ANGELES.

THE THEME OF THE WINNING 15-MINUTE SPEECH DELIVERED BY CLUB TREASURER PHOEBE CARSWELL LAST NIGHT WAS "WE CAN PROSPER TOGETHER".

IT WAS THE UNANIMOUS CHOICE OF THE PANEL OF JUDGES HEADED BY RADIO PERSONALITY JAY COBB OF WVDM.

BELLVALE CLUB PRESIDENT MONICA TAYLOR SAID THE $1500 WOULD BE DONATED TO THE URBAN DEVELOPMENT FUND OF BELLVALE.

TEN FINALISTS HAD BEEN CHOSEN FROM 400 ENTRIES JUDGED DURING THE THREE-DAY CONVENTION. SECOND PRIZE WENT TO THE LOS ANGELES ENTRY AND THIRD TO THE SAN DIEGO ENTRY.

-000-

Review Of the Release:

The release was prepared in broadcast format that maximized its chance to find its way onto the airwaves at a small station, less so at a larger venue. It was correctly submitted on the club's letterhead, was properly dated, and the name and number of the person to contact was accurately indicated.

This substance of the release was important, so it would have been serviced to the media in a timely fashion, as is the case for all news material. Feature – puff – material does not have such strong time components.

The release was only fairly well-written but that is okay, as very few broadcasters will accept copy as is. They will almost always rewrite it in the format of the show it is to be aired on, in the style of the talent and, of course, according to the importance of the material.

Note: a cover letter to the station would request a follow up interview with the prize winner and/or the club president an appropriate show.

Additional Story-Development Ideas:

The important lesson to remember is realizing that many possibilities exist for additional exposure on the women's club *beyond* that initial news release to the media.

If this was your public relations project, you could attempt follow-up coverage by the media by implementing any or all of the following ideas:

- A feature article about the prize-winning club member.

- Offer to have the essay read live on TV or radio by the winner, accompanied by the club president.

- Have the club officers visit a redevelopment project for coverage of their donation actually being used.

- Approach a ranking elected official and suggest a proclamation or resolution for the Club.

- Create or add to an existing newsletter a feature story on the award – it will be a 'keeper'.

You can conjure up other ways to legitimately capitalize on this honor - all to the good of the club's image.

The main point to remember is there are always more public relations opportunities available than first meets your eye.

Watch for them.

18. 10 Local Radio Guidelines

1. Supply copy to the Program Director far in advance as feasible. Provide news releases to News Editors a week or more in advance, if possible.

2. Triple-space on 81" x 11" white paper, one side only. Start one-third down the page, leaving ample margins at sides and bottom.

3. Insert name of organization, address, telephone number and contact name at the top of each item.

4. Give complete and correct news - all the fact, all dates.

5. Make an appointment at the station in advance. ·

6. If an interview is arranged, be punctual.

7. Write your copy more informally than you would in a newspaper release - use let's instead of let us.

8. Provide a brief biographical sketch of any interviewee; along with a list of points to be covered, plus the phonetic pronunciation of a tough name.

9. If you are obtaining public service spots, time spots to run ten seconds, 25 words; twenty seconds, 50 words, or 60 seconds, 150 words. Use simple, descriptive words that form a picture for the listener.

10. Accept graciously the help of the radio station personnel in improving your copy.

19. 10 Guidelines for Local Cable Television

1. Determine who should receive the information or release, the proper format and the deadline.

2. Familiarize yourself with what airtime is available and go after it with valid news or feature material, or to book someone for an interview or discussion show. Some stations have Directors of Public Services or Community Services for free public service announcements - PSA's – for non-profit organizations.

3. Insure that written copy is suited to visual aids such as slides or film and gain clearance to use them.

4. For public service cable television spots, ensure that the copy is written for a slower pace than for radio: 'about' 20 words for ten seconds, 40 words for twenty seconds, and 125 words for sixty seconds.

5. Provide one slide or photograph for each 10-second spot, two for a 20-second spot, and so on.

6. Ask for public service time only for valid events for the public good, not for every small function.

7. Do not operate at cross-purposes by 'commercializing' any organization and its services or products.

8. Ensure that the on-air appearance is absolutely the best it can be for your client or employer. Advise men to wear dark suits and solid ties, and women to wear suits or dresses of dark colors or pastels and to avoid non-contrasting or busy patterns.

9. Cooperate with directors and managers during the visit to the station; learn what they need and then fill that need with your client or employer.

10. If you advertise, the broadcast medium you call on for free airtime should get its fair share of revenue.

20. Public Service Announcements – PSA's

Public Service Announcements – PSA's – are free offerings extended to charitable and civic groups to promote their special activities and causes. Both broadcast venues of radio and cable television provide this as a service to the communities in which they operate.

PSA's will help to fulfill the corporate responsibility of the sponsoring organization and of the broadcast outlet. The public relations practitioner who utilizes this opportunity for free is also providing a service to the community for his or her employer or client.

The Federal Communications Commission until recently required broadcast outlets to provide Free community service air time which was then part of the FCC considerations during license extension or granting processes. Now, it is primarily voluntary on the part of the outlets.

Well-written spots, with quality supporting graphics for TV, that are both timely and appropriate have an excellent chance of being accepted by the Director of Public or Community Services at a broadcast outlet.

Radio Cable TV PSA's are usually from 10-to-30 seconds in length, although they may extend to a full minute in rare circumstances. Well-produced documentary style public service programs can be 5, 30 or 60-minutes in length, depending on the subject matter and its relevance to the public interest. These are generally shown on educational or specialty channels.

Broadcast outlets will assist in the process if you provide scripts for rewrite and/or suggestions, quality support materials such as audiotapes for radio and slides, video and film for TV. They will also help prep and guide an executive booked by the PR practitioner to appear in the PSA.

PSA's are not inclusive of profit centers except when they are directly involved in a charitable or civic cause and the content is non-commercial in nature. For example, the president of a commercial enterprise can be featured and even identified with his or her company as long as the content of the PSA deals with the cause.

Newspapers will publish publicity about a charitable or civic event or cause if it is presented in an acceptable manner. Often a newspaper will cover an important event or activity that occurs within its circulation and coverage areas. Another venue within newspapers and magazines are the 'listings' and 'things to do' sections.

A review of the guidelines in the section titled "Local Radio and Cable TV" will give the tips and counseling important to any appearance by the PR practitioner's employer or client, including how to service the material.

Also important is to learn the standards and practices of the broadcast outlet and abide by them. In that way, PR practitioners won't miss out on the free opportunities of PSA's.

Here are some guidelines to follow for radio PSA's:

- Create spots from 10 or 30 seconds long and only rarely 60 seconds, or longer
- Write a strong opening with credible information presented in a conversational style
- Use appropriate background music when appropriate
- Ensure that a professional announcer or nice sounding volunteer reads the message on air
- Focus the message on key points, don't leave essential information out
- Make the spot clear, concise and, hopefully memorable.

For television, 10, 30 and 60-second PSA's are the norm, although occasionally you will see five-minute, 15-minute or even 30-minute programs dedicated to public service. Documentaries that are well-produced have a shot at gaining TV airtime.

The proper use of free cable TV time will maximize your overall effort for the non-profit institution, or organization.

Make it simple for the TV station to assist you by providing scripts, slides, audio or visual aids, or special instructions or requests.

You also may be required to prepare an executive for a TV speech, or panel discussion, or simple appearance.

PSA's are not generally offered to profit-centers except when they are involved with a charity, and rarely in a newspaper. Although they will run an article and listing, they consider Public Service Announcements as advertisements and secondary in value to paid ads.

Most local newspapers are community-oriented and will print most charity, civic or non-profit institution releases, as long as they fit into the prescribed standards discussed on these pages.

Investigate the possibilities of this free method of gaining exposure for your particular cause through the careful use of PSA's by bonding with the media decision-makers and showing them that you understand their journalistic standards and constraints.

Remember that broadcast or print outlets that grant you PSA time should be considered for advertising when the budget allows. It is not necessary but in reality it is a good *quid pro quo* that opens doors in the future.

PSA Sample Request - Newspaper:

LETTERHEAD OF THE ORGANIZATION

FOR IMMEDIATE RELEASE   Further Information:
Mailed January 20, 2002   Jim Rice 800- 555-1212
                                                                            Publicity Director
PUBLIC SERVICE ANNOUNCEMENT

EXPERIENCED CAMP COUNSELORS ARE BEING SOUGHT BY THE MERRY HEART

CAMPGROUNDS IN NEVEILL, CA. TO ATTEND A SERIES OF SEMINARS DURING

THE WEEK OF MARCH 5TH THROUGH 10TH. THE SEMINARS WILL PREPARE THEM

FOR THE MONTH LONG 100TH ANNIVERSARY CELLEBRATION OF THE NATIONAL

CAMPERS ASSOCIATION IN AUGUST. INTERESTED ADULTS OVER 21 CAN APPLY

BY CONTACTING JIM KAYS AT MERRY HEART CAMPGROUNDS, 122 OLD

BRICKTOWN ROAD IN NEVILLE OR BY CALLING 1-800-5455-1212.

012002   -000-

PSA Sample Request - Radio:

LETTERHEAD OF THE ORGANIZATION

FOR IMMEDIATE RELEASE   Further Information:

Mailed February 20, 2002   Jim Rice 800-555-1212
                                                                            Publicity Director

PUBLIC SERVICE ANNOUNCEMENT

Time: 20 seconds. Words: 42

EXPERIENCED CAMP COUNSELORS INTERESTED IN SEMINARS THE WEEK OF MARCH 15-TO-20 TO PREPARE FOR THE NATIONAL CAMPERS ASSOCIATION 100TH ANNIVERSARY CELEBRATION IN AUGUST SHOULD APPLY TO JIM KAYS AT MERRY HEART CAMPGROUNDS IN NEVILLE OR AT 1-800-555-1212. CALL JANICE SMYTHE AT WRRR-FM FOR MORE DETAILS.

-ooo-

PSA Sample Request - Television:

LETTERHEAD OF ORGANIZATION

FOR IMMEDIATE RELEASE

Mailed March 1, 2002

PUBLIC SERVICE ANNOUNCEMENT

Time: 20 seconds. Words: 34. Slides: 3.

VIDEO	AUDIO
Slide No. 1 – camper in water Announcer:	AUGUST 2002 MARKS THE 100TH ANNIVERSARY OF THE NATIONAL CAMPERS' ASSOCIATION.
Slide No. 2 – group of counselors Announcer:	EXPERIENCED LOCAL CAMP COUNSELORS ARE CORDIALLY INVITED TO PARTICIPATE . . .
Slide No. 3 - shot of Campgrounds Announcer:	AT THE BEAUTIFUL AND SPACIOUS MERRY HEART CAMPGROUNDS FROM MARCH 15TH-TO-20TH. CALL 1-973-5551212 TODAY FOR INFORMATION!

-ooo-

21. 10 Tips for PSA Announcements

1. Keep text for radio within 10 or 30-second limits.

2. Keep text for television within 10, 30 or 60-second limits.

3. Write a strong opening and closing.

4. Focus only on the main points.

5. Provide scripts and audio-visual aids for back-up.

6. Prep executives doing an announcement about their appearance and delivery.

7. Keep newspaper releases of PSA nature within prescribed standards.

8. For-profit entities requesting a PSA must use the non-profit tie-in as the main focus.

9. Investigate the availability of documentaries from your 'home office.'

10. Make sure the PSA is 'timely' for every media outlet.

22. 10 Tips for Placing Broadcast Publicity

1. Determine availability of airtime for news releases, submission guidelines for prepared materials, and standards for requesting coverage from each outlet.

2. Familiarize yourself with what constitutes proper on-air material, how to write it and how to tailor it to specific news slots or programming.

3. Determine the reach area, audience demographics and relative public influence of each outlet.

4. Provide cassettes according to each outlet's standards, and ensure that a signed release (permission to air) has been obtained from all who participate in your submissions.

5. Do not cross-purpose advertising or promotional material with news or feature presentations, arrange for interviews or appearances at the outlet, and prepare the interviewer and the interviewee with all pertinent current information.

6. Provide information in advance on the main story lines, biographical information about the on-air subject, and background materials to the reporter/interviewer.

7. Honor all deadlines imposed by the outlet by being on time, by submitting materials on time, and by understanding the pressure of on-air reporting.

8. For television, the on air guest should wear apparel in pastels or dark colors with little or no contrast; avoid bright whites, and avoid 'busy' patterns.

9. Request Public Service Announcements - PSA's - on radio for charity or civic endeavors according to each outlet's guidelines, be informative and factual in the messaging, and be

honest and straightforward in your appeal.

10. Request PSA's on local radio or cable television according to established guidelines in a similar with acceptable audio or video footage or slides; or request the station to film the spots for you as part of its public service.

23. *Arranging Interviews*

Interviews with the media can be valuable by gaining good exposure if the subject – your client or employer -knows and understands all of the pertinent information, can deliver it in a winsome and convincing manner, and has a positive perspective and point-of-view.

The Appointment:

To arrange for a convenient but timely interview with a reporter or columnist, call the pertinent media person and present him or her with reasons and background information, or provide it through a pitch letter and fact sheet alerting him or her as to why they should want to do the interview.

Preparing the Interviewee:

Educate yourself to the basics about the person and his or her subject and the topics to be discussed. Collect materials for the interviewer, including general resume data and background, copies of previous publicity, *etc.* Do a mock interview asking key questions and helping the client or employer to refine the answers. Instruct the subject to be alert for twists or unexpected questions and answer carefully. Tell her/him to shy from guesswork and simply indicate an answer or comment will be forthcoming later. Tell the subject to always be courteous and calm and to never argue with the media.

Prepping the Interviewer:

Prepare suggested questions in advance and forward to the interviewer along with the background materials.

Keep the suggestions timely and aimed at the points you wish to be made by your client or employer. Stick to what would be relevant to the readers of the publication or listeners to the broadcast outlet.

Do not hover over the interviewer during the interview.

Getting the Facts Yourself

When interviewing a client or employer for an article that you intend to write, take notes and underline highlights, key words, phrases and facts. Take direct quotes and modify them for the actual story with the subject's permission. Use a tape recorder to assure accuracy, if necessary.

24. *Writing the Article*

Review and organize your notes after the interview unless you immediately do the article. Check on any questionable points or quotes. Allow your client or employer the literary license to change the article as he or she sees fit (if you wish to keep a good relationship) before submitting to the media.

Then observe the following methods in consummating your article.

Writing The Lead:

There are many ways to write an article but the straightforward manner is usually best. Find the key point(s) from the interview and begin. This could be the most important quotes or facts, or both. Identify the subject by name and title early on, adding pertinent facts and quotes in descending order of importance: the pyramid approach.

Note: copy editors will cut copy from the bottom and will seldom rewrite a submitted PR article.

Dos And Don'ts:

- Do get titles, names and quotes accurately.

- Don't insert yourself as the interviewer into the copy.

- Do write: "He said" and not "When asked, he said."

- Keep it simple.

- Let the subject review the material for accuracy before submitting it to the media.

Perspectives:

- The interviewee's opinions are valid and must be the focus.

- The interviewer's opinions are inescapable but should not shape or influence the story.

- When writing the article, let quotes speak for themselves.

- Avoid adjectives or editorializing like *he said seriously* or *he emphasized*.

- Avoid use of descriptive overkill like the interviewee is *marvelous* or *compassionate* even if she/he is.

PR Emphasis:

Do not spoil your article by overdoing your special interest in it. Mention your organization once in full in the lead and maybe once or twice by reference but don't overdo it. After using the full name of the organization, use the initials from then on in future references: *i.e.* American Cancer Society (ACS).

Be sure to mail, fax or e-mail the published article or interview to a select editor and include your client's company or organization contact person if appropriate. Time the release so that all members of interested media have a chance to print or air it at the same time, unless you target it to one select media outlet.

25. 10 Guidelines for a Media Conference

Preparation is the best method to ensure that your media conference will be successful. The 'press party' should include commentary by the key involved individuals, handouts that summarize the mission of the event, and management by the public relations practitioner, from inception through follow-up *post mortem*.

Here are 10 guidelines to follow for conducting a media conference:

1. Only call a media conference when the news content – 'peg' - warrants it.

2. Don't play favorites - invite all concerned media to the press conference.

3. Invite the media to press parties at least two days in advance.

4. Make certain there is a solid news peg and not just bridge-building, provide media kits to every attendee with correct names/titles, read some of their stuff in advance to familiarize yourself with them.

5. Don't pressure the media to attend your events, persuade them that it is in the best interest of their readers and them. This will help establish your own credibility.

6. Critique a media member one-on-one first when necessary. Don't complain publicly or to others. If you strike out while attempting to favorably influence, try again. Only go to the media person's superior if absolutely necessary and you have a good case to make to complain about coverage or lack of coverage.

7. Supply only accurate, timely and newsworthy items to the media.

8. Do not visit a newsroom or station uninvited, call for an appointment.

9. Thank the media for coverage 'privately' (they are, or should be, just doing their job).

10. Do not send gifts or attempt to 'comp' the media unless you learn it is appropriate and acceptable to them. A sincere offer to buy lunch is enough of a gesture.

Bonus Tips: Learn what works and what doesn't, continuously improve your media conferencing skills, call your contacts personally and through e-mail or fax to invite them to the conference, and remember to follow up with e-mail or fax to all of your invitees – and then hope for the best re coverage.

26. *10 Tips for Publicity Photographs*

1. Retain the best and most-dependable freelance photographer available within your budget and then learn to work closely with him/her on photo assignments.

2. Do not send the media inferior photos, and no instant pictures that are not of high-resolution and quality; do not expect the return of photos unless you obtain specific approval in advance.

3. Send only glossy prints in good condition, either in black-and-white or in color that can be converted by the publication.

4. Send 8 x 10 or 5 x 7-inch photographs or smaller head shots, depending on the requirements for publication; it is easy to reduce a photo than to enlarge it.

5. Pose photographs professionally, with subjects either looking at each other or at the camera, but not a mixture. Insure that the background is appropriate and uncluttered; use five or fewer persons in the photo unless you have prior approval for more from the publication.

6. Write and attach captions in the style of the publications that are accepting the photographs; identify subjects from left to right with full names and titles and give a brief description of the activity; indicate if the photo and caption accompanies the article at the top of the page.

7. Most posed photos are boring so show some action or uniqueness; for example, the award of a standard-size $10,000 check to an organization is boring but the award of $10,000 check is not.

8. When a publication assigns a photographer, be sure the shoot is set up properly and on time and let the professional do his/her thing but don't be timid about suggestions.

9. When you forward photos to a publication, label the back with the first two words of the caption, writing lightly in pencil so as not to damage or scratch the front surface.

10. You may ask a qualified photographer to volunteer services and save your program some money but do *not* sacrifice the potential of gaining media exposure unless you can deliver quality photos on time.

27. *Word of Mouth - the Best and the Worst Advertising*

Rumor control and word-of-mouth are important parts of crisis-problem management and public relations. What employees, executives, vendors, customers or clients, the general public and the media say about your client or employer and their product or service will directly impact their ability to succeed.

Word-of-mouth is the best and the worst form of advertising. Can you control it? To some extent if you try hard with proven strategic PR methods. These include the following techniques:

- Obtain complete details from all sources and determine what is accurate and what is not.

- Translate those facts into a pertinent vehicle such as a media release, a fact sheet, a newsletter, a letter to various publics of interest, a speech by a key executive, a hotline telephone team to answer pertinent questions - whatever will carry the true message to the publics of interest.

- Ensure that the media has accurate details and insist on corrections when applicable and ask that the morgue files carry the corrections so erroneous information is not reprinted.

28. Persuasion is the Art of PR

A personal vignette • • •

Persuasion is a much better tool than being adversarial in the practice of PR. In fact, persuasion is the art of public relations. And it is far more enjoyable to be positive rather than negative.

We deal with a certain unnamed wealthy client. He consistently challenges my low-key style and calls me "too nice a guy", as if that was a bad thing to be.

I listen until he cools off and then respond that it is me who keeps coming, me who tells him when he's wrong, me who refuses to do his bidding if it is unethical, and me who he usually calls to help solve his problems.

He usually sees the light and I manage to keep intact my dignity and my monthly fee; when he doesn't I bug out - until the next time he calls. Is it worth it? Sometimes yes, sometimes no.

29. Impressions

The important result for any form of communications in journalism, public relations or advertising is the final and lasting impression you make on your publics of interest.

A great example of a clear, positive and lasting impression is from Nike in its advertising campaigns of recent years.

The simple appearance of the words *Just do it* immediately elicits visions of athletic shoes. The simple checkmark logo in the ads or printed on a shirt engender the same subliminal response.

How is this possible? First, it is a clever and carefully crafted slogan and symbol. Second, it has been reinforced with thousands of repetitions in multiple advertising vehicles: television commercials, print ads and billboards, and on apparel and accessories. Third, it has been endorsed by famed athletes like Michael Jordan and by struggling lay persons like you and me, each of us pursuing an endeavor that is best served if we simply just do it, like Nike says.

Chapter Two

Product Publicity

1. Esoteric and Similar, Too

Publicity campaigns aimed at a product launch or as part of any direct marketing campaign designed for a specific product or service are more esoteric than the general publicity guidelines previously discussed. At the same time they are similar in many ways, too.

An analysis of the PR world surrounding this category leads to this simple and obvious question: would you like to expand the volume of business for your client or employer? Of course you would!

You can let thousands of people know about your product, your service, your store or facility or yourself through the relatively inexpensive venues of publicity. If you want to increase sales or sales potentials, you can enhance the possibilities for your client or employer through publicity.

You don't have to climb a flagpole or hire a dancing bear to attract attention and sales. In fact, through simple telephone contact, follow up letter and fact sheet, and a working knowledge of the tools and techniques of publicity, you can accomplish your goals.

What product or business are you involved with that needs more clients or customers? You might have a neighborhood store, or you might be seeking exposure for a celebrity or politician.

Maybe you have a new invention that you can't get marketed or a recently released line of designer furniture that you want to increase sales on.

How are you presently getting to customers? You may be advertising in newspapers and magazines or trade journals or you may be relying on a distribution agreement to retail the products your plant manufactures.

Perhaps you're an author depending on a publishing house to promote your book, but it seems to be *waning. Or* you could be a young comic, trying to develop new material to further your performing career and bring it to a new level.

Regardless of your business or enterprise, free publicity is available to you. And you don't need any particular background or training to do it. What you do 'need is the belief in yourself and your product and the diligence and perseverance to continue when one idea doesn't pan out.

Take a look at the variety of types of publicity. Whether you want a local increase in sales, or national fame, free publicity is available to you.

2. Again, What is Publicity?

Publicity is making something known to the public, spreading information to the general, local or national markets. It is information with a news value used to attract public attention or support. And all of this occurs at relatively inexpensively, depending on the skill of the public relations practitioner.

Everybody needs publicity to succeed. Business owners, organization heads, politicians, manufacturers, celebrities, Detroit automobile producers, *et al,* all employ publicity to further their causes and gain attention.

And publicity isn't limited to large organizations. Small committees and enterprises use the local newspapers to publicize events and endeavors.

Publicity differs from advertising because it is free. Although some groups or individuals do trade tickets or services for free *mention in* publications, generally publicity is newsworthy copy that a publication produces.

Publicity is a form of promotion, although promoting a product or service may require other efforts that cost the company money. Good publicity is one of the best ways to let people know you have a worthwhile business.

3. Know Your Product or Service

In order to gain publicity, the public relations practitioner must be thoroughly familiar with the product, service or business that you are promoting - you are the best one to describe the benefits and features.

If you want to publicize something else regarding the same client or employer, talk to everyone involved and get all the facts and details.

Consider the radius of your market. If you are representing or have your own local business such as a retail store or service shop, most of your customers are from the surrounding five miles. If you are located in a large city, you may have a larger radius, but at the same time, there may be stiffer competition.

Your enterprise might be regional or statewide and your clients may come from hundreds of miles, either in person or by telephone or in increasing numbers, via the Internet and e-mail, to avail themselves of your services. And, if you are a large manufacturer, your clients and customers may come from the entire United States--or you may have a worldwide audience.

Profile your customers. Who are they and what do they do? If you have a service, how often is this service used? If you have a product, is it something that is bought again and again, or is it a lifetime purchase? How much do your customers pay for your products and are you competitive wit# the other manufacturers of the same products? If you have an unusual product, are you reaching the widest audience you can?

4. Survey the Market(s)

What do the customers want? Sometimes, the least expensive price is not the most important element. With today's packaging, many customers expect and will pay for things elaborately packaged.

Where do these people go to buy your products? Are they sold at retail outlets or through trade publications or magazines? Or, are they special items available from mail order or from certain regions of the nation or world?

Finally, why do your customers buy this particular service or product, or use the particular business you have? An architectural design studio produces blueprints for architects to construct buildings for homeowners and industry. But your product may be aimed at a less precise group of people, somewhat hard to define.

You can discover what consumers want from surveys. You can get copies of surveys from special companies that conduct surveys, or you can do your own. The best place to conduct a survey is at a trade show for your product. You might run a drawing and ask people to fill in information. You can have cards printed with boxes to check easily so people will spend the time to answer your questions.

Manufacturers use surveys with warranties. Appliance makers often include a few questions along with the warranty that the consumer sends back.

Most major manufacturers have their own teams of product testing. Toymakers bring in children and watch their reactions. Book publishers have people look at covers and decide which they'd buy, and car manufacturers run surveys and opinion testing before they determine style and pricing.

Before you seek publicity or even advertise, know the product. Become familiar with the people who buy your product or service, and have a full understanding of the general competition and the full scope of marketability.

5. Where to Publicize

Depending on your product, you have a full gamut of possibilities for advertising without paying--free publicity. Deciding on the type of media is as important as knowing your product and the people who buy.

As a manufacturer, you want to let retailers know of your product. The trade magazines would be a good place for new products and comparisons of product reliability.

If you want to publicize directly to the general public national publications, metropolitan newspapers and Sunday supplements are ways to tap into the market.

For a local enterprise - either a profitable business or a charity or community service - the local newspapers are certainly the best resources to obtain frequent free publicity placement.

Once your product or news is of national importance, the television and radio can be good sources of publicity. Even the local public stations produce interesting shows about local people and products.

For international significance, the newspaper syndicates and wire services provide the publicity you'll need.

Don't go for the biggest first; move up to the larger markets. Start with the local news, then expand as your product interest grows.

6. Write Newsworthy Material

In order to qualify for publicity, your information must be newsworthy. Anything published in the newspapers, magazines or trade journals must be important to readers-either as information for an event, or interesting insights in the industry.

You may have a new product or product line that can be publicized in magazines. If not, you need to come up with unique angles to get the publicity you seek for your client or employer.

An unusual background for the inventor of the product or owner of the manufacturing plant may make good news for the new product. Or you may need to come up with fresh ideas for your service. For example, a short item about famous people using the service is noteworthy, or an unusual combination in the owner's biography may make a good story.

Some businesses produce literature that points out facts of the particular industry--either historical or contemporary. For example, a television news feature was done a group of companies that check the quality of houses for interested buyers. Or, a pamphlet on cutting costs on building an addition onto your house is a natural for a construction company.

7. Seek the Best Angle

What is unusual about your product or service that can become newsworthy? Even if nothing stands out at first, you'll find you can think of the best angle that deems it worthwhile from a publicity point-of-view.

What about anecdotes? Failure stories can be as entertaining as success tales. How people have trouble getting their businesses off the ground can be newsworthy.

And don't forget simple endurance. A business that's been profitable for twenty-five years is a sure bet for local newspapers.

If you want to publicize an event, consider the radius of the participants. A national trade convention should receive national interest in the magazines and other publications geared towards that particular industry. More local events can be publicized in metropolitan newspapers.

The most local events can be publicized by flyers and notices, or through the schools. Look for common trends in your product or service. Think often about what makes it different from the other thousands of products and services. Make lists, List the features of what you want to publicize; list the people who use the product or service; list why people use it.

What do you come up with? Do more young people use it? Do more women, or members of special groups? You may use an angle of publicizing a person not in your typical consumer group purchasing or using your product or service.

The most important consideration in choosing an angle is to make your item newsworthy, so the editor of the publication will print it.

8. *Making Contact*

Whether you are sending products, media kits or news releases, the most important element in getting them publicized is to send it to the right editor or broadcaster. If it doesn't reach that person's desk, it may well end up in the wastebasket.

When you decide on the media market you want to publicize in, contact the people who will make it happen on a local level. A small medium-sized newspaper will have a features editor or a specific person who takes care of the notice you want to place. Call up the publication to obtain that person's name. Then send in the notice.

A larger metropolitan newspaper is a busy place. Consider the section you'll want your story to appear in. Many newspapers have entertainment, travel, business, sports, and food sections, *et al*. Contact the appropriate editor.

Editors rarely have time to accept cold calls that are soliciting publicity, so you might try first to talk to the assistant. Speak briefly, introduce yourself, and say you'll send in a news release – then do it.

For a radio message, contact the program director, or assistant. Make enough telephone calls to be sure you have the correct name of the person at the publication or broadcast outlet to send your release to.

Television programming directors may be more difficult to reach; use perseverance. With active pursuit, you can get your message through to anyone.

9. *Trades and National Magazines*

The most worthwhile connections for promoting a new product are with the editors of trade magazines or with national magazines that have a new products section. You may want to send a sample or a photograph or drawing of the product. Include all pertinent facts and features.

Magazine editors can also be difficult to reach-but try. If you can speak directly to the person who handles new products, try it. If not, be sure to contact the person who does handle the feature angle that you have chosen.

As soon as you've contacted the right person to use your material, send it out immediately. If you have arranged a personal appointment, follow up with a short note that confirms the date and time.

A few days after you send out your materials, call that person again. Simply ask if the information was received; don't push for a commitment to run the release. By pointing attention to the materials, you have a better chance.

Before you send the information and graphics electronically, be certain they accept them and that your formats are compatible.

10. News Releases

News releases - press releases - are the most important selling tool of publicity. For success, the release must capture the editor's attention, be precise and easy to read and understand for the targeted public.

A news release can go to just one newspaper or many publications at once. It can be a product release, a community notice about a special sale, or information about a promotion.

Or the material can be labeled and submitted as an op-ed opinion piece that is by-lined by the client or employer, along with her or his photograph. There are many opportunities for releases that will build the credibility and exposure of the client or employer and by inference the product or service.

The same standard format is used for every type of news, whether an executive promotion in the trade magazines, or a local event such as an author signing books at a neighborhood bookstore, *et al.* The public relations practitioner will have multiple subjects for every client or employer.

If you want your notice to get into a special edition of a publication, be aware of the deadlines. Sunday editions generally have more readers than daily editions: find out when your release must be received by the editor.

Never mix publicity with advertising. If your newspaper features specific businesses in special industry supplements, you may be chosen because you advertise. But otherwise, editors frown on any releases that merely imitate advertising and are not newsworthy.

Don't embarrass yourself by sending anything not newsworthy. Not only will your release be thrown away, you will destroy any chance you had for subsequent placement through that particular editor.

11. Preparing the Product Release

As previously discussed, keep the news release to one page or as brief as possible. Type it clearly on white bond paper, double-spaced, and never send it with typographical errors. Since the release might be published exactly as it is received, particularly by smaller publications, be certain the copy is professional and 'worthy' of the editor's consideration.

At the top left, put your name and address and the phone number you can be reached at during business hours. In full capital letters at the right should appear 'for Immediate Release' or on or after" a listed date. Editors will respect your legitimate release date.

Use a headline appropriate to the event or topic, and keep it short - just like newspaper headings. Capitalize the letters and underline the headline.

Start the copy with a dateline, which is the city and date. Then write the rest within a few paragraphs. Include the important information in the standard who, what, when and where. Use good English, but don't run on with unimportant adjectives or boring information. You can

Capitalize the first letters of your new product or program, or for important events such as a Discount Days Gala event.

If you have a release to send to many publications at the same time, make sure each copy is clear and looks like the original.

Include a brief cover letter to the appropriate editor. Be cordial and keep it short. If your product is convenient to mail, you may include a sample if the editor is amenable.

Watch the publications and clip the printed publicity yourself or use a clipping service. Do not ask the publications to send you copies.

12. Promotional Literature

You can publicize your service or product with a pamphlet or booklet. Topical subjects such as saving energy or cutting costs are always newsworthy. Naming new trends or buying habits can equally be publicized.

Take a look at the magazines and trade journals in your area of endeavor. Are there special sections for interesting tidbits of the industry? Maybe there's a section for new products, or even a section that compares products.

Does your product or service have something special that competitors don't? Maybe yours is the best--and "best" is newsworthy. Does yours have the longest resiliency, or is it made from the best materials? Maybe your service is noted for complete satisfaction or reliability.

These aspects are especially important for the big manufacturers. Trade journals cater to the special industries and those in the trade always want to consider the best product investment, especially after spending many thousands of dollars on its development.

An oil company sends out free booklets on maintaining your car; a travel agent prints a brochure on the most beautiful vacation spots; a dry cleaners gives out a flyer on getting out stains as soon as they happen.

What promotional literature can you tie into your business? And it doesn't need to be product oriented. Some large companies produce tips on employee relations or benefits. Many print their own in-house publications.

Any special message booklet is a public service and is worthy of free publicity. Some interesting information can make a good feature if followed up by a reporter. Or you may write your own feature for magazines.

You can get your literature designed and printed by a local Printer at minimum cost. Don't go for an elaborate four-color booklet unless you can afford to.

Consider what you can get at the least expense and then work from there. From a small investment, you may get thousands of dollars worth of free publicity.

Always include the name and address and business number of your enterprise on the brochure, and offer copies for the general public as a free give-away or as a bonus for services.

13. Pitch and Query Letters

As discussed in a previous section, pitch and query letters can open the gates to exposure. For products or services, when you don't have a specific news release or a special booklet to publicize your enterprise, you may solicit publicity with a letter to the editor of the section that suits your endeavor.

Rather than providing complete information, suggest the practicality and timeliness of a feature or article on your business or the owner of the business. Some people or organizations are famous in their own right and start side businesses or enterprises. For example, celebrities open restaurants or community theaters; financiers donate art collections; a local orphanage may raise a phenomenal amount of money for a special cause.

A pitch letter is a highly motivating letter to get the editor interested in the topic that will benefit your cause. Type it on letterhead and send it personally to the editor, or e-mail if you know that is acceptable and will be read. You might call in advance and use e-mail as a follow up.

Get right to the point. Present the topic and the angle immediately. Then, support the worthiness with some poignant information concerning the topic.

Send copies of local publicity if you're building to a national level, or send copies of other news features that relate directly to your person or product. Don't deluge the editor with too many clippings or an overload of information. A few choice tidbits will suffice to get that person's interest in doing a feature. Close your letter with a mention of calling that person and then follow up with a telephone call a few days later.

14. Use of the Telephone

The most important tool to the publicist is still the telephone (even more than e-mail). People who make their livelihoods with publicity make calls all day long. And persistence is the greatest attribute but not to the point of annoyance.

Use a soft-sell approach on the phone, it's a great way to make and keep contact with important people in the media.   Just one phone call may seal up a lifetime business relationship with someone who will provide you with many thousands of dollars worth of relatively free and hopefully believable publicity in the media.

A telephone call is the most efficient means of reaching somebody up close and personal to introduce yourself and your mission, and firming up a contact for follow through. Don't be afraid of calling people and don't be shy in asserting yourself.

If you have a clear idea about your product or service and believe in what you're selling, your tone of voice will be the best selling feature. Know your facts and present them clearly.

If you are working for a specific person or trying to get a meeting for the owner of your company, know when you can set up an appointment and settle on it immediately. Don't forget business lunches--a great way to sell yourself or your product in a relaxed atmosphere. Follow up with a memo that same day to confirm the date and time of the meeting.

When you meet with rejection, don't take it to heart, there are many ways you can make solid connections and a few no's shouldn't stop you.

15. Column Releases

Some trade 'journals have specific columns written by a reporter that run weekly or monthly. If you have a newsworthy item for a column, you can build up a working rapport with the writer and supply material from time to time.

The entertainment trade papers have daily columns that keep celebrities in the limelight. Metropolitan newspapers run daily columns that mention politicians. And industry publications have columns that pertain to a certain aspect of your enterprise.

When you write a column release, copy the style of the person doing the column and use the format of the standard news release. Clearly label it for what it is and render it for 'exclusive use' by the columnist you contacted.

Don't be shy about forwarding info to columnists, they are always looking for solid material.

16. Media Kits

The media (press) kit is made up to publicize a new product or product line, service or program, or an individual who is being promoted. They kits may be put together for a general conference or one to be conducted at a trade show or convention.

Generally, a press kit includes biographies and fact sheets, with a news release photographs with captions attached.

Copies of previous articles and/or clippings are enclosed--anything pertinent to the item you want publicized. An entertainer's schedule and promotional photos would be included if the conference is about an upcoming tour or engagement.

The press kit is usually in a folder or envelope and is handy to send to publications or for press conferences or to give information to the local media.

Use your imagination when you write the column release, and don't get discouraged if it's passed by. Keep building relationships with the columnists and you'll get your news publicized.

17. The Biography

A bio of a personality, whether for a famous celebrity or the president/CEO of your company, is fact and not hype and should be treated thusly. It usually is included in press kits for background information and as a resource of material.

Although important information concerning the person's career should be included, make it informative and interesting to read. Many editors or reporters will use that information in a news story or feature. It should be single spaced, and never make it more than two pages, even if the person deserves a full book.   Regardless of the scope of your news or feature article or conference, photographs are will be an asset to the submission.

New product releases always include a photo(s), whether it be an expensive professional shot that can be used later for advertising, or a simple black and white photo, it should be clear and uncluttered with extraneous objects.

Generally for a small business, the black and white glossy photo is your best bet. Use a professional photographer for the shoot – he or she will be certain the product is captured on film in its best light. High contrast photos are the best for newspapers and magazines. If your product is mainly light colored, it will stand out on a black background, and vice versa. Never use a 'busy' background.

Always have the photos professionally duplicated and of the highest quality. Forget about anything that closely resembles amateur work or the editor won't take your release seriously. Have the photos printed on 5-x-7 or 8-x-10-inch paper and be sure to enclose a cardboard backing when you send them through the mail with the news release and/or caption.

18. Merchandising the Publicity

When you do get coverage from your efforts, clip those pieces from the publications and exploit them. You may have seen this done in restaurants. They often enlarge and mount (favorable) restaurant reviews and post them in windows to attract and potential customers. This is good merchandizing.

Good publicity in one form may lead to a wider scope of publicity in a larger publication. You can use local newspaper clippings for pitching a feature in a national magazine. And you can use write-ups in large circulation publications to give credentials for a television appearance.

Many businesses exploit reviews. Look at the back of books; they list the quotations from reviewers to promote the product. And films do that too. How many times have you seen a film advertised by quotations from famous film reviewers?

What can you do to use the publicity at its best and spread its effects as widely as possible? Take a look at your metropolitan newspaper. In the features section, there are often stories about interesting people and their enterprises. With a little ingenuity, this coverage can go national.

An obvious way to use good publicity is simply to photocopy it and send it as a direct mail piece to your customers or to include it in your brochures. Even a stack of flyers at the counter can promote your business.

How far do you want to go?

19. Promotion and PR

In most cases, you can use the normal media channels to get the publicity you need for your product or service. And, although you don't need to come up with schemes to get attention, they do work.

Sometimes promotion departments of manufacturers stage marathon events or contests with their products, especially with toys and games and these events generate ample publicity. For example, apparel-companies may sponsor athletic events and manufacturers of motorcycles may opt to sponsor races.

Although promotional schemes do cost money to stage, the efforts usually pay off in a long run with the number of customers sold on the product. For local coverage, charity drives and dinners are good ways to get in the paper. Some enterprises strive for a more national coverage with special prizes connected to sports events.

If you are clever enough and there is no big news break that day, you may get your scheme on television. Even local footage reaches thousands and thousands of people.

What promotional gimmicks can you devise that can provide a return on your original investment? How is your product or service used that can commercially be exploited by you through publicity? Can you keep going with it - making it an annual event, drawing customers from near and far?

20. Retaining Other Pros

What if you don't want to do the publicity yourself? If your product or service is a natural for free publicity, you can hire a niche company or professional to help with PR and promotion.

There are many freelancers with their own clients that they already promote and publicize. They've already broken the ice with the editors and the media and can get releases printed if you can't. Tap into them whenever appropriate and pass the costs on to your client or employer.

If you want to hire someone for a special project, get a pro who has the contacts and who specializes in your product line. If you're a celebrity, use someone who has a reputation in the entertainment industry. If you are a manufacturer with new appliances, likewise consider a person with expertise in that field.

Check out the person or firm. Talk to other clients and find out what has been done for them. Have they increased their sales or public exposure?

Investigate the reputation with people in the media you want to publicize in, and be sure there is a clean slate with the local business associations. Then work efficiently with the person who will handle your publicity.

Communicate effectively and be sure your ideas are understood. Listen well and absorb any ideas thrown your way. Between the two of you, you can come up with an excellent publicity campaign that will make your business boom.

21. Just Do It!

The wonderful thing about free publicity is that you have nothing to lose. Make a few phone calls, send a few personal letters and maybe invest in quick-printing of news releases and you can reap many times your investment through additional sales and orders.

Whether you have an international personality to publicize or a community barbecue, you can get that inform in front of the public at minimum expense by asking and answering the following questions:

What is unique about your service or product?

- Is it the best, or one of the best?
- Is it the most used?
- Is the most durable (longest lasting)?
- Do customers return time and again (rate of retention)?

Then, consider all of the angles, reconsider them and then promote them!

- Be sure to make solid contacts and be thorough with your follow-ups.
- Be polite and efficient to create effective business relations.
- Exploit your own publicity by posting it in the store or rewrite it for wider distribution.
- Go as far as you can with your ideas – they don't cost much.

22. *Associated Costs*

The costs associated with publicity include the proportionate time spent by the practitioner on behalf of his or her client or employer seeking to write, place and monitor publicity, the costs for mailing or for a wire service, the cost for a clipping service or subscriptions to publications, and other miscellaneous expenses such as for telephone and fax.

The space occupied by the publicity can be measured exactly and then compared to the cost for the same space in advertising. This would indicate the comparative costs and show the savings of publicity over advertising. In most cases, publicity will prove to be highly advantageous.

Besides being more cost-effective, well-written publicity can have more influence on the reader who is pre-conditioned to believe what he or she reads in the newspaper .

23. *Both PR and Ads Have a Place*

Both publicity and advertising have their place in a strategic marketing and public relations plan. The wise practitioner selects the venues that will do the most good in fulfilling the mission of the client or employer, weighing costs vs. potential impacts. In the end, those techniques and tools that work best are the ones that should be repeated in quest of fulfilling the mission.

Both general and product publicity are dependent on creativity matched with strict procedures that rely on tactics and techniques, and a special bonding with members of the media that will establish trust and result in access. That said, access will lead to publication or air time only if the material is judged by the print editor or broadcast director to be both newsworthy and of interest to readers or listeners.

Nothing in business is totally without cost, not even relatively free publicity. The costs to the employer or client are for the time of the professional public relations practitioner and the associated costs of servicing via e-mail, fax or public relations wire service, and then following up with the media. Clipping services are expensive but not when compared to tracking 'hits' in the media, and far more efficient than combing through newspapers and magazines.

To quantify the value received from publicity: measure the column inches devoted to your release then compare it to the advertising costs for the same space. If your release is given 10 inches in a daily newspaper and the advertising cost per-inch is $50 then you received a comparative value of $500 for your client.

Section Three

Chapter One

Crisis-Problem Communications

1. What is Doable, What is Not

Dealing with crisis-problem management requires that the public relations strategist and the client or employer involved both understand and agree upon three basic 'what' elements.

For example:

- What is doable and what is not?

- What is correct and what is not?

- What is of service to the mission of neutralizing, mitigating or eliminating the problem and what is not?

That said, the ensuing rapid-response crisis-problem action plan must include delineation of three basic 'who' elements of the situation:

- Who is to direct the command-center?
  The best scenario is that the top decision maker and the PR strategist operate in tandem.

- Who fills spots in the chain-of-command?
  This must be established to determine who will be the public, media and internal spokesperson(s).

- Who will develop a fact sheet specific to the incident or event?
  Compilation of background information, a news release from the client's point-of-view and biographical information about the executives involved are all necessary to give the media appropriate background.

This should all be accomplished in a professional manner without misleading or misinforming anyone about anything, especially the media and its honorable participants.

2. A Mosaic of Five Basic Elements

The 'mosaic' designed by the Prather Group to deal with citizen opposition to a project such as a business expansion or relocation into a resistant community or a negative event such as pollution or an accident includes the following five basic elements:

1. Those who are solidly aligned with your mission.
   They should be informed and kept close to the action by inviting them to meetings and sharing information with them so as to cement the relationship.

2. Those who are leaning toward your mission.
   They should be informed and cultivated to shore up their support.

3. Those who are in the middle and have not made up their minds about your mission.
   They should be informed, cultivated and motivated in order to gain their support.

4. Those who are leaning against your mission.
   They should be lobbied by appropriate supporters and informed, cultivated and motivated in an appropriate fashion without applying undue pressure.

5. Those who are strongly opposed to your mission.
   They should be ignored as much as possible and not motivated to take action that will oppose the mission because of undue pressure or negative tactics.

It is important to take a whole-world approach to your publics of interest during a crisis-problem and then to isolate and approach each one in a common sense manner.

Remember, first do no harm – don't tick off anyone and inspire him or her to take action against your employer or client –or yourself.

3. A Published Article on the Subject

The following by-lined editorial published in *CORPORATE INSIGHTS* reflects on both the practice and science of PR in regards to management of crises as viewed by The Prather Group.

Trends 2000 • • • Crisis Communications Tactics Vital to PR Strategy

By Jack Prather

There has been a quantum growth in demand by business and industry for strategic public relations services during the last quarter of a century.

The practice of PR will remain both a management and a marketing function. The science of public relations will continue to evolve, and tactics and techniques will continue to be refined well into the new millennium.
Electronic communications will mature and become even faster and more complex, but public

relations professionals will retain their basic objectives: to provide insight on an organization's point-of-view and image, and to communicate both in a manner that will favorably influence publics of interest.

The PR pro will continue to work alongside marketing professionals to develop cutting-edge communications strategies for management and sales executives, with a level of confidentiality similar to lawyer-client privilege.

Three mainstays of public relations services have remained the same for more than 50 years: media relations, publicity and promotion.

A critical fourth element with its own set of tactics and standards has evolved: crisis-problem communications management.

That key element is the most sensitive because it usually revolves around a situation or accident that can cause irreparable damage to an organization or business, often unfairly.

To deal with the crisis, an advance plan of action must be formulated that includes a rapid-response team to draft a fact sheet, a news release and the official organization or company position to be submitted for publication or airing to the media only if the crisis is or soon will be publicly known. In some instances it is best to seize the moment and put forth the materials before the media or public discovers the crisis. This is called *controlling the message*.

The objective of the public relations professional is to neutralize or minimize damage to the organization or business as much as possible without misleading or misinforming customers or clients, the media, the public, or even its own employees. Tough tasks, to be sure.

Consistent standards must be established and maintained throughout the crisis. A healthy guideline is to put forth nothing that is illegal, immoral, unethical or untrue.

A designated primary spokesperson should handle all contact with the media and the public, and all members of the response team should be in possession of the same factual information. Lines of communication to the media and public should be kept open, as information is best coming from the source directly to them.

Rumor control is a critical element in handling communications before, during and after the crisis. Follow-ups to correct the record, to memorialize the best possible scenario and to maintain trust with the media are all essential.

Advance and ongoing media relations efforts will have provide a base from which the public relations professional can tap into an established trust and rapport with editors, columnists, writers and broadcasters in a time of crisis. This will be good for the practitioner as well as for the organization or business represented.

The PR pro must continue to fashion credible and timely releases about the products or services of the client or employer and invite coverage regardless of the treatment during a crisis.

For special events and activities, the pro must remain sensitive to the crisis and its ramifications and handle inquiries and comments with great care to make the situation better and not worse.

Trust and truth are the ties that bind. They are what make PR efforts believable and acceptable to the media, customers or clients, and the general public, especially in the 21st century.

4. *Influencing Publics of Interest*

Every company or organization will face a crisis or problem at some point and unfortunately many escalate to become full-blown crises. What the company or organization does to solve each crisis will influence all of its publics of interest either favorably or unfavorably.

The vehicles for reaching the publics consists of multiple communications techniques that will determine both the short and long-range impacts and the eventual costs to repair the damage for the company or organization.

It is in these crisis modes that a well-trained *strategic* public relations practitioner can and should be the centerpiece for action.

The practitioner, with support from the rest of the management team, can apply proven crisis-management techniques that can turn negatives – even severe ones – into positives. However, this requires designating the practitioner to take charge of the formation and implementation of short and long-range action plans.

5. *10 Thing the PR Practioner Can Do*

1. Create an advance crisis action plan
2. Help to oversee the rapid-response team
3. Create and disperse statements to the media and public
4. Compile pertinent fact sheets to ensure correctness
5. Prepare news releases for immediate or timed release
6. Write letters stating the company or organization official position
7. Arrange interviews with key area newspaper outlets
8. Book key executives on radio and television news and interview shows
9. Develop timelines and to address the crisis until resolved
10. Do a follow-up *post mortem*

6. *The Specific Point of View*

The communications should be geared to inform and persuade the public, the media, the employee base, the vendors and especially the customers or clients, and to steer them to a specific point of view favorable to the company or organization.

The experienced practitioner will present the facts and scenarios of what happened to cause the crisis in the best possible light without misleading, misinforming or misrepresenting anything to anybody.

It is immeasurably better to react to a tough question with "no comment" or "I'll get back to you" than to fudge the facts.

It is important to immediately address a crisis in the early stages. The public relations practitioner in charge must take the initiative and contact the media to help control and/or correct the message and information flow.

7. *10 Guidelines to Action*

1. Have management and key involved personnel fully prepared and available to talk with the media in non-conflicting terms where appropriate and possible.

2. Give out facts and reports on what occurred and its impact. Don't speculate. Include information on what safety and security measures were in effect and the past record of the company. Add in company background materials.

3. If the media arrives on site, provide a locale for interviews and use of a telephone. Be cooperative but do not lose control of your side of the story.

4. Check out all rumors with management and clarify with the media. Prepare fact sheets and position papers that reflect the company position in the best possible light without misleading or misinforming anyone.

5. Establish a crisis control team of management, involved personnel who are cleared by management and the public relations internal or external professional.

6. Inform employees and customers/clients who are directly involved in or affected by the crisis or problem, either in groups by supervisors or through letters or a newsletter. Reporting the facts will help control harmful rumors.

7. Continue monitoring the crisis and its aftermath. Prepare releases or fact sheets for the media and involved parties about the recovery effort and success.

8. Review media coverage of the crisis and correct errors in reporting via telephone calls or letters. Do not be overly critical of the media. Help them do a good job!

9. Review all procedures and actions so that everyone is prepared the next time a crisis or problem occurs.

10. Report all final findings to the team involved with resolution of the crisis or problem

Chapter Two

Community Relations

1. Reasons to Participate

Every business, organization and institution should participate in the affairs of their community of service, especially in light of September 11, 2001.

Here are three especially valid reasons:

1. It is the right thing to do

2. It will fulfill an important responsibility

3. It will bring deserved rewards and recognitions back to the participant.

2. Constantly Seeking Support

The civic and charity organizations and programs in all communities are constantly seeking support, and the goodwill and improved image of those who are actively involved and those who aren't become sharply defined.

The resultant goodwill, personal bonding and networking opportunities that will result from meaningful and well-intended community relations activity often translates into increased access, sales, political favors and positive word-of-mouth advertising.

Within the case profiles of the 'ski area and theme park' and 'luxury hotel' are samples of community relations activities by The Prather Group for its clients.

3. 10 Community Relations Activities

There are many activities that can be devised to successfully implement community relations programs for a client or employer, including:

1. Sponsoring a youth league sports team

2. Donating damaged or close-out goods to charities

3. Honoring charity requests with cash or a certificate for goods or services

4. Hosting a charity event at your business, if appropriate

5. Offering senior citizen discounts

6. Advertising in school yearbooks and event ad booklets

7. Hiring local youth, seniors or handicapped for the summer

8. Sponsoring management or supervisory employees into organizations

9. Attend and sponsor others to attend local events

10. Attending business, governmental and school board meetings

4. Taking Responsibility

In most instances the chief executive officer or president of a business or the executive director of an organization will assume the critical role of the point-person for the community relations programs and the public relations practitioner – either an employee or consultant – will fulfill the important but secondary role in all public appearances and visible activities. The consultant or employee does have the responsibility of keeping the point-person on track so the right organizations are supported and the right events are sponsored.

All of the efforts will combine to establish positive links with the community and will result in a return-on-investment that is clearly beneficial even though it might not be exactly quantified.

5. A Community Relations Example

Following is an example (case profile) of the first quarter of a 12-month community relations program for a hospital.

The *theme* and intent of the program was to position the hospital as a "Good Neighbor" so it would become even more the health institution of choice within its service area (see demographic attachments).

The *goal* of the program was to promote a team spirit among the varied factions of the hospital, including employees, doctors, volunteers and board members, and have that momentum carry through to the community and its leaders.

The ultimate *objective* of the program was to enhance the image of the hospital to all publics of interest and thereby boost patient use.

The *Action Plan* was put into motion with full approvals from the Administrator and the Board of Trustees. It was scheduled to continue unabated through the end of year one whereupon a *post mortem* analysis would determine the plan for the following year and beyond.

The *budget* approved for the first quarter of the 12-month plan (see attachment) was adhered to exactly.

The *results* after one quarter of activity included increased involvement by all concerned, enhanced media exposure and support, and most-importantly public acceptance that resulted in an increase in occupancy of four percent for the three-months of activity. This was a return-on-investment that surpassed the original forecast of three percent.

The *forecast* for the remainder of the year is for ever-increasing acceptance and occupancy as the program builds momentum.

The *program elements* implemented under the guidelines of the original proposal met most of the stated activities and objectives, including the following:

- Formation of a PR committee including management, the board, employees, volunteers

- A "Good Neighbor News" newsletter mailed bi-monthly to the community of service

- A brochure distributed for pick-up at area businesses and doctors offices

- "I'm A Good Neighbor" buttons with the hospital logo for employees, trustees, volunteers

- Appearances by management and board members at key civic and business events

- Participation in or sponsorship of community projects and special events

- Media releases and interviews in area publications and on broadcast media

Results included the following activities in the first quarter of activity:

Media -

- Obtained a series of 90-second public service announcements from two local radio stations and one cable-TV station. The spots were recorded by a member of the medical staff, a Trustee, an employee, an Auxiliary Club member and a volunteer.

- Met with the local daily newspaper to successfully pitch a series of hospital news and feature releases, and requested and gained positive editorial commentary on the Good Neighbor program (see clip copies attached).

- Wrote and placed a feature story about three long-time elderly volunteers of the hospital in an area magazine, a feature article and photos about the new ER unit, and articles about hospital participation in the 'Great American Smoke-Out' and the new hospital pediatric wing, and arranged a 30-minute cable-TV interview with the Board president on local healthcare issues.

Internal Relations -

- Signed up employees to various PR and special event committees
- Obtained volunteers for promotional assignments
- Established an at-cost in-house PR photographer
- Created a rapid-response for information to and from management
- Arranged for medical staff participation in PR activities
- Arranged for Women's Auxiliary special event participation
- Created an internal employees monthly bulletin

Printed Materials -

- Published the first external newsletter
- Published the first two employees newsletters
- Created boilerplate design template for PR promotional flyers
- Published a low-cost but quality brochure for patients, doctors' offices and pharmacies
- Produced signs for use internally and on the grounds re the good neighbor theme
- Produced "I'm a Good Neighbor" buttons with hospital logo

Summary: Various factions of the hospital family - trustees, doctors, employees, Auxiliary members, volunteers, *etc.* - have participated *en masse* in the new program and have asked for it to continue.

Thus far the community relations program has been highly successful in meeting its goals of increased occupancy and public image enhancement and is moving into a new quarter with increased involvement by all publics of interest and consistent attention from the media.

All of this was attained within budget.

6. Employee Relations, Too

A business will benefit from active internal and external relations programs that involve base line employees a well as managers where appropriate. They should be encouraged or sponsored into joining civic and business organizations and to participate in community affairs, then recognized for their good work by management.

Following are some of the ways for a business to relate to its employees and get them involved both internally and externally. Of course, many more are discussed in other chapters of this guidebook.

- Underwrite the dues for employees to join service clubs (Rotary, Kiwanis, *etc.*)
- Form a Speaker's Bureau and prepare the speaker to address organizations
- Start an "Employee of the Month" (and year) program
- Train managers to attend high school and college career days
- Hold quarterly or semi-annual functions for employees and their families
- Present employees with a Christmas gift or bonus
- Provide a free turkey to employees on Thanksgiving Day
- Create a summer student jobs program
- Adopt a county or stretch of state highway (for clean-up)

Chapter Three

Special Events

1. A Unique Place

Special events have a unique place in the hearts of any public relations practitioner. They can be the source of great success and pride, or . . . well, did you ever throw a party and no one came?

Special events can be great fun but *always* create anxiety. The fun comes from the promise of an exciting function that features activities or entertainment that allows a client's clients to mingle with existing or potential customers while promoting their company or organization.

And then there is that special *high* that comes at the conclusion of a successful event.

The anxiety stems from the absolute requirement for careful planning, attention to detail and timely implementation. All are critical in the world of special events.

Whether the function is a fund-raising dinner for a not-for-profit organization, a sales promotion at a mall, a charity softball game, or a celebrity appearance, pay attention to the *Three D's: detail, deadline and delivery!*

The Special Event Checklist in this book will prove invaluable to the chairperson and committee for a special event. Use it from inception through post-event evaluation to keep all on track.

2. Determine the Objective and Budget

After the chairperson and committee members' specific responsibilities have been assigned, the objective of the event should be determined. Then, care should be given to estimating attendance based on previous functions, or by using collective common sense.

Remember that it is better to overestimate than to underestimate attendance, especially if you are arranging for the food and beverage, the latter of which may be returned if unused and unopened.

A budget should be assigned to cover all of the key elements needed in a successful program: advertising, printed materials, the invitation, mailing costs, the menu, the site costs and miscellaneous expenses. Payment to vendors should be according to parameters established when making the arrangements.

If the event were planned to be a fundraiser, the objective would be to earn enough profit to make the event worthwhile. If it were planned to be simply a promotional activity, then the goal would be to conduct the function cost-efficiently and gain as much goodwill as is possible.

3. Committee Leaders Must Do Their Jobs

The event chairperson should insure that committee leaders all do their jobs because any breakdown in one area affects all other areas. That is why regular meetings and use of the checklist are so critical.

It is important to remember that the universal honoring of timelines and deadlines by each member of the committee and all involved in the event are extremely important to the ultimate result.

Finally, post-event evaluation and summaries will help insure that your next special event will be even more successful.

See the Special Events Checklist in the section devoted to custom PR forms.

4. Budgets Count

An event must be conducted with an overall budget that includes all cost items: from location to food and beverage, from sound and lighting equipment to set up charges, from entertainment to emcee. Every expense must be considered in advance so there are no surprises when the bills come due.

One person with at least some basic cost accounting experience should be selected to oversee the budget through the entire process.

Common sense projections of how much money can be raised by the event and how much money it will cost to put on are two vital questions to consider. An organization attempting to raise funds at an event must expend existing funds carefully and wisely or it could end up in the red.

As in a business, the objective of a charity event is to make as much money for the organization as is possible, as well as to publicize and promote it. Businesses practices therefore should be applied to each investment along the way. Ask about each purchase or rental: is it at the best price, is it necessary and is it right? Then invest in the program accordingly.

PR Tip: Ensure that an event suits the image of the organization.

Chapter Four

Sales Promotion

1. Many Areas to Consider

There is no specific definition of sales promotion. The term interprets as any means of increasing sales through standard PR techniques such as promotion events, publicity, advertising, direct mail or signing.

There are many areas of sales promotion to consider, including these 10:

1. Direct mail incentives

2. Point of purchase (POP) displays

3. Contests

4. Special events

5. Specialty advertising/sale days

6. Celebrity appearances

7. Product demonstrations

8. Premium giveaways*

9. VIP customer listings

10. Closeouts

*According to PRSA's prize-winning publication, Public Relations TACTICS of February 2002, Counselor Magazine named the top 10 promotional products, imprinted items that are commonly dispensed at shows and expositions, *etc.* They are: tote-bags, calendars, key tags, Tee-shirts, rulers, matchbooks, mugs, magnets, writing instruments and caps. They have been constants in the promotions industry for as long as this author has practiced PR.

2. 10 Tips for Merchants

1. Keep signing, literature and advertising consistent in theme and style.

2. Advertise in strength, when business is good.

3. Use a media mix of print, broadcast and direct mail.

4. Maintain a good community image through participation in charity and civic projects.

5. Utilize cooperative advertising.

6. Keep pace with new marketing trends in your line(s).

7. Hold special events or sale days.

8. Keep your brochures, flyers, *etc.* up-to-date and distributed properly.

9. Make sure your displays are modern and change according to seasons, trends, *etc.*

10. Regularly evaluate your advertising and promotion expenditures and fund accordingly.

3. *10 Tips for Community Relations*

1. Sponsor employees or business associates into charitable organizations and create a budget for participation in events and sponsorships.

2. Sponsor employees or business associates into civic and business organizations and create a budget for participation in the organizations' activities.

3. Host on-site or sponsor a charity or civic fund-raising event.

4. Participate in local affairs such as joining or supporting organizations and attending functions.

5. Hire local youths or college-students in interns or in work-study programs when possible.

6. Organize employees for blood drives, clothing drives and other community oriented endeavors.

7. Create an appropriate public service advertising budget for charity, civic and school publications.

8. Sponsor a boy or girl's youth league sports team.

9. Donate damaged or closed-out goods to charities and fund-raising auctions.

10. Provide on-site tours and luncheons, or a special event, for senior citizens.

4. *Desktop Printing*

The small business owner would be wise to investigate the newest desktop printing software and examine if he or she, or an employee, is capable of following it to design and produce quality printed promotional material.

Until recently, professional looking type was solely the domain of those with high-end phototypesetting equipment. It required not only the know-how to operate the equipment but a precise understanding of how to properly spec the type to fit the available space. With these skills came an understanding of the subtleties that create eye-appealing and readable type.

The layman needed no knowledge of what made good looking type; just about everything was typeset and designed by a professional and the rest of the universe was limited to typewriters or word processors connected to clunky dot matrix printers. But those were the days of yore.

Just a decade ago most PC users thought they could publish anything using Desktop Publishing (DTP). It was partially true as the need for costly photo-typesetting equipment was indeed eliminated. What happened (and in some cases continues) is that small businesses produced mountains of laser printed clutter that can confuse and disturb the reader and is often passed over. Among the unsatisfactory and common results were smudging, less than precise reproduction on newspaper print, blurring – examples abound. The inferior reproduction reduces the chance of the message being read and absorbed by the target.

Advanced software and PC's rule the scene now and the average person is no longer bound to the standard typewriter or early computer equipment.

Small business owners should learn desktop publishing properly and fully or count on a graphics professional for assistance to design and produce documents such as letters, ads, flyers, brochures, newsletters – whatever is needed to influence potential customers.

5. Trade Shows and Expositions

Small business owners can benefit from trade shows and expositions on many fronts: to learn about new products and innovations at an industry event or to see what the competition is doing and to show off his or her own wares at an appropriate event.

Another opportunity is for the exhibitor to enhance its relationship with the media through arranged or by-chance interviews with industry publication reporters at the booth.

Better yet, the exhibitor can book a private room for a media conference and reception to introduce a new product or announce a major newsworthy item such as a merger, acquisition, ownership change, CEO or president change, *etc.* Be prepared with product displays, media kits and prepared remarks and expect incisive questions from the press.

Choose the right events to participate in and make certain the booth is in prime condition and updated, and that printed materials, signing and incentives such as contests or gifts are prepared early in the game.

Attempt to get a choice location for the booth, although choices are often made through random placement, first come first served or seniority in participation. Read the event instructions and follow the rules from shipping the booth to breakdown and removal very carefully.

The budget must include the costs for the event including booth set-up, break-down, construction, electrical, telephone, *etc.*, all materials, all expenses for attending personnel including travel, food, miscellaneous, and ancillary event costs such as for a media conference.

The most important element often ignored by exhibitors is follow-up. You must contact your contacts and follow-through on their post-show interest or the event will not be cost-effective and your return-on-investment will be minimized.

Chapter Five

Reader Preference Survey

1. What are the Publications of Interest?

A survey of existing and potential customers for the PR practitioner's employer or client can determine their reliance on and rating of key industry publications. This will provide valuable guidelines to help the practitioner decide which outlets are the most effective for advertising and publicizing the company or organization they represent.

Among the benefits from a well-crafted reader-preference survey will be:

- Insights into how the main target audiences are influenced by and rate publications

- An increased awareness of the company or organization by those surveyed

- Valuable additions to the mailing list from those surveyed

The first step is for the practitioner, in concert with the marketing and sales department, to create the mailing list from a combination of existing and potential customers. The list should be large enough to provide quality results and small enough to be manageable.

2. Letter to the Decision-Maker

To do a survey of a customer or client's industry reading preferences, first craft the survey and a cover letter to be sent to key decision-makers asking them to participate. It could be to the owner, president, marketing manager – whoever handles the advertising decisions and budget approvals.

The tone of the letter should be courteous and professional, and should express thanks in advance to those who complete and return the survey. It should clearly state the deadline for return.

A promotional item to inspire participation should be included or sent later under separate cover.

This small but valuable research effort will identify which publications are read by and most influence the advertiser. This information, as well as reader demographics, areas of circulation, cost-per-reader, total circulation and competitor advertising, will be used to determine publications in which to invest advertising dollars.

The ratings from the 1-to10 point system (see custom form) will indicate strongly which publications are influencing the industry leaders the most and, equally important, persuading them the least! This information will guide the practitioner in selecting the best publications for your advertising and publicity.

3. 10 Steps to Follow

To initiate the survey the following steps should be followed:

1. Reproduce sufficient quantities of the custom form titled Customer/Client Survey
2. Create and produce the cover letter
3. Create and produce the survey questions
4. Produce a return response mechanism, a postage-paid envelope or reply card
5. Label the envelopes with the names, titles and addresses of targets on the mailing list.
6. Add in a note about or send under separate cover an incentive promotional gift item
7. Designate a point-person to receive and tabulate the responses
8. Prepare a report on the results for management and marketing/sales
9. Send thank you notes to the participants
10. Make your advertising recommendations accordingly

Note: In most cases, the evaluations will be clear. In others, interpretations will be needed to account for deviations from the norm or commentaries contained in responses to the survey.

4. Internal Marketing Audit

Outside customer surveys of various types can be important tools for gathering pertinent information that can guide the practitioner in planning future programs for a business but not the only ones.

An internal audit of the advertising programs (and dollar investment) used in the past will also provide valuable information on how to proceed in the future. An analysis of the advertising and marketing programs will reveal their relative success or failure - or something in-between – and lead to more effective ones in the future.

The internal audit should take into account a company or organization's sales and revenues, profits and losses, marketing history and current plans, budget histories, recent successes and failures, known positives and negatives of products or services, development plans, management attitudes, and employee satisfaction, retention and attitudes, *etc.*

The more effective the advertising and marketing is the better will be a company's position in the marketplace. To successfully accomplish an internal marketing audit, evaluate the following:

*   The status of each product line
*   The competitive status of each product line
*   Current advertising and marketing efforts and budget

- Total investment dollars and resources necessary to reach stated goals

- The status of the marketing and sales team

5. *Providing Insights and Input*

Key executives, customers, vendors and select employees can all provide insights and input during the internal audit, not only to determine the statistical overviews but how they all actually *feel* about the company or organization. They can be reached via personal interviews, surveys and through in-house focus groups.

The external audit requires understanding just what it will take to attain the goals of a company or organization.

Key elements that must be understood are:

- What are the target markets and the publics of interest?

- What are the methods available to reach and influence them?

- Who are the key competitors and how they and the industry in general doing?

- How is the business or organization and products or services perceived by target markets

- How to compare the data with past or future audits

6. *Industry Experts and Consultants*

The external audit process can determine the current status and trends within the industry by also seeking the opinions of industry experts and consultants and by closely evaluating the products, services, marketing efforts and relative successes of key competitors.

Public Focus Groups can be assembled and designed for input on existing and new products and services to help guide the decision-making process.

All of the research can be managed by the trained public relations practitioner, in concert with experts in the fields, marketing professionals or more formally in collaboration with a qualified research firm. This choice depends on the scope and depth of the mission.

It is essential to find an expert researcher who is well informed and cost-conscious, and who will work alongside the PR practitioner each step of the way to jointly develop an effective action plan within an affordable budget.

The public relations practitioner should attempt to learn as much about research as is possible, not to upstage the researcher but to work better with him or her, and to learn more about the process for future research projects.

Chapter Six

Direct Mail Basics

1. Basic Objectives

The basics of successful direct mail programs for a company or organization dictate that they must be efficient, well produced and stylish to be cost-effective.

The public relations practitioner must fully understand the process in order to initiate and oversee a successful program from conception through budgeting through implementation through _post mortem_ analysis through follow-up activity.

Three basic objectives of a direct mail program are to sell, promote or help brand a product or service, and three basic principals are that it should be targeted to the right publics at the right time with the right printed material.

Direct mail is also used to promote community relations ventures such as special events, or for communications to help ameliorate a crisis or problem. The PR practitioner, in conjunction with the management and marketing teams, should establish the standard of response required.

2. 'ROI' is the Key

Return-on-investment (ROI) is the key to any marketing communications program, including direct-mail, be it for the short range benefit of gaining sales leads or closures, or branding a product or service to targeted publics of interest.

Direct mail can employ a wide range of printed materials, including a brochure and reply mechanism such as a card or coupon, a flyer promoting a sales special, a price list or technical sheet, a survey to be completed and returned, or a credibility building flyer, letter or newsletter.

Many direct mail experts plan for a response of at least one percent to be break-even, two percent to be better than break-even, and three percent or more to be successful. There are many variables in this equation such as the cost of the program that will determine the ROI. However, ROI is not the only consideration: success often depends on whether or not the program increased sales, provided leads or helped to effectively brand the product or service.

3. Specialists Can Help

Research firms and specialists should be retained to help design and implement a direct mail campaign, including identifying markets most likely respond favorably to a direct mail piece.

Researchers can also help to geographically target appropriate recipients, establish program objectives, set response goals, determine the type of piece(s) to be produced, suggest budgets for production, handling and postage, prepare a schedule, design follow-up procedures, evaluate the results and propose follow-up activities. The follow-ups will be cost-efficient if all returns for any reason are culled from the next mailing and potential new recipients are added to the list by the firm doing the work in conjunction with the public relations consultant or employee.

Research professionals can also organize and conduct focus groups to forecast the viability of a product or service and indicate if it can be successfully marketed or branded via direct mail.

4. Melding Techniques

Research will determine where direct mail will be going and what will be mailed. This should be viewed as an important part of any integrated marketing communications plan that melds public relations and advertising techniques in order to accomplish a company or organization goal.

Direct mail employs its own in-depth science and these few basic notes will begin the journey toward understanding and implementing programs that will work for the PR practitioner who either opts to go it alone or who chooses to retain a professional in that field. In either case, the public relations pro would be wise to study the subject so expenditures can be made wisely and outside resources retained as needed to fulfill the research mission.

5. 10 Tips for Direct Mail

1. Create and produce an attractive and efficient mailing package of the main piece, envelope and response-mechanism.

2. Research and plan for all costs, including for postage and handling, list-acquisition, printing of the package, and follow-up tracking and analysis.

3. Determine the objectives of the program as to inquiries, leads or sales desired.

4. Evaluate the predicted percentage-of-response ratios according to industry standards for the type of direct mail program that is implemented.

5. Research the target lists to ensure the addresses and zip codes are valid to the mission.

6. Remove all unopened or mislabeled returns from future mailings.

7. Review current innovations, available direct mail services and modern techniques.

8. Consider adding promotional items and incentives to the package to attract interest.

9. Understand the differences between cold canvassing and prime mailing to known prospects and gear to your mission and budget accordingly.

10. Research cost-efficient use of zip codes, pre-sorting, posting and bulk rates where suited for mailings; third class mail is cheaper but not suited to many direct mailing campaigns.

Section Four

Chapter One

Advertising Support

1. A Major Support Vehicle

Advertising is the major support vehicle for the strategic public relations and marketing program and vice-versa. Both elements of the strategic plan must work in tandem to create synergy and become successful.

Creating and placing stylish and informative advertisements in the right publications at the right time and within budget will help to fulfill strategic public relations missions and objectives, including generating sales leads and orders, and ultimately revenues and profits.

A balanced mix of creative, institutional, informational and direct-sell advertising can attain great results and help brand a company, product or service. It will also help to result in fulfill objectives and realize a good return-on-investment (ROI) of advertising dollars.

All of the strategic marketing communications programs should be *filial*, with a consistent style, look, and theme or motto throughout. Each element should complement each other element for synergism, as multiple exposure equals remembrance.

The industry standard for numbers of messages necessary to retain a company, product or service is nine so repeated messages with a consistent look will work best on the memory bank. This messaging mix will include advertising, publicity, direct mail, signage, promotion, printed materials, *etc. Note: Advertising forms are located in the forms section at the end of this book.*

2. Preparing for the Ad Campaign

To prepare for the advertising campaign, ad sales kits and editorial calendars should be acquired from each of the publications under consideration in order to build a timely and effective schedule for the client or employer.

The Insert Order Form should be reproduced and used by the in-house agency with final artwork of advertisements submitted for publication, coupled with a cover letter on official agency letterhead.

The form indicates the type of ad (display or classified) and if it is for specific placement or ROP (run of the press). The insertion dates, ad size, description, and other instructions are among the other key requirements.

3. Payment Methods

Most publications require advance payment until credit is established. Both external and in-house agencies are entitled to the standard agency commission (SAC) of 15 percent for ad placements, although commissions can vary from publication to publication. The net 85 percent due to the publication reflects either a profit of 15 percent for the outside agency or a savings of 15 percent for the in-house agency's employer. If the publication allows a two percent pre-pay discount, it should be deducted from the cost after the SAC deduction.

Some publications have non-commissionable rates that must be paid in full by the agency. An outside agency would then bill the client that amount plus the standard 17.65 percent commission (deduct 15 percent to return to the original figure.) An in-house agency would bill the employer at cost and note the 15 percent savings on the invoice.

It is wise to build good relations with ad reps and to cultivate editors if the plan is to submit publicity material. When an ad appears, an agency can purchase reprints for distribution to customers and for sales portfolios, *etc.*

4. Media Ad Impact

Any publication that features an advertisement placed by a PR practitioner must be an instrument for lead-generation and eventual sales in order to be deemed effective.

Any publication that is effective must also provide a profitable return-on-investment (ROI) in order for it to be deemed successful!

How are these complex standards of effect and success measured?

One method is to compile the total number of leads generated, the volume of sales, and the total revenue produced. In this way, statistical measures of the effect of an ad and of the publication in which it appeared can be compiled and analyzed.

More important, however, is the return-on-investment, which can be measured by comparing the gross revenue income resulting from an ad to its total cost for production and placement.

The Media Impact form provides the format and methods to determine these two important results: the cost-per-inquiry and the ROI:

1) For the "cost-per-inquiry", divide the total ad cost by the number of inquiries. For example, if the ad production and placement cost $1,000 and generated 200 inquiries, then the cost-per-inquiry would be $5 (1,000 divided by 200).

2) For the "ROI", divide the total gross revenues in sales resulting from the ad by the total ad cost. For example, if the gross sales totaled $20,000 and the ad cost $1,000, then the ROI would be 20-to-1 (20,000 divided by 1,000).

It should be noted that sales resulting from inquiries could result long after the ad appears. Therefore, credit must be given for continuing leads generated from a specific ad and its host publication.

There are also qualitative ways to measure the apparent value of an individual outlet, including the publication's integrity and production standards, placement of ancillary publicity or listings, and advantageous ad placement (far-forward and on the right-hand page, for example).

However, what matters in the final analysis is: *which ad in which publication produced the most revenue and profit.*

The ads and publications that best fit that final analysis are the ones that should find a permanent location on the ad calendar.

5. *Media Ad Comparisons*

Media comparisons will assess the performance of an advertisement in each of the trade publications it appeared in. This will guide the decision as to which specific outlets to choose for future placement and will provide a strong element to long-range planning by the PR practitioner.

The practitioner should review the following ad forms in this book for the total picture:

1) Media Ad Impact
2) Media Calendar
3) Advertising Budget
4) Media Ad Comparisons.

The forms collectively will provide statistical information and analyses necessary to make informed decisions on pending advertising selections and campaigns. The Advertising Insert Order form will assist making the ad placements.

The Media Ad Comparisons form is designed to hold information on seven trade publications. Simply use additional copies of the reproducible form to measure even more outlets.

The form will provide a quick-glance overview of the ads' performances. The name of each publication is followed by the date(s) the ad appeared and the official circulation, then lists the total number of inquiries the ad generated, the volume of sales that resulted, and the total gross revenues of income the company realized from those sales.

The line that lists ad rates and cost-per-thousand tells the relative expense for each publication. Compare that to the inquiries and revenues generated and a clear picture emerges of the performances of each of the publications that featured the same ad the same amount of times.

To calculate the cost-per-thousand for each publication, enter the cost for identical space in each of the outlets and divide that number into the total circulation broken down into thousands.

For example:

If a 2-column x 8-inch ad in Publication 1 costs $3,000 and the circulation is 30,000, then the cost-per-thousand would be: $3,000 divided by 30, or $100-per-thousand.

If the same ad in Publication 2 costs $5,000 and the circulation is 18,000, then the cost-per-thousand would be: $5,000 divided by 18, or $277.77 per-thousand.

The cost-per-thousand for the outlets can be measured by employing the same formula. There is no way of measuring the effects of the proposed ads until after they appear but the practitioner can figure relative costs.

Every informational byte is helpful in assessing the advertising plan and gaining a tactical edge on your competition.

6. Media Ad Schedule

A tremendous amount of advertising data can be accumulated on the Media Schedule information-gathering form. Key elements can then be transferred to a calendar spreadsheet for general review within the practitioner's company or organization marketing department, and ultimately by management.

A fine-point writing instrument and careful input of the information will provide one all-encompassing vehicle on which to record and share the many details of the advertising programs. The form for this is easily reproducible for continued schedule maintenance and tracking.

Next to each item in the first column that begins with the name of the publication, simply enter the correct detail. For the 'key code', insert the correct number from the key code legend that appears near the end of document. The letters A-through-I represent informational areas outlined in the letter code section. For example: size information should be entered under the calendar month during which the ad will appear.

Two more examples are: C (key #) and D (insert order #) should be entered in the allocated space under the calendar month during which the advertisement will be published.

The trade publications are indicated by month, but weekly or daily publications should be listed by exact date.

Special issues, where applicable, should be labeled by their particular theme or focus name. Attach information or explanation sheets to the forms wherever they are necessary.

Broadcast advertising on local radio and cable television outlets can also be efficiently tracked on a detailed calendar sheet that includes the following information elements:

- Each broadcast outlet's call letters and name

- The sales representative's name and telephone number

- The number of spots booked on each outlet

- The length of each spot: 30-second or 60-second

- The dates and times the spots are scheduled to run.

- The reach (coverage area) of the outlet

- The estimated numbers of viewers or listeners

- The cost-per-spot and total cost per-outlet

- The cost for production

- The total broadcast budget amount.

- The availability of PSA's (free public service announcements).

The public relations practitioner's job is to oversee the in-house or external agency's advertising and marketing communications efforts. They will be greatly enhanced if there are detailed print and broadcast records of all placements and their costs.

7. Advertising Budget

Determining the amount of investment for an initial advertising campaign is a difficult job, not only because the return-on-investment (ROI) cannot be measured until after the fact but because there are so many other places to spend ad funds.

However, the practitioner must bite the bullet and invest in advertising if he or she wishes to claim a significant portion of the market in which the company or organization operates.

There are several methods to determine just how much should be invested in advertising. Those with experience in advertising can determine which publications and which advertisements worked in the past, and then build on them for the present and future. And those with external ad agencies can follow the recommendations of the 'experts'. The funds dedicated to advertising will in large part be dictated by the previous ROI.

Novices should avoid a scattergun approach to advertising. They should utilize the various forms and plan a professional approach to their business marketing programs. This will eliminate much of the waste associated with a lack of planning.

Many established businesses allocate three percent of their gross sales to advertising. A newcomer to the ad world might determine a set annual affordable sum, or a fixed percentage of estimated revenues, broken down into quarterly expenditures.

Whatever advertising budget the practitioner decides upon, he or she must make certain it is spent as wisely as possible.

If there is a strong season for the company or organization to advertise, then do it after research and planning.

If there is a certain event meaningful to the company or organization, such as an exhibition or show, then increase the advertising just prior to or during the early stages of the event.

Common sense will dictate how ad funds should be spent. The tracking forms will give structure to the programs and help the practitioner to avoid improper decision-making.

The Quarterly Budget form includes allocations for print advertising and production, broadcast advertising and production, public relations support advertising and applicable fees and expenses.

It also includes budget amounts for direct mail and telemarketing, which must create their own sub-budgets. For example, direct mail has many associated costs, such as for mailing lists, postage and handling, printed pieces, reply mechanisms and premium costs.

Proper advertising will be one of the most solid vehicles to increase sales and profits. And when paired with publicity and other public relations vehicles, it will serve as an anchor, too.

Many firms use three percent of the gross as their yardstick for determining how much to spend in these areas. Others spend as much as 25 percent, and realize profits because of it. Others spend little or nothing, but only rarely does that make sense in this competitive and highly-communicative world.

The public relations novice or those doing their own advertising should spend according to their own budget availabilities.

They also should consider the advice of those in the know: the experienced public relations and advertising professionals in their midst.

PR practitioners must understand the principles of advertising if they wish to satisfy the complete marketing needs of their clients or employers.

PR Note: Publicity is inherently more believable than advertising.

Chapter Two

e-Mail and the Internet

1. Fulfilling Needs

The escalating use of e-mail for advertising and publicity reflects the fast-paced society we all live in that requires instant gratification in virtually everything, including the need to sell and buy products and services and dispense information. Well done, the e-mail and the Internet fulfill those needs.

Electronic mail outpaces regular mail (now known as 'snail mail') hands down. And 'spam' is so much frowned upon that it is now ranked below telemarketing during dinnertime.

You can sell products or provide info directly, or refer recipients to your website if you can get them to open your e-mail transmission.

Proper use of e-mail and Internet advertising and promotion are incumbent on the public relations consultant who most often must work in concert with an expert in the electronic communications fields.

Whether you are dispensing a sales pitch, a newsletter, a news article or a memo, e-mail is the fastest method both internally and externally.

Brokers can advise their clients as to what's happening in the markets . . . fundraisers can promote their upcoming special event . . . a company can announce a major new product or promotion . . . the potentials are enormous.

2. Staggering Numbers

The numbers are staggering. According to the Nielsen/Net Ratings, Internet usage rose 15 percent from 2000 to 2001 in the United States - to more than 115 million users.

Users are becoming inured to the pitfalls of the Internet because it is such a vital tool. Ever more sophisticated, they are avoiding the viruses spread with bad intentions and greater remedies are being developed to control the problem.

3. A Significant Resource, Not a Panacea

The Internet should be viewed as a marketing and public relations resource and not a panacea. It is true that you can use the net to showcase your own website to promote your products or services, online advertising and e-mail messaging of a commercial or personal nature.

That said, a report issued by the PR Newswire on February 6, 2002, does give Internet advertising a high mark. It said:

"In a joint presentation to agency and corporate advertising executives, the Advertising Research Foundation (ARP), the Interactive Advertising Bureau (IAB), the MSN@ network of Internet services from Microsoft Corp., and researcher Rex Briggs today announced the results of groundbreaking new research that validates the importance of online advertising."

It continued: "The culmination of a yearlong investigation of the relative effectiveness or and synergies between online and traditional media advertising, the research found that online advertising's share in the media mix can have a significant increase in the effectiveness of an overall advertising campaign."

4. 10 tips for Internet Advertising

Here are 10 tips for the PR practitioner re the Internet and e-mail:

1. Build an e-mail address book of customers or clients for sales campaigns or information transmission

2. Purchase lists of targeted and qualified addressees who opted to be included

3. Employ clever and well-produced e-mail to reach them

4. Develop a deployment tracking system to track numbers of recipients and opened e-mail

5. Do not allow 'spamming' (mass unsolicited messaging) to taint your professional endeavors

6. Respond to inquiries or sales commitments on the same day or as soon as possible

7. If immediate fulfillment is impossible, advise the sender ASAP when it will be done

8. Install and continuously upgrade anti-virus software

9. Obtain the services as needed of an Internet professional for training and service

10. Learn from your mistakes and do not repeat them; do not give up – you need the Internet and e-mail.

Marketing Reality: Consultants who treat their clients fairly and honestly will soon learn that and they will be their best sources of advertising through good word-of-mouth. The opposite is also true.

Chapter Three

Doing Your Own Newsletters

1. Controlling the Message

Controlling the message is important to companies and organizations that wish to influence target audiences, employees and others. The clever use of newsletters by public relations practitioners for a business or organizations or for themselves can accomplish just that.

Newsletters can express opinion, build goodwill and morale, promote products and services, tout management, communicate in crises, enhance morale, and be informative and interesting, too.

However, this just doesn't happen. Newsletters need style and substance, elements that require hard work, creativity and an appropriate investment of funds.

Newsletters can control the message like no other outlet or venue and, used properly and wisely, it can be a major toll in the public relations practitioner's arsenal.

And it now can be sold electronically over the Internet or via direct mail that boosts its potential circulation enormously.

2. Follow Simple Steps

The newsletter instructions and form in this book will assist the PR practitioner to create or reformat a company or organizational newsletter. It provides an important checklist for setting deadlines, determining subject material, assigning tasks for editing, graphics, printing, distribution, *etc.*

If the newsletter is to be published entirely in-house, then following the simple steps will provide a solid foundation. If outside professional assistance is required, then it will be helpful to designate appropriate individual internal responsibilities.

First, a newsletter committee should be formed and a chairperson selected. Then the editor and supervisors should be designated according to their abilities to manage the following:

- Articles and features
- Editorials and commentary
- Assignments and material management
- Personals and letters

- Photography and graphics
- Layout and design
- Editing and headlining
- Printing and distribution

Other important tasks to fulfill in order to establish a solid foundation for the newsletter include:

- Selection of an appealing and appropriate newsletter name
- Establishment of a budget for production and distribution
- Planning publication dates as quarterly, monthly, annually or semi-annually
- Determining objectives for the newsletter
- Deciding on the number of pages and the total copies required
- Arranging for the method and outlet for printing
- Establishing and monitoring all deadlines
- Planning methods of distribution via mail, handout, electronic or POP displays

3. *Specialized Information in Your Newsletter*

The continuing expansion and diversion of businesses, organizations, manufacturers, arts and crafts enthusiasts, sports fans, and hobbyists, *et al*, into more and more specialized areas of endeavor has enhanced the need for more information via print or electronic newsletters. Publishing your own newsletter may provide a potentially effective vehicle for you to cash in on the ever-expanding markets for specialized information.

You can write and produce your own newsletter from your home or office with a low overhead and potential for high returns. Weekly, monthly or bi-monthly newsletter subscription rates can range in subscription costs, depending on the content, quality and delivery mechanism: Internet or mail.

Do your homework and scout the competition, then price your newsletter accordingly. You can always upgrade the newsletter and its cost as you satisfy your readers. Just a few hundred subscribers will bring in substantial earnings.

There are no tried and true methods of making a newsletter successful, but if you investigate your own market thoroughly and are cautious in your moves, you can make turn it into a sound profit center year after year.

You don't have to be a famous business consultant or an insider on the stock market to produce a newsletter. There are many that cater to all types of businesses and organizations, sports, arts and crafts, health, housing or moneymaking ideas.

The most important aspect of creating a successful newsletter is the market. You need to research who will buy the subscription and how much they are willing to pay. But there are sound methods of testing the market so you can be sure to come out ahead and establish yourself in your own field of professional interest through the interesting format of your own newsletter.

If you have a special interest that has a broad following, you might find that a newsletter will be readily accepted and flourish.

What interests or hobbies have you been involved with that can make a lively income for you? If you follow the steps and carefully consider your market, there is no reason why you can't get into the newsletter business too.

4. *What Should a Newsletter Do?*

As you move forward in developing your own newsletter, remember that it should be a special and timely report on a subject that you fully understand. It will become a personalized and concise statement that helps to establish you as an expert (or player) who is thoroughly familiar with that specific field or endeavor.

The beautiful part is that you will totally control the message.

Newsletters are maintained solely by subscriptions; there is no advertising. Most are printed within low budget means and range from two to eight pages, rarely more.

The specialized information in newsletters is current and some of it usually cannot be found elsewhere. They are a logical extension to trade journals and magazines.

Aimed at a select group of subscribers, they often contain inside information, hot tips, speculation, opinion pieces and news scoops that then become old news in subsequent publications within the trade.

Newsletters are not distributed at newsstands nor are they meant for the mass market. In fact, the average number of potential readers of newsletters in any one field is relatively small.

Because of their specific information, newsletters can command a fairly high subscription fee and eventually result in handsome profits. Businesses can afford to spend the money to inform their executives with the top-rate inside information you will provide.

Primarily through the Internet, there are now thousands of newsletters being published and distributed in the United States. But there is room for thousands more.

Because of specialized markets, there is often acceptable competition among newsletters, and there is a continuously rising trend toward subscribing to numerous ones. Nobody wants to miss out on industry news and, hopefully, your opinion and take on the industry involved.

Note: The Prather Group will be launching a newsletter in 2003.

5. Why Are Newsletters So Popular?

With all the print media and Internet visual communications in this country, you might think there is a saturated market in newsletters. That seems especially true when it comes to general interest mass-market publications.

However, the need for specific information in specialized fields is constantly increasing. Questions abound: How can I beat the competition? How does world events and business news affect my industry? Will a union strike on the other side of the nation or world cause us to raise our prices? What are our competitors up to?

The focus of the newsletter is success: in business, in hobbies, health and in happiness. The information contained in the newsletters motivates readers to follow the advice. What are the best investments? Where are the trade shows? How can I get an edge on winning contests?

There is an endless need for specific knowledge in every field of endeavor. Since there is a high standard of competition within every aspect of our modern life, people search for ways to be in the know, and use that information effectively.

One of the reasons subscription prices can stay high is because people are paying for the knowledge and what might be gained by it. If a two hundred dollar newsletter saves a company thousands of dollars in excellent advice, then it is well worth the price.

6. What it Takes

You can start a newsletter by yourself; you don't need a large staff. A desk at home, a computer and a telephone are all the basic tools you need to create a newsletter. Even when you get into computerized labels and mass mailings, you still will not need a large space to operate.

You don't need to invest a lot of money to begin a simple newsletter. You will need to invest in Internet or direct-mail advertising to introduce your NL to potential subscribers.

And of course you need to spend some money on getting the first newsletter printed. However, your return-on-investment will make it all worthwhile.

7. What to Write About

The topic you choose has got to be your major interest. You'll be living with it day in and day out for years, so you need to be devoted to the subject. Usually, it's not hard. You probably already have a chosen field of endeavor, or have developed a keen interest in a special hobby or sport. Writing a newsletter is only one more way to demonstrate your interest.

Read any newsletters you can find. What do they talk about? How much do they cost? How long have they been in business? You might want to talk to some publishers to learn how they started and what troubles they encountered. Consider paying a small consulting fee for their advice.

Take a look at all the trade magazines of the topic you'd like to work with. Find out if there are any newsletters already existing in that field. But don't worry--there is usually room for more if you keep to another aspect of the business or endeavor.

Keep up with the current trends in health, money, sports, or social events and styles. What's new with the young people or the elderly? There are many retired people actively pursuing hundreds of various interests. How can you tap into that market?

8. Who Will Subscribe?

The first place to test who will subscribe to your very own newsletter is to ask associates and colleagues – not for their subscription, just for their input. Ask what they think about your ideas? How much would they pay for a newsletter delivered to their office via Internet or direct mail? What subjects are they interested in?

The target you're aiming at is anyone who will benefit from the information you have. Not only are people in a specific profession hungry for news, there are people in all sorts of related jobs and organizations seeking specialized knowledge.

Everyone is interested in making or saving money. Although you don't have to focus on investments -there are many such newsletters already- you can point out the benefits of your inside tips on how to find the easiest or the least expensive direct-to-the-source methods of attaining savings.

Generally, your target audience will be limited but even a small percentage of it will make your newsletter profitable. Successful topics include new trends in your subject matter where those involved can't get enough information.

Depending on the subject you choose, tap into those potential subscribers who are hungry for what's new. But remember to write only about what you know and express opinions that you can back up.

9. What to Name Your NL

The title in the masthead (top) of the newsletter is the most visual aspect of the publication. It reflects the content and it reflects you.

What title is best for your newsletter? If you are well-known in your field, you can use your own name. Or, think of a few titles that indicate the topic, or use a catch-phrase that sums up the endeavor. Two-word titles work well.

You might use an action title if you're going after sports, or a title that includes the word "money" if that's a main focus of your subject.

Make up a few titles of your own. How do they compare with the titles of other newsletters?

Which rings true for your enterprise?

Check at the library to be sure your title is original and doesn't duplicate other publications currently on the market. The title is your trademark.

Although newsletters require very little graphic design, illustrations, or an art director on staff, you may want to consult a professional designer to help you with the prototype.

Since the title of the newsletter is so important, it would be worthwhile to have it designed. You'll only need to pay a one-time fee, and you can use it forevermore.

The logo can be very simple. If you have a title that doesn't use your name, you might have a company name under or above the title in small print. Although most publications don't place the address under the title, newsletters often do, so potential subscribers know where to write.

Another aspect of the title at the top of the publication is the date and the issue number. These should be considered in the original design. Since a newsletter has timely information, the date of the issue should be easy to find.

If the newsletter is top of the line, use the best design and reproduction techniques for the logo and the pages with four-colors, if affordable and within budget. If the newsletter were designed to be low-tech because of limited funds, then an elaborate logo would look out of place. In that case, print in one or two-colors and keep the look as homespun and fresh as the news you'll be publishing.

Avoid fancy type styles or those that are hard to read. And don't go overboard with a clever or cute design. Something simple and clear is what you should be after.

10. Style and Format

The most economical way of publishing and servicing your newsletter is via your computer and via e-mail. Or, have it printed on one or two 11 x 17 inch pages, printed on both sides and folded. This will give you a small booklet of four or eight pages in a standard 8 1/2 x 11 inch size. (There are several other sizes and formats you can consider.)

You might consider having it three-hole punched. It doesn't cost much to have this done at the printers and this format could be an added feature to encourage subscribers to save the valuable information.

Any graphics should be kept simple, but don't be afraid to use subheads to break up the copy. A few words capitalized or in a larger or darker print help the reader identify the information, and make it easier to read.

Keep enough white space to encourage reading, but fill the pages to make the subscriber feel the newsletter fulfills its promises.

11. *What to Include*

Consider a copy format that is divided by types of information. For example, you can have a section labeled profiles, another on upcoming events. Perhaps you have a calendar of shows, conventions, or seminars that would concern readers.

There might be sections on various industry policies or unwritten rules. Past events and history are always good fillers. And don't forget humor. Although your newsletter is serious, potent information, no field of endeavor is without its light side.

Don't lock yourself into a format you can't always fulfill. Rather, have these sections available for you to use or not as each issue is developed.

And always include subscription information. Your own newsletter is the best way to promote increased subscriptions.

12. *Finding Out the Facts*

Your first few issues won't lack for information because you already have pages of information in your memory bank and files to publish. But after that, you'll need renewable sources of copy.

The Internet is a prime source for you to discover what's new in the industry, as well as all of the pertinent printed trade and specialty publications.

Your associates and colleagues are of course prime sources of inside information within the field you write about. Renew and make new contacts, they'll be invaluable for acquiring information.

Are there any correspondents you can use in other parts of the country to give you facts? Perhaps you can work out a financial arrangement with an insider for important information you want to include.

Interviews are important ways to get vital information. If you can't contact the people in the high places, such as presidents or directors, remember that their assistants can be just as valuable for acquiring information.

New trends are found by talking to the workers or the participants. An employee might describe the wonders of a new machine; an athlete may praise some new equipment. And you don't have to travel to see these people. A good phone voice can unlock many doors.

Don't overlook the obvious: public relations professionals have a lot of information to disperse. Creating a good rapport with a PR pro can get you constant timely advice and specialized information.

Talk to people who will be open to sharing their wisdom and who know the products or services you are offering. What they know can fill pages of newsletters.

Follow up on the articles presented in the trade publications. You might be able to use some more in-depth aspects of the same topics they publish. Can you talk to the people they interview? Perhaps you can critique some controversial subject and get someone to present an opposite opinion.

The newsletter is a personal forum. That means that you are welcome to give your personal comments and opinions on anything. However, they can't be egotistical or narrow-minded or you'll lose subscribers.

Trade shows and conventions are your gold. Every person who displays or attends the show is interested in the subject. You could virtually interview everyone and get a complete overview of the industry.

If you are working with a sports topic, meets and events are the place you need to be. Talk to people who arrange them and the broadcasters--they have a lot of background knowledge. You might be able to feature events regularly in the newsletter.

Where are the people who subscribe to the newsletter? What events happen in their towns? If you are writing about an industry, where are the main manufacturing plants? Have their local newspapers written about public opinions about those plants, such as pollution or high employment?

If you have a topic that requires a certain environment, how do the local towns cater to the enthusiasts--especially during a main event?

13. *Writing Copy*

In this publication, you are the authority. Use strong and direct statements with an active voice. Although you are often offering opinion, the content should be factual.

Your readers are intelligent, and experts in the same field you are writing about. You'll need to back up your statements with research. A rule of thumb is that three concurring sources make your conclusions factual.

Become a polished writer - your copy must be easy to read and understand. It should be exciting, filled with lots of bits of information.

The main thrust of the newsletter is enthusiasm. Your subscribers are into the subject you are writing about. Don't be afraid to let them know you love the topic as much as they do. Go ahead--get excited.

If you have chosen a technical subject, you'll need to be an expert in the field. If you are not, have somebody you can call at any time to confirm fact. After all, your newsletter is geared towards the experts, so you have to pull through.

You don't have to do all the writing yourself. You can employ free lancers who collect or write material for the newsletter. The financial arrangement is negotiable but keep in mind that high-quality skills and expert knowledge usually come at a cost.

The success of the newsletter lies with the quality of information you have. Not the quality of writing--the quality of information. If a reader can review an entire copy and say, "I know that," you're not coming through with inside information or new trends.

Quality of information is the dozens of little tidbits of information, expert advice, and tips for success. That is the core of the newsletter, and should be the core of your own interests. That is why you have a unique knowledge to offer, and why your newsletter will be successful.

What interests you? You are the best judge of lively topics, and are the best critic of the newsletter. If you subscribed to this publication, would this be what you'd expect? Are you delivering the full potential of the subject matter?

Above all, is the information practical? Can a person reading the newsletter gain from having acquired that information? Although you are publishing the newsletter for a select group of people, you should direct it to each individual person.

The personal approach is the best attitude to take in both gathering information and in writing copy. Since the newsletter is an informal publication, the copy should read informally--as though you just heard the hot news and are writing it quickly for your best friend to profit by.

14. Getting Ready for Distribution

Once you have all your copy and advance design ideas completed, you or an assistant needs to enter it on your computer for a disc to go to the printer or for electronic servicing to subscribers. Make the final copy as perfect as possible as any errors will reflect on your credibility.

The first few newsletters you publish will require a lot of trial and error with copy and layout. You'll need to decide how many spaces to leave between the end of a paragraph and the beginning of a subhead, how many spaces to indent, and how big the margins will be.

Think about what is important to the format. Some newsletters use italics or underlined words to emphasize the importance. And some of these overuse these methods. Always let good taste dictate the layout and style of your publication.

A whole line taken up by a few words or the last half of a hyphenated word is called a widow. These look sloppy in any type of publication, so you may rewrite the paragraph to extend or shorten that sentence.

Be careful about carry-overs to the next page. It's very awkward to hyphenate at the bottom of a page, or have only one line at the top of the next, then space for a subhead. As you get more adept at preparing copy, you'll be able to write to fit. And that looks good.

The basic standard for a newsletter is clarity. Can you read the type? Are the ideas well presented and easy to understand? Do the subheads provide an interest level that will motivate the majority of readers?

The final disc copy must be exactly what your want printed or mistakes will be memorialized and haunt you forever. If printing, photo offset is the least expensive way to produce multiple copies. The pages must be clean and the designer should indicate a second color (or more) with an overlay, a sheet of tracing paper taped to the copy with printer's instructions written on it and sections circled that need special attention.

15. *Printing*

As stated, the least expensive and most practical method to print your newsletter is at an instant printer using photo-offset. These small local businesses can print, collate, fold and stuff into envelopes, all for a reasonable price.

Or you can electronically distribute it on the Internet - or, a combination of both.

If you want to use color in the newsletter, design a customized masthead and border design and print in advance in huge quantities or format it on your computer. The content can be added as it is developed.

Don't go to the expense of elaborate printing until your subscription volume is high and you advance into a highly professional and artistic format. Almost all publications, including newspapers, books and magazines, are printed from disc or scanned material, so compare investments in money and time and act accordingly.

If your subscription list is large and the newsletter is successful, you can afford excellent printers or specialty PR houses that will handle the entire job from copy input to layout to printing to labeling to mailing.

Or you can get advice from a consultant on how to create and distribute your newsletter via Internet.

16. *How Often to Publish*

There are a lot of factors to consider when deciding upon a publication schedule. The main ones are determining how often you should produce a newsletter based on current or future demand from subscribers?

Work backwards from the date you want a subscriber to receive the newsletter. It needs to be in the mail a few days before that. Understand that, it will take the printer about 10 working days to deliver the final printed newsletter to you. Then figure out how long will it take you to compile the content and either produce the copy or disc for the printer or retain someone to do it for you; and finalize the design and layout by yourself or through the help of a specialist.

How long will it take you to research and write material for your newsletter? This may be a deciding factor in the size of the publication. Perhaps you'd prefer to get a four-page newsletter out every other week rather than an eight-page newsletter out every month.

If your topic is filled with today's news, then you'll want to get that out to your subscribers as fast as possible. Or, your NL can be done bi-monthly or even quarterly. Be careful with infrequent mailings, however, because the subscribers may forget about it: out of sight, out of mind. There is not much call for a small newsletter published only a few times a year.

You must deliver the newsletter on a regular basis. Whatever production schedule you've decided on, keep to it. Later, when it's successful, you may step up the production and publish more frequently.

17. Getting Subscribers

Think about where the people who would want your newsletter are and make a concerted effort to find them.

Do you have access to mailing lists directly related to your subject matter? Maybe you already have a small business selling information, or have access to a customer list of people who buy similar information.

You can purchase mailing lists that have every demographic breakdown you can imagine. What is the profile of your potential subscribers? Think about those people, and write down their attributes. Write down the age group, sex, education level, income, where they live, perhaps the type of housing accommodation they have. A good list broker can work out the best lists to give you results.

A sure way to build up a potential subscriber mailing list is with a drawing at a trade show or convention. You can have cards printed up for people to fill in their names and addresses. All attendees would be interested in the subject matter of your newsletter.

You can take out display ads in the trade magazines that cater to the topic you are pursuing. Include the full details of your newsletter, or use a leader to get inquiries, and send the details later. Especially with the prices of newsletters, you may want to prepare and send out literature and samples rather than go for a low response.

Prepare a direct mail piece that describes the benefits and features of your newsletter and pushes for subscription. You can offer a special free booklet to new subscribers, or a discount. You may include a sample newsletter in the direct mail piece to show how worthwhile the publication is.

Selling newsletters, like any other direct mail or publishing enterprise, takes a lot of testing. You need to test the initial response to the idea of the topic; and the response to the first few newsletters produced.

Pricing is always a tricky aspect of selling information. How high can you price your newsletter and still keep the number of subscribers to make it profitable? You'll find through testing that there's a plateau, and subscriptions will fall off when the price gets too high.

Frequency of publication is also important. Although you may be able to prepare and publish a weekly newsletter, your subscribers may not be able to keep up with reading it, and prefer a monthly subscription.

Any good mailing list should be used over and over. If you know you have a list of prime targets for your newsletter, don't-stop with one mailing. Follow through with subsequent offers at certain intervals to catch those who couldn't decide the first time.

18. Mailing the Newsletter

You can use computer services in your town to have labels printed up or, if you're only dealing in a small quantity, you can have mailing lists photocopied onto address labels. After your first success, and after you've paid your initial investment and you've got enough money to expand, make things easy on yourself.

The most sophisticated and the easiest method of delivery to subscribers is by Internet but hard copies are often more desirable because they are retained. Computers are so commercially popular and cost-effective that they are within almost anybody's budget so that delivery method is more and more the delivery vehicle of choice.

If the mail is pre-sorted by zip code, you can use a bulk rate for mailing and save money. If your newsletter can meet the specifications, you might even be able to get a special second-class rate permit for educational material. Talk with the postal workers to find out what you need to do to comply with these special rates.

19. Record-Keeping

You can keep complete and accurate accounts of your newsletter business by yourself. It's basically broken down into two areas: how much you spend, and how much you make. If you keep track of all your expenses, you'll have an easy time of it at tax time.

Open up a business checking account at your bank. Get to know the bank manager - you may already.

Although you can start and maintain a newsletter within a low budget, be sure to figure your costs and risks before you invest too much money, and be sure of a back up to be able to fulfill all the subscriptions.

Maintaining your subscription lists is a task that needs diligence and a head for details. Since each subscriber starts at a different issue, you need to create and continue a method of keeping track of expiring subscriptions.

You'll want to write a standard appeal for renewal to be sent out in plenty of time for subscribers to renew. And you'll have to follow up for those who choose not to renew at the end of their present subscriptions.

The best advice is to get the best advice. Who can help you set up a subscription system? Maybe somebody local is expert at that. Find out who handles subscriptions at a nearby publications and talk to that person.

20. What's Legal and What's Not

Although any business in the United States is subject to the Federal Trade Commission's regulations, a newsletter business is simpler. You don't need a license but you should consult with your local Sales Tax office for acquiring a resale tax permit.

The content of the newsletter must be documented by facts if you get into any dispute. If you don't border on libel, you should have no problem with any lawsuits for the content of your publication.

However, you should consult your attorney if there are any problems with copyright, confidentiality or access to news, and read over the section libel in this book.

If you write with integrity, independent of any payoffs by companies or individuals, you'll have no trouble with being on the wrong side of the law.

21. Success is Your Goal

Writing and publishing a newsletter is a challenging and exciting way to express your views and news. Success in this venture will give you prestige and acknowledgement in your profession.

You can start the business with virtually no overhead and a small amount of capital, and you can build up to making impressive profits.

Most newsletters have a built-in market and the people who subscribe to it will pay high prices for the information you have. Tap into the market and reap those profits.

There is little news you can't find out about in this day and age of the Internet with its vast source materials.

There is no industry or type of endeavor in this country today that doesn't have a large group of enthusiasts. How can you find out what they want to know? This is a good place to exploit your resources and use your background to good advantage.

The actual task of researching, writing, and having a newsletter published really not that difficult. There are .no secrets or special tricks or skills you need besides a penchant for writing and reporting and a good nose for the getting the best prices for production and printing.

What is important is for the point-person to come up with an idea for a newsletter that will sell to a select group that currently receives little or no specialized information on its area of interest from any other published source.

22. Go Ahead and Try

You no doubt already have some ideas, so go ahead and try a sample newsletter and test it with 25 or 50 potential subscribers that you know and ask for input.

A good initial response to the test will provide a pretty good indication that the rest of your market will like it too and success is just around the corner. A negative response will send you back to the drawing boards but don't give up, simply refine it and massage it until you get it right.

If you need specialized legal advice or assistance on this subject, the services of an attorney with the right credentials is recommended.

23. Play It Straight

Remember that when you publish a newsletter its content is memorialized in print for all time so be especially careful with the material.

All newsletter content should be grammar and spell-checked, all names should be checked for correct spelling, and all facts should be carefully researched.

Pay special attention to the section on libel in this book and be sure to never defame anyone, any company or any organization.

Newsletter editors who correct honest mistakes in a subsequent edition are off the hook for most legal actions and complaints by readers or the subjects in the material.

Play it straight and you will take much of the anxiety out of publishing your newsletter.

PR Tip: A good newsletter is terse, lucid, factual, interesting and appealing to the eye.

Section Five

Chapter One

College Fundraising and PR

By Dr. Robert F. Prather, Ph. D

Dr. Prather recently completed a three-year term as presiding officer of the Foundation for Independent Higher Education in Washington D.C. and been president of the Texas Independent College Fund for 10 years. He has won four national awards for fundraising excellence. He received his bachelor's degree in journalism from Ohio University and master or arts and doctor of education degrees from Columbia University Teachers College. He is the brother of the author.

1. Overview

Good public relations helps lead to good fundraising. Great public relations helps lead to great fundraising. My experience in fundraising for independent colleges can serve as a template for virtually any type of development work for non-profit organizations.

There are many definitions of fundraising but the following two are perhaps better than the others. One is by Harold Seymour in his book Designs for Fundraising that is considered to be the bible of fund raising. In it he says: "Development (fundraising) is the planned promotion of understanding, participation and support."

The other is by Henry A. Rosso, founder of The Fundraising School who said: "Fundraising is the gentle art of teaching the joy of giving".

Thus, you have one practical definition and one philosophical definition. Both come into play in successful presentations to prospective donors. There is joy in giving, there is joy in asking and there is joy in receiving.

The joy will come more often if the ask is backed up by solid research and planning.

Virtually every 501(c)(3) non-profit organization has a genuine need for more funds in order to meet its mission. Many thousands of small non-profits, while desperately needing additional financial support, do not have the resources to hire a full-time development professional or even a part-time person. Thus, the executive director adds this critical function to his/her agenda. Many of these agencies do have limited funds to engage a consultant on a retainer. A PR consultant who also knows fundraising is doubly valuable.

Because adequate financial support has a great deal to do with the quality of services offered, not to mention the survival of the organization, executives of non-profits are quick to listen when someone suggests ways in which additional dollars can be raised.

Public relations consultants who can offer their non-profit clients and prospective clients advice and counsel in the area of generating funds will find themselves vastly more marketable and increasingly more indispensable.

Long-term relationships are more likely to evolve when the client sees the consultant helping to bring in additional resources on a consistent basis.

2. The Foundation Center

The Foundation Center in New York City defines a foundation as: "A non-governmental, non-profit organization with its own funds (usually from a single source, either as an individual, family or corporation) and program managed by its own trustees and directors that was established to maintain or aid educational, social, charitable, religious or other activities serving the common welfare, primarily by make grants to other non-profit organizations."

The Foundation Center, located at 79 Fifth Avenue, New York NY 10003, publishes many invaluable general research directories, subject directories and guidebooks, manuals and report. Among the most valuable are The Foundation Directory that has information on the 10,000 largest foundations, and The National Directory of Corporate Giving that highlights giving by 1900 company sponsored foundations, plus more than 1000 giving programs.

Located in NYC, Washington D.C., Atlanta, Cleveland and San Francisco, The Foundation Center also has cooperating collections in every state and Puerto Rico.

3. Planning

The most successful fundraising programs are planned very carefully. This planning process is concerned not only with the asking for support, but also with increasing the chances or receiving meaningful support. The chances increase when the prospective donor not only understands, but also is moved to action and involvement by the organization's mission and accomplishments.

The largest gifts often will come from those who participate in the organization by being on the Board or doing volunteer work. Thus, a plan must be developed to broaden the base of volunteer participants.

Perhaps the key factor in the success or failure of a non-profit organization is the Board of

Directors. A strong, involved, giving and positive Board with committed board members can and will make all the difference.

My organization, The Texas Independent College Fund, has a "Commitment To Serve" that all prospective Board members are asked to sign.

4. Commitment to Serve

In accepting the honor and responsibility of serving on the Board of Directors of the Texas Independent College Fund, the members in Texas must take the following pledge.

Something of this nature would work for almost all non-profit organizations in their cultivation of board members. It follows:

I agree to the following standards:

- That I will be actively involved in attracting financial support for the Fund and its member colleges.

- That I will act as an ambassador of independent higher education in Texas.

- That I will attend, to the best of my ability, the annual meeting, regional committee meetings and meetings of committees on which I serve.

- That I will share with the Fund's president ideas as to how the Fund might be more successful.

- That I will, in line with my capabilities and my other commitments, make an annual personal financial investment in the Fund and thus in its member colleges and the students they serve.

5. Primary Purpose

The primary function of fundraising for the involved person or staff is to open the way for others to have the opportunity to share their resources with the institution, including:

- Individuals
- Corporations.
- Foundations.
- Churches and synagogues.
- Clubs and organizations.
- Federal government.
- State government.
- County government.

6. 10 % Give 80-90 %

Experience has shown that in virtually all fundraising campaigns, 80 to 90 percent of the dollars realized will come from 10 percent or less of the donors.

A careful analysis and understanding of that statement show that it is incumbent on the fundraising and PR professionals to identify those key prospects and develop a plan for approaching them, as well as following through with the mass of smaller donors.

And they comprise the segment that will repeat gifting annually.

7. Five Steps to Attracting Gifts

Basically, there are five steps in the process of attracting major gifts for colleges and universities:

1. Identification
2. Cultivation
3. Planning the Approach
4. Asking for the Gift
5. Follow-Up.

The identification process involves research, research and more research.   This is best done by having those who are closest to the organization collaborate to identify potential contacts of financial substance that might have some kind of linkage with the organization and thus be candidates for major support.

The next step is to find out as much as possible about and cultivating the prospect(s). This can be done by speaking with those familiar with them, searching the Internet, studying directories in the public library, reviewing profiles in the business media, of scanning local and regional newspapers, business publications and magazines.

Corporations can be researched in the net and in Dun & Bradstreet and Standard & Poors publications, as well in business publications.

Foundations can be researched through the Foundation Director and state foundation directories and publications of the Foundation Center.

Governmental funding opportunities can be obtained by contacting local, state and national governmental entities, including congressional delegations.

The cultivation of prospects, both major and otherwise, should be an ongoing process. Those who are served by and involved with the organization must be kept informed about the progress, the dreams and the aspirations of the organization and of the people in charge.

This can be accomplished through many techniques such as newsletters, personal Letters, newspaper feature articles, TV or radio Items - PSA's , telephone contact and website promotion

The best prospects are those who care enough about the 'non-profit' to give it some of their valuable time and expertise on a volunteer basis.

It follows that methods should be sought that will involve as many people as possible in helping the organization in ways other than providing support.

8. Planning is Important

The planning of the approach phase is extremely important. Success in fundraising generally occurs when the right person is asking the right person for the right-sized gift for the right reason at the right time

Remember that people give to people. The most meaningful gifts, generally speaking, will be given when a prospective donor is asked by someone he/she respects highly for whatever reason, be it financial or political clout, academic or athletic achievements, reputation in the community, or simply through the treasured bond of friendship.

9. Research is Important, Too

Research on the prospect(s) should include speaking with those who know him or her best. This will often reveal what aspect of the organization's activities is most likely to be of appeal to that person.

An example: if it is known that the prospect has a deep love for children and the organization is a hospital and funds are needed in the pediatrics area, then the donor should be given an opportunity to share his resources with the hospital by providing support specifically for pediatrics, thereby helping the children of the community for years to come.

The asking for a gift is what it's all about! If proper homework has been done in terms of identification, cultivation and planning the approach, then the asking part should be fun.

Unfortunately, many people assigned to a fundraising task find it difficult or distasteful to ask for money. The important thing for each fundraiser to remember is that the appeal is NOT personal.

The request by a fundraiser is made on behalf of a worthwhile organization that is attempting to help the community, people who need their help.

Remember: by asking for involvement, the fundraiser is also giving the prospective donor an opportunity to do something good with the money he or she has managed to accumulate over years - or stands guardian over for a business entity.

Never forget that fundraisers are also providing a meaningful service for the prospective donor.

10. Don't Ignore the Donor

A cardinal sin in fundraising is to ignore the donor once the gift is made. When this happens, it doesn't take long for the donor to come to the conclusion that he or she has been used and that all the organization cared about was the donation.

A proven and basic rule of fund-raising is that the best prospects are those who have given before. So don't ignore them and violate that rule.

Any meaningful fund-raising campaign should not ignore the smaller donor, either.   A broad-base of support is important to an organization, both in terms of the dollars realized and in terms of the number of friends generated during the fundraising process.

Word-of-mouth is important and the friends of the organization can and will continue to be invaluable in many ways during future campaigns years if they are handle correctly.

The history of fundraising has countless examples of individuals who made very small gifts for years and then, all of a sudden and basically out of the blue, made a major gift to the organization.

For this to happen the entire development process has to be in place and abided by. The young development professional will be wise to study the process closely and act accordingly.

11. Seven Specifics in Planning

There must be a planned effort in terms of both small and large donors. Seven specifics tasks important to the fundraiser and public relations consultant are:

1. Goals.

2. Timetables

3. Frequency.

4. Methods of appeal*.

5. Use of volunteers.

6. Use of staff.

7. Use of directors

> (*examples: semi-annual letter, auction, personal visits, Monte Carlo Night, $100 a plate dinner, *etc.*)

The structure of the campaign is customarily as follows:

- Chairperson

- Vice-chairpersons

- Captains

- Workers to make calls in person/on telephone

- Public relations support agency or consultant.

12. Sophisticated Programs in Other Areas

More sophisticated development programs will functions in areas other than just the annual giving by individuals, including:

- Solicitation of foundations
  (they exist to give away money)

- Solicitation of corporations
  (many have extensive giving programs)

- Proposals to governmental entities
  (research is available to discern them)

- Planned giving opportunities from individuals
  (wills, annuity programs, etc.)

13. The Public Relations Link

There is a close link between the public relations and fundraising efforts of an organization. Non-profits that present an image (accurate or not) of being unsuccessful or uninspired will find it exceedingly difficult to convince people to give to their cause. That is where public relations enters the fundraising picture.

The consultant responsible for both the development and the PR efforts has a real advantage as she or he can easily ensure that both elements complement each other. When the development and public relations efforts come from difference sources it becomes imperative that the entities work closely together to create synergy.

A fundraising campaign of any magnitude depends to a significant degree on the quality of the written materials developed in support of the program. The basic brochures, the appeal letters, the training materials for the volunteers must all be first class and reinforce the image of the non-profit as an essential, successful organization. This is an important portion of the PR consultant or employee's job.

The consultant who does his/her job well in both the public relations and fundraising areas for a client will gain great personal satisfaction, acclaim from those in the know and the reputation of being a winner. That reputation will help immeasurably as the PR fundraising professional attempts to draw even more donors into the fold and with future clients, as well.

PR techniques are called upon throughout the fundraising process and each practitioner must understand its relevance for the organization, the mission and the aims and goals of the college. A review of this entire volume will provide fundraisers the information they need to fulfill publicity, promotion, support materials, consultation and assistance, problem management functions, *et al.*

Tip: Visit major book websites such as Amazon or Barnes and Noble and search for published works on the subjects of fundraising and public relations.

14. *Fundraising in Review*

- Take the initiative in suggesting to clients and prospective clients that you be the consultant for their fundraising as well as for their public relations efforts. Note: generally, consultants work on a set fee structure and *not* for a percentage of the funds raised.

- Consider the possibility of spending a day 'picking the brain' of a respected and successful professional fundraiser in your area. Most colleges have at least one development professional on their staff, as do many hospitals. Offering to pay her or him a consultant's fee for the day may be well worth the expenditure and a nice goodwill gesture.

- As is true when consulting in public relations, it is essential when consulting in fundraising that you present an image of a professional who is both competent and optimistic. You need to cultivate your clients to want to follow your lead and direction.

- One of the most important concepts to remember in fundraising is that people give to people and people give for people. Therefore, it is critical that the right person be asking the right person to make the gift. This is especially true in relation to the major gifts.

- The professional fundraiser knows there is a lot of back scratching involved in the obtaining of the larger gifts. In other words, "you give to my charity and I'll give to yours". Many wealthy individuals have a lot of 'markers' out among their friends. Hopefully, you can convince them to call them in on behalf of your organization.

- In a fundraising campaign, the chief fundraiser (the hired hand) stays in the background. In the public eye are – and should be - the volunteer leaders of the effort. The campaign structure should have the most respected individual associated with the non-profit as the chairperson and other highly-respected members of the community leading positions within various divisions.

- The most important question that must be asked during the planning and execution of any fundraising program is: "Why should anyone give their hard-earned dollars to this particular cause?" The answer must be expressed in familiar 'people terms' and not in 'building terms', 'budget terms' or any other terms. The answer will form the philosophical base of the campaign.

- Beware of the client or volunteer worker who promotes the idea that "We need $50,000 so let's ask 5,000 people to give $10 each." While this may sound reasonable, it almost never works. As pointed out earlier, 80 to 90 percent of the funds in any campaign will normally come from 10 percent or less of the donors. You *must* also seek major gifts!

- Fundraising works from the inside out. The executive director, the staff and the board of directors of the non-profit organization's campaign must and should give to the program first to set the standard.

- Set reasonable goals. Because the client needs $100,000 doesn't mean that it's possible to raise that amount. What you don't need is an unsuccessful campaign. Success breeds success. Set a goal that will take a lot of effort to reach, but that can be reached within the time frame set, and do your best to keep 'on target' throughout the campaign.

Bonus Tip: Develop and utilize the best possible print materials within your budget and internal/external resources to help you solicit gifts.

15. *Avoid Annoying Habits*

The kiss of death for the practitioner who refuses to learn the basics is to adopt annoying habits. Remember, first impressions do count and so does integrity.

Here are some of the nettlesome mistakes made by novices:

- Sending requests or attempting to make contact with the wrong person or with to someone with the wrong title and name spelling,

- Not taking no for an answer,

- Pretending the call is for some purpose other than fundraising,

- Insisting on seeing the foundation or corporate head who will only refer you to the human resources or other decision-maker, and who probably knows little about the programs,

- Using the old line: "I happened to be passing by and wanted to bring you up to date on our activities",

- Making a cold call with no advance notice or contact and expecting a positive response,

- Providing no proposal or program outline and asking the potential donor what to do to obtain funding,

- Failing to do homework (research) prior to contacting as potential donor source,

- Failing to understand and respect grant-making criteria,

- Asking for funding not covered by the grant,

- Faking the depth of a relationship with a funding source to staff or other contacts,

- Padding project budgets or omitting pertinent facts in reports,

- Being too aggressive or inappropriately friendly with a funding contact,

- Not understanding that charisma is no substitute for integrity.

Remember: Fundraising professionals should develop both their re-active and pro-active public relations skills.

16. Direct Mail: A Strong Tool

There are many tools important to fundraising: surveys and polls, sales pitches and presentations, information dissemination and lobbying, *et al.* But direct mail emerges as perhaps the strongest tool for the PR consultant and development officer to employ in a fundraising campaign.

1. A fundraising direct mail 'piece' usually consists of the following elements:

2. A letter of explanation of appeal from a key organization player.

3. A well-written and produced brochure.

4. A simple response mechanism – a return envelope or postcard.

Production of the material should be with attractive colors or in an efficient black-and-white format with consistent type and copy style, plus a professional look that reflects the 'class' of the mail.

Consultants must ensure that the piece does not fall into the 'round-file' syndrome that befalls most ill-conceived and poorly executed direct-mail pieces.

When constructing your budget for direct mail, you must consider production, postage, handling, mailing lists, writing and all other out of pocket expenses.

On all budget items, do not under-estimate costs or necessary investments in time and effort but do learn how to figure all costs and all how-to procedures so you can present and defend your expenditures!

17. Prime Mailing Results Can Soar

A 'cold canvass' can result in a dismal one percent showing or more standard, two to three percent return. However, by using a 'prime' mailing list of prospects that are known can elevate the results five or more.

The Proper use of zip codes, pre-sorting, proper posting and bulk rates where suitable in a particular mailing can result in high efficiency and lower overall costs.

Third Class mail is cheaper but slower than First Class mail. However, an attractive piece mailed Third Class can have an excellent effect when the recipient realizes you spent as little money as possible to reach him with your fundraising appeal.

18. Acquiring the Lists

Good mailing lists can be acquired for from 40-to-70 dollars-per-thousand or more, depending on the demographics of the addressees and other factors. The more specialized your requirements, the more difficulty in obtaining the lists and the more expensive.

Check your lists regularly and remove the names of returns and keep track of all positive responders. There are many good direct mail houses and new standard and electronic methods of utilizing direct mail and e-mail. The bottom line: it is up to you to research them and utilize them as needed.

19. 10 Tips For Direct Mail

1. Create an attractive, efficient and comprehensive piece.

2. Use colors or efficient black and white format.

3. Use consistent type and copy style.

4. Consider all expenses, including for postage and handling, mailing list costs, printing costs, *etc.*

5. Consider the percentage-of-return ratios for cold canvas vs. prime list mailing and expense differentials.

6. Use zip codes and pre-sort opportunities for savings where appropriate.

7. Investigate various classes and bulk rates, for each mailing.

8. Remove all returns from future mailings.

9. Add names and addresses and record positive results received for future mailings.

10. Read up on innovations, new companies, and methods of utilizing direct mail.

20. Case Profile: Exciting a Donor

A Fortune 500 company had been giving operating support to the Texas Independent College Fund for many years and I/we had begun to count on it.

However, the support was dwindling and was slated to be discontinued within one year.

The Question: What to do?

The Answer: Find a new approach that would excite the donor!

Photographs in the annual report of the donor company revealed there was not a single member of a minority on the top management team.

That was it: we would help them move into the 21st century in a beneficial way.

We submitted a proposal that pointed out the importance for the donor to have minorities represented in top management, and a method of getting top minority students into the pipeline for consideration.

The proposal was simply this: the donor would give 16 minority students $5,000 scholarships each in both their junior and senior years, a paid internship between those years and a two-year contract for a managerial-level job upon graduation.

It seemed to be an excellent deal for all parties involved.

It turned out to be. The donor signed on with a grant of $165,000 and an indication that the amount might double in two years if the program proved successful.

The donor and the fund manager met to iron out the details and the rest is history.

Chapter Two

Non-Profits and PR

By Monica Prather, M.E.

Monica Prather, M.E., president/CEO United Cerebral Palsy of Tarrant County, Texas, was a finalist for The Most Influential Women In Texas Award in 2001 and was named Outstanding Woman of Fort Worth in 2002. She also has won the National United Cerebral Palsy Association Program of the Year Award in 2000, its Outstanding Executive for Customer Responsiveness in 1999, the 2000 Tribute Award from the state Association, and the first Leadership Award from United Way in 1989. She earned a Masters in Education at Edinboro State University and was graduated *cum laude* from California State University in Pennsylvania. She is the sister-in-law of the author.

1. *One is a Guide for Others*

The fundraising action planning, implementation and public relations support for one non-profit agency can be used as a guide for others, and it is in this spirit that I discuss my efforts with Cerebral Palsy. It is essential that any professional fundraiser develop basic philosophies.

I offer the following 10 basic philosophies developed during 28 satisfying years in the non-profit field in hopes they will help guide those wishing to shore up their fundraising and public relations skills. This same set of philosophies will work in virtually any fundraising or PR endeavor.

2. 10 Basic Philosophies

1) You must believe in what you are doing.

2) Your plans and actions must meet a specific need or needs.

3) Be sure to network and collaborate with others in your efforts.

4) Follow-up on positive results, nothing succeeds like success.

5) Involve others – all people enjoy being part of success.

6) Maintain integrity and strive for excellence.

7) Promote your successes appropriately – do not be afraid to toot your own horn.

8) Tell your story and include compelling measurable outcomes, including to the media.

9) Remember 'WIIFM' – everyone concerned wants to know "what's in it for me?"

10) Build relationships and partnerships – it's all about people!

3. Experience Counts

I have had the privilege of providing services to people with disabilities for 28 years. There were no friends or family members with disabilities, I just felt drawn to the field and have loved it ever since. Experience counts! It builds credibility.

It is so important to do what you love, not only for your own happiness and professional satisfaction, but because it is a necessary ingredient for success.

Experience will help to solidify your personal belief in your missions and your passion for your work will come through and will compel others to join you.

4. Success is No Accident

Six years ago when I began my position as President & CEO of United Cerebral Palsy of Tarrant County in Fort Worth, Texas, our budget was $300,000+ and our client base was 800. The community was not aware of us and we had a lot of work to do. Today, the budget is at $1,500,000 and we serve 2,500 individuals with a variety of disabilities. The agency has won three national awards in three consecutive years and has established a reputation for excellence that has been consistently recognized on a local, state and national level.

This did not happen be accident, but by design and hard work. There are so many things an agency needs to have in place to be successful: a solid and clear mission, skilled and dedicated staff, solid programs, name recognition, strong board and supportive donors. However, like anything else, you have to learn to walk before you can run. Most importantly, in order to have a successful fundraising or public relations program, you have to have a story to tell and successes under your belt.

5. *A Clear and Compelling Mission*

United Cerebral Palsy of Tarrant County has a clear and compelling mission, which is to advance the independence of people with disabilities. It has been our guiding light that we turn to whenever we have decisions to make.

Developing this mission was especially important in light of the fact that 20 percent of the population has some form of disability and by the year 2010 that number is expected to exceed 30 percent. We must meet that need with continued and aggressive programs.

6. *The First Two Steps*

The first step was to develop a competent, highly motivated staff, which is a critical ingredient for building excellent programs. Morale had been low, and there was an absence of team spirit and sense of purpose. The process of turning it around took approximately two years. During that time we experienced an 80 percent turnover in personnel! As change became obvious many staff members did not accept the change so they left. Others resisted supervision and dug their heels in until they were asked to leave. As turnover took place we hired the most skilled and self-motivated people we could find to begin the building process.

The next step was to build solid programs that would fill a need in the community. At the time our programs included case management, a social program, and respite care. Many of our clients started with us as children and now were adults. They were graduating from school and had nowhere to go. Some of them had gone to other organizations for help and were labeled unemployable. They and their parents were desperate and called on us for help. We determined that there was a large demand for an employment program to assist people with disabilities to find jobs in the community.

7. *A Strong Program*

A request for proposals for organizations interested in starting an employment program came to our attention and we wrote a grant that was funded. We set out to develop a strong program that would provide excellent service.

That was a turning point in our agency's history because it helped us to start an employment program that would help two hundred people a year to realize their dream of finding a job, impact one hundred and fifty businesses, and win a national award.

The next program we initiated was home modification. Many people in the community who had a disability from birth or an acquired disability were concerned that they would not be able to live at home because their homes were not accessible.

We responded to an RFP (request for proposals) from the Texas Department of Housing and Urban Affairs and were awarded a grant to modify homes for people with disabilities.

8. *Important to Tell the Story*

As program successes grew we continually updated our list of accomplishments and incorporated it into our corporate sponsor packet along with copies of our newsletter and newspaper articles. It is extremely important to tell your story and make the community aware of what you are doing. If you don't do it, who will?

We started to receive many positive comments about what we were doing and began to build our base of donors who were attracted to our mission and excited about our story. We included a special page in our newsletter to let the community know that we proudly recognize our corporate sponsors and appreciate the part they play in making these successes possible. People want to be a part of success.

9. *Networking with Other Organizations*

One of the strategies we used to get the word out about what we were doing was to make a concerted effort to network with other community organizations. Each staff member was encouraged to join and participate in appropriate groups.

This participation proved to be very helpful in making sure others knew of our services. It also helped for us to know of other services that were available in the community. Attending regular meetings and becoming active members helped to build relationships and collaborations. These collaborations are generally required when seeking funds from foundations as well as corporations.

During the next few years other programs were initiated as we became aware of unmet needs. They included personal assistance service, homemaker service, and habilation. Since many of our consumers were now employed they were interested in getting a home. Through our networking efforts with our state organization we became aware of the opportunity to develop a Home of Your Own program (HOYO). This would require securing start up funding to enable us to provide assistance to people with disabilities, who were first-time home-buyers.

10. *Complications of Home Owning*

There are many complications in gaining mortgages and therefore very few people with disabilities are homeowners. Traditional mortgage products have requirements they usually can't meet. For instance, a credit history is necessary and the person must have money in the bank. People with disabilities who receive social security or social security disability income can lose their benefits if they have money in the bank, and they frequently don't use credit cards or have a traditional credit history.

Fannie Mae developed its Home Choice mortgage product specifically for people with disabilities who purchase a home through a HOYO program. They will count social security benefits as income and will also allow rent payments, cable bills, utilities, etc. in assessing a person's credit.

11. Community Development

The Sid Richardson Foundation in Fort Worth is very interested in community development. We met with them to seek start-up funding for this program and were thrilled to receive a grant to support it for two years. Although we were venturing into a new area, we were able to show our successful history with the home modification program.

We had also networked and collaborated with the housing organizations in our county who had asked UCP-TC to be the lead agency for the new Home Of Your Own program, which they felt was important to our community. The letters of support from these organizations was very important to the successful outcome of our application.

When the program was initiated we worked with Fannie Mae, the Fort Worth Mayor's office, the Sid Richardson Foundation, the Fort Worth Housing Consortium, State Senator Mike Moncrief, and other state officials to hold a press conference at City Hall to announce the new program. Invitations were sent to the media, public officials, public organizations and nonprofits. More than eighty people attended the press conference, which was covered by newspapers, radio and TV.

The publicity generated a lot of interest and referrals from people interested in the program. It also resulted in significant notice from the community that began to see UCP-TC in a new way.

12. Housewarming Press Conference

A few months later, when our first family closed on their home, a "housewarming press conference" was held in their driveway. The newspaper story included a large picture of the mother with her one-year old son who is blind and has cerebral palsy. They have two young daughters and were hoping to buy a home. When their new son was born, his medical bills and equipment needs dashed their hopes until they heard about our program.

This family's story is so compelling and they were so thrilled to be able to have a home. The article became part of our corporate fundraising package and generated significant support for our services.

13. Getting Grants

The City of Fort Worth has been interested in community development and took note of our new Home Of Your Own Program. They provided a grant in the amount of $90,000 to cover down payment and closing costs for people with disabilities who have low incomes to assist them in buying their first home. Recently, City Council approved an additional $180,000 for the same purpose to assist our consumers who are waiting to purchase a home through the HOYO program.

We are collaborating with the City of Fort Worth and building relationships. A grant opportunity presented itself to forge a new collaborative effort together through the Department of Housing and Urban Development. Last March we were advised that we would receive a two-year grant in the amount of $150,000 to initiate a Fair Housing program.

The purpose of the program is to advise the community of civil rights protections regarding housing discrimination and to provide information and support to individuals who file a complaint with the Fort Worth Human Relations Commission.

14. Work Incentives

Last year, Congress initiated work incentives for people with disabilities who receive social security or social security disability income. The Social Security Administration sent out an RFP for benefits planning and outreach programs so people with disabilities could receive information about the new incentives and have an individual plan to assist them in seeking employment. We had learned about this new program through our national organization, United Cerebral Palsy Associations in Washington, D.C.

Since we operated an employment program for five years and were aware of the importance of this new initiative, we were very interested in applying. We knew that it would be very difficult to get the grant since it required a strong network and demonstrated collaborations. We were thrilled to get a call from the Social Security Administration advising us that we had scored high and asking us if we would take on 12 counties, rather than the nine we had applied for. We said yes and got off the phone jumping and hollering in excitement.

This new federal grant has been very well received. Our program manager and benefits specialists are charged with speaking to groups all over the 12-county area to spread the word about the new work incentives and the services that are available. Many people really want to work, but they are afraid that they will lose their benefits and possibly lose a new job and have nothing. Whenever our staff members speak, individuals with disabilities and parents come over to talk with them to learn more about how this will impact their own situation.

This Social Security grant will result in more than $1,000,000 in funding over a five-year period to serve a 12-county area. These facts are at the top of our list of accomplishments and when we speak with current or potential funders or corporate sponsors our excitement and passion for what we do comes shining through.

15. A Strong Board

A strong board of directors is vitally important to the success of any nonprofit. During this time of growth we had a core of dedicated board members who were committed to the agency and its mission. We knew that we needed to recruit additional board members from various fields and employed a variety of PR techniques to do just that.

We were also in need of high-powered community leaders to help us with raising the funds we need to do the job. We had to build our agency, its programs and successes in order to gain their respect and attention.

Strategic public relations techniques helped us to publicize, promote and bolster the image of our agency and this contributed greatly to our success in cultivating and signing on board members and gaining respect in the communities we service.

Now when we ask someone to join our board they know why we are proud of our agency and the important need it serves in our community. We are happy that 10 individuals joined our board in the last year. They have brought so much and tell us that they have gained so much.

16. A Wonderful Team

Our wonderful team, which includes our dedicated board members, talented staff and terrific consumers, is excited about our accomplishments and our donors are excited too.

This positive energy is contagious and people want to become a part of it and our future.

Young development professionals should develop the personality and energy to develop the same excitement and, hopefully, have the same sort of results.

17. Making a Difference, Creating Awareness

It was exciting seeing how our work was making a difference in the quality of life for many families.

One young woman we worked with had been in a car accident that resulted in severe disabilities requiring the use of a wheelchair. There was only one bathroom in their home and that was upstairs. Her husband had to come home from work just to carry her up the stairs to use the bathroom.

Our solution for her and the family was to turn one of the downstairs rooms into a master bedroom and built on an accessible bathroom. She was able to take a shower and use the sink by herself. A ramp going into the backyard made it possible for her to go outside and be with her children. A second ramp allowed her to go from the house to the garage to get into her car.

It was the right thing to do but, as is so often the case, we realized great PR for our efforts. We included a story about this program in our newsletter and submitted an article that was published in the local newspaper.

This exciting program attracted a lot of attention and the resultant publicity increased community awareness about UCP-TC and its vital services.

Fundraising Axiom: **The key to successful fundraising is asking the right person for the right gift at the right time in the right way.**

18. *Tips From Monica and Bob Prather*

Ten Reminders for the Experienced	Ten Tips for Newcomers
Stay young, fresh, and vibrant.	Believe in yourself as others have.
Take time to smell the roses.	Allow others to enjoy the gift of giving.
Focus, focus, focus!	Understand rejections are not personal.
Believe in your importance to the cause.	Learn from others and attend workshops.
Network, network, network.	Be donor driven, understand their needs.
Share your expertise with newcomers.	Research, research, research.
Strengthen your board.	Write thank you letters immediately.
Find new solutions to old problems.	Make time for proposals, personal calls.
Be a friend-raiser as well as a fund-raiser.	Create a fundraising plan, stick to it.
Applaud when you pull in a big gift.	Trust in your cause, it'll show.

Good luck to all you experienced hands, and especially to you newcomers, in all of your fundraising and public relations efforts!

- Monica and Bob Prather

Chapter Three

PR for the Political Candidate

1. Integrity and Honesty Required

Integrity and honesty are required for the public relations consultant within the political arena and it is up to he or she to attempt to keep the candidate on the straight and narrow. A hard task? Yes. Doable? To some degree. Worth it? Oh, yeah.

No public relations area is more sensitive to the need for efficient and plausible programs than for that of a grassroots political candidate. It is in that first attempt at politics or during the re-election effort that integrity and honesty in communications are absolutely necessary.

Blatant untruths by a candidate or his spokespersons will be unmasked by the opposition or the media and will boomerang on the culprit in a highly negative manner.

Conversely, when a candidate and his campaign team gain a reputation for integrity, honesty and fairness, this will help override the unsavory accusations and attacks that might be mounted by the opposition, and sometimes by an unfriendly media.

2. Rules of the Game

The PR consultant for a candidate must remember the many rules of the game. Traditional guidelines for mounting an effective campaign dictate that it closely mirror who the candidate is and what he or she stands for.

The candidate's agenda must be intelligently shared with the public via the media, the necessary vehicle for every political campaign. If the themes and missions of the candidate are not clearly elucidated during the election season then the candidate will be out in the cold when Election Day rolls around.

Media releases and publicity events including press conferences, as well as printed materials and advertising, must all portray the candidate in a consistent and credible manner or they will turn out to be counter-productive, if not immediately then sometime in the future.

The PR/campaign advisers must be straight with the public/media or the candidate's credibility will suffer.

3. Someone is Always Watching

In this day and age of electronic media, 30-second sound bites, political analysis and in-depth coverage on every level from local to national, suspicion and doubt toward politicians are universal.

At the grassroots level, new candidates who espouse programs and policies that are doable and which they eventually initiate after being elected will be fueling re-election down the line. They will succeed more often than those who do not implement their campaign promises.

Remember, there is always someone watching and who will call on an elected official to explain broken promises. Both the media and opposition keep records well and no doubt will cite broken promises during the term of service and a subsequent election campaign.

4. *Theme and Tone*

The theme and tone of a political campaign is often set or heavily influenced by the public relations advisor or manager. The PR person, at whatever level of influence and regardless of whether he or she is on the payroll, should develop a bottom line of compromise and never, ever, go below that standard. And that bottom line should be quite high, as the standards in political public elations – and politics – are always under great scrutiny.

The reputation of being a 'bad guy' (or gal) can thwart or cripple a political campaign and candidate. This does not mean that solid negative campaigning on the opposition's weaknesses is unethical or unscrupulous. Real charges with credible back-up often are necessary to unseat an incumbent or to retain an office. The point is: charges must be legitimate, well thought-out, and documented satisfactorily.

The days of rumor-mongering, name-calling and political assassination have given way to a more sophisticated manner of negative campaigning, usually citing the opposition's record or comments (mostly by lifting out of context). The voting public is simply too intelligent and too cynical, to fall for the old-style politics of personal attack without foundation. That now backfires more often than it works.

5. *Best Possible Assists*

To succeed in political public relations is to supply your candidate with the best possible assists with the media, as well as in publicity and advertising, themes and slogans, printed materials, surveys, speeches, media relations, personal appearance scheduling and preparation, and volunteer management and training.

Releases to the media must be timed appropriately, and must contain some valid news peg - or they will be tossed into the circular file by the media. Accessibility to the media is a must. Local radio and television stations should be in possession of a full resume, including political, civic and business accomplishments of the candidate.

Print media should be supplied with a sharp, clear, 8" x 10" black-and-white photo of the candidate and perhaps a family photo. Television might be able to use a good a color photo.

6. 10 Things to do for Your Candidate

1. Make a list of appropriate public functions the candidate should attend.

2. Compile a roster of media reporters, columnists, interviewers, editors and news directors.

3. Do background research on the opposition candidate(s).

4. Get copies of all newspaper, magazine and broadcast interviews about the opposition.

5. Write speeches and briefs that are effective and handout copies to the media and attendees.

6. Compile a complete media kit with photo(s) for media handout.

7. Obtain media endorsements of your candidate.

8. Arrange for testimonials and endorsements.

9. Arrange for someone to accompany the candidate to all events.

10. Correct all media mistakes in a professional manner.

7. More Rules to Remember

The media will be negatively influenced by pressure, false or misleading information, missing out on a release or event because of oversight in alerting them, harassment to cover a candidate, unjust criticism or false charges of unfairness and generally boorish behavior.

In their zeal to promote a specific candidate, many volunteers and even some professionals overstep the boundaries with their partisan points of view. Working in a political camp can skew good judgment but a real pro will avoid self-victimization by being above the fray.

8. 10 More Tips for the Political PR Consultant

1. Create a publicity kit on the candidate for the media (with sample copies) containing:
   a. Resume of the candidate
   b. Head-shot photograph and one or two feature photographs
   c. Printed materials on the candidate (brochure, flyer, handout materials
   d. Copies of articles or scripts favorable to the candidate
   e. Enduring position papers or statements
   f. Endorsements

2. Write and produce position papers, or statements, that will endure:
   a. On leading issues of the campaign
   b. On candidate's stand re these issues
   c. On opposition's stand, with critique (if pertinent)
   d. Rebuttals to opposition charges or statements

3. Obtain endorsements of the candidate in written or broadcast form (examples):
    e. From leading party officials
    f. From leading citizens
    g. From opposition party (if apropos)
    h. From union, business, civic, or church leader(s)
    i. Local, regional or state office holders (elected or appointed)
    j. From media where possible

5. Produce an inclusive brochure or flyer about the candidate with as much quality as budget permits:
    a. Include personal/political/career background
    b. Photo of candidate/family (if apropos)
    c. Statements of positions on leading issues
    d. Campaign promises that can be kept
    e. Reasons to vote for the candidate - carefully document into fact sheet

6. Produce releases and a media strategy for the candidate:
    a. On leading issues
    b. On campaign promises
    c. On opposition positions (document them)
    d. Aimed toward specialty interests (senior citizens, veteran groups, *etc.*)
    e. In defense of criticism
    f. On speeches by the candidate

7. Look after the candidate:
    a. Arrange the schedule for the candidate
    b. Appear at all major public (and some private) functions
    c. Be aware of all joint appearances of candidates
    d. At meetings and interviews
    e. Arrange visits to sites such as nursing homes, children's hospitals, *etc.*

9. Produce speeches for the candidate:
    a. On leading issues
    b. On specialty causes (senior citizens, veterans, taxes, *etc.*)
    c. On general 'good guy' themes like political integrity, patriotism, *etc.*

10. Develop a consistent theme and slogan for the candidate:
    a. To be used in advertising - typestyle, certain wording, *etc.*
    b. To be used on all printed materials (consistent type style, color, *etc.)*

9. Remember Your Role

Your main role as PR adviser is to make the candidate look good. You should ensure that the candidate thanks all those responsible for helping: volunteers, election-day workers and staff. Thank you notes should be sent to media members who were fair or generous in their coverage.

Courtesy counts in maintaining long-term relationships.

Chapter Four

PR in the Entertainment Industry

1. *The Need for Public Relations*

Intertwined in the fascinating but complicated world of entertainment is a need for public relations that is often overdone but always necessary. The good PR adviser to an entertainer will strike a balance of what the traffic will bear in gaining publicity in the print and broadcast media and what pertinent and appropriate promotional activities can and should be arranged.

All of this requires planning and implementation from the PR professional and the rest of the entertainer's management team.

All entertainers (and entertainment venues) must have solid advance publicity for an upcoming appearance and it is the PR adviser's role to assure it is done to the maximum and correctly.

The adviser also must plan for and implement consistent exposure to build the image of the client and to keep him or her fresh in the public mind.

PR professionals must already have established -or quickly build- solid media relations with entertainment reviewers, reporters and editors. They also must further their client's career by arranging promotional tours or appearances in dynamic venues that will enhance their image, reputation and public (fan) acceptance.

2. *Special Handling*

Special handling and advice from trustworthy advisers are also enormously important for the entertainer who not only has to face competition but his or her own fears. The mental drains are great and many stars quickly burn out, including from self-inflicted excesses.

Truly successful and therefore invaluable PR counselors help to quell or mitigate bad publicity and take a major role in counseling the client to stop the abuses before the career is wrecked.

Even Chairman of the Board Frank Sinatra had high-paid public relations experts working to keep his name in the forefront, to deal with controversies and protect his reputation, and to publicize his appearances, movies and recordings.

All of the young stars of today, from hip-hop artists to actors, have brought PR and publicity professionals in their retinue in ever-expanding numbers. They generate the fire that illuminates their clients, much as fabled publicist Lee Solters did successfully for Sinatra for many years.

3. The Unknown Need PR

The relatively unknown entertainer has trouble affording promotional costs but every one certainly needs public relations for many reasons, including development of his or her career until they attain stardom.

A first step is to develop a publicity kit and promotional materials that can be serviced to the media, talent-bookers and event managers. It should consist of:

- Photographs/black-and-white and color
- Resume of career with all appropriate performing credits
- Copies of favorable reviews
- A release that can be updated or rewritten for each appearance
- Information of how to contact you or the manager/agent
- Demo tapes or records
- Your business card

4. Key Advice from a PR Pro

The public relations and promotion professional will not only handle publicity and promotional tasks but will offer advice to the entertainer and the manager or agent about how to deal with the media, including reviewers, reporters, interviewers, *etc.*

The PR professional on the team should do research by reading entertainment trade publications and major newspapers to see what the competition is doing and to note names of reviewers or reporters to contact now or in the future. She/he should also become familiar with television and radio reviewers and entertainment reporters and their shows.

PR advice to the entertainer or manager would include:

- Trends in the entertainment world pertinent to the entertainer
- Tips on friendly and unfriendly or aggressive reviewers, reporters and columnists
- Suggesting appearances at fundraisers, autograph sessions, record-signings, *etc.*
- Updates on the competition

5. PR Fees Can Vary

In this day and age of electronics and a high level of leisure and entertainment outlets there are thousands of highly talented performers with relatively low visibility. It is the PR counselor's job to increase the entertainer's visibility to the public, bookers and media.

But what is the pay standard for the PR professional? Generally, fees for this type of PR work can range from a flat salary to a monthly consulting fee to a percentage of the entertainer's income. Or payment can be by agreement beforehand for a specific appearance or event. Remuneration can vary greatly and often depends on the established bond, the continued success of the relationship and the generosity of the performer or the management decision-maker.

Many times PR professionals are permanent employees but this swings up and down depending on the success of the entertainer over a certain period of time. Individual public relations counselors who join the team fulltime often become personally close and valuable to the performer because of the nature of the business that requires extensive travel and time demands.

6. 10 Tips for Entertainment PR

1. Prepare a publicity kit with all essential inclusions and keep material updated

2. Submit new photographs and updates periodically to the media

3. Use attractive photos and well-written copy for ads, brochures and flyers

4. Distribute information re upcoming appearances to the media

5. Invite booking agents and entertainment room managers to performances

6. Establish relationships with reviewers, reporters and editors

7. Invite key media members to performances as your guest

8. Publicize, advertise and promote each performance

9. Arrange for the entertainer to make special charity and other public appearances

10. Insure that signs and flyers or brochures are available at each appearance beforehand

PR Tip: Your job in PR is to make the entertainer, the politician or the client, whoever he or she may be, look good. If you look good and enjoy yourself in the process, more power to you!

Section Six

Chapter One

Forming an In-House PR Agency

1. An Effective Solution

Strategic public relations programs and the marketing and advertising requirements that accompany them are often too confusing, elusive and demanding for the management team of a business or organization to deal with effectively.

Trapped in this scenario, the team turns by default to an outside agency for assistance, even when that is not really the best or most cost-efficient path. Of course, an external agency often is the best course of action. How to decide which route to take is a difficult process.

An effective solution that can potentially save a business up to 17 percent on advertising is the creation of an in-house public relations agency managed by a knowledgeable PR employee or outside consultant. It is up to the decision-makers to consider this move in full.

A practitioner versed in the basics of public relations and advertising can be promoted from within or hired to create and manage a new in-house agency, with assistance and direction from the guidelines, tips, case histories, forms and insights presented within this kit.

Bonus: Increased marketing and advertising successes gained for a business through its new internal agency will eventually enhance the practitioner's position and standing with the employer and lead to increases in budgeting for marketing (and for the practitioner's salary).

2. Real and Perceived Value

The new in-house agency will allow the marketing, advertising and public relations programs and activities to be formalized and give them increased real and perceived value to all concerned. And the properly run in-house agency will gain a solid return-on-investment (ROI) for the employer – the ultimate goal, of course.

The PR professional in-house would coordinate all activities from outside agencies and resources necessary to fill in the gaps and complete the marketing mosaic.

This in-house agency can save the employer or client on advertising costs that include the standard agency commission (SAC) of 15 percent and a 2 percent pre-pay reduction where applicable for a potential savings of up to 17 percent.

This savings will be realized in magazines and newspapers that charge standard agency commissions of 15 percent and perhaps the two percent prepay option. Reductions of the commissions from radio and television rates to the internal agency can also be factored in. In the broadcast industry, negotiation is often a vital factor.

By forging action plans that are within a proper budget, a talented and dedicated PR practitioner can craft a scenario in-house or work closely and in an appropriate manner with an outside agency and its reps, as outlined in the next chapter. This will lead to a lasting and mutually rewarding relationship for all concerned.

3. *The First Steps*

An important first step for the internal agency point-person is to contact all appropriate media outlets for their policies and rates, deadlines, ad production and placement deadlines and the editorial calendar.

Next, the practitioner should over the creation or redesign of the company logo, typestyle, colors and motto/slogan of the company or organization.

Continuing, he or she should write and design advertisements for individual placements or for an ad campaign in concert with management and the sales executive.

Important, too, is the creation of a traditional kit of PR and sales materials that includes articles about the business or organization, fact sheets, bios/photos of key executives, appropriate printed materials such as brochures and newsletters, and sales sheets.

All material for the new agency should be professionally produced and neatly arranged in a pocket folder. This kit would be used in many ways to promote the company and gear up for advertising and publicity campaigns.

The professional image established through an internal agency, and the new materials, will help to position the employer or client (and the PR practitioner) in a positive light with customers or clients and the media.

4. *10 Involvements for the Practitioner*

Ten areas in which the public relations practitioner agency point-person should become involved include:

1. Obtaining complete advertising kits from key print and broadcast venues

2. Evaluating ads and promotional materials of key competitors

3. Insuring that the employer's website is current and dynamic

4. Enrolling the employer or client in appropriate associations and organizations

5. Subscribing to publications of interest

6. Arranging participation in key shows and exhibitions

7. Providing creative input to the internal sales team

8. Handling crisis-problem management

9. Tracking and quelling harmful rumors

10. Working closely with management and the sales department

The responsibilities are lengthy and complex but each one is necessary in order to fulfill the obligations of the position assumed when you create an internal public relations agency.

All of the strategic advertising, marketing and programs and activities under the PR practitioner for an employer should be coordinated within appropriate time frames so that synergy and positive return-on-investment result.

The point-person, whether it is an employee or a consultant, should operate under the premise that it is for his or her own business.

5. *Gaining Clout Through a Title*

An appropriate title is essential for the PR practitioner or consultant for a specific employer or client because it will provide a measure of *clout* with outside agencies and professionals, the media, and internally with management and staff.

A title can also help boost the practitioner's self-esteem and regard by industry with contemporaries and could and should result in increased earning potential for that point-person.

The practitioner will get more attention and access by being identified as one of the following: Public Relations Manager or Director, Corporate Communications Manager or Director, Media Manager or Director – the point is clear. Just remember that the title should be appropriate to the person and the mission.

6. *Evaluating the Agency*

After the first six months or year of operation, the internal agency should be running smoothly and the savings on ad commissions and perhaps prepay can be evaluated.

Along the way, the point-person will be building relationships with ad reps, as well as with the traditional media contacts. And he or she will be getting a 'whole-world' view of the potentials of advertising, marketing and public relations.

7. 10 Guidelines to Follow

Following are 10 basic guidelines that businesses, organizations and practitioners who understand and agree with the value of establishing an in-house PR agency should follow:

1) Thoroughly review the guidelines, tips and case histories so there is a clear understanding of the value, complexity, potential and scope of public relations in order to make an informed decision about creating a new in-house agency.

2) Insure that there is or will be an appropriate employee or dedicated consultant versed in creating, managing and implementing the responsibilities required of the point-person for the agency.

3) Acquire and use public relations and advertising tools from many professional sources, including the forms in this kit, to establish the agency in for full service and not solely for the potential savings of advertising dollars.

4) Create a credible, appropriate and previously unclaimed agency name; for example, "The Millco Agency" could represent The Miller Company.

5) Register the agency name with the County Clerk, who will then advertise it in the 'New Business' section of a local newspaper to make it official.

6) Develop a logo and reproduce it internally or through a local printer for multiple uses. The logo for the Millco Agency could include the initials TMA followed by the company's address, telephone and fax numbers, and e-mail address. The PR practitioner would be identified as the agency PR manager or director.

7) Create an appealing stationery package of letterhead, envelopes, business cards and advertising insert order forms for appropriate use.

8) Select an appropriate title for the practitioner who manages the in-house agency so as to enhance her or his clout internally, increase chances to gain better access with the media and outside agencies and resources – and boost self-esteem.

9) Place the logo and company or organization I.D. on each of the forms within this kit so they may be used by the in-house agency whenever needed.

10) Maintain complete financial records and keep track of commissions saved through use of the advertising discounts offered to the in-house agency by the media.

NOTE: The custom forms included at the end of <u>All PR is Local</u>@ are for purchasers of the book to use for an internal public relations agency representing their employer, clients or selves. The forms provided are for unlimited use by the purchaser only. Reproduction of the forms for redistribution or sale is strictly prohibited and a violation of law.

Chapter Two

The In-House Agency In Detail

1. A Detailed Review

The general standards and guidelines of the past chapter are necessary to understand and embrace if a practitioner wishes to create an internal agency for a business or if the owner wants to start one on his/her own.

This chapter presents a more detailed and specific review of the in-house agency and its primary advantage, the potential of saving up to 17 percent in advertising costs, 15 percent on standard agency commission (SAC) and two percent for pre-pay wherever that policy applies.

Deciding whether or not to form an internal PR agency begins with a key question: with the high prices of placing ads today, why not save from 15-to-17 percent on your investment if you can? It isn't for every business or every practitioner but, where and when it fits, it can save a substantial amount of money over the course of time.

2. No Special Secret

There is no special secret to placing advertisements in magazines, tabloids and newspapers. The only costs to the owner or the PR practitioner are the time and effort expended to learn the ropes in order to claim the discounts traditionally given to advertising agencies as commissions, and deservedly so if they do the work.

If you don't have the ability or resources to create your own ads in-house, a common situation, you can rely on an external resource to do that work. You will still profit up to 17 percent from your own agency's *placement* of the ads. Some outlets provide lesser agency discounts – as low as nine percent - but 15 percent is the standard agency commission within the industry, with two percent discount for pre-pay where policy dictates.)

The practitioner or owner, whoever is the agency decision-maker, must determine the budget, research the best potential advertising outlets, plan the ad campaign, work with layout artists and copywriters to produce effective ads, and then place the ads.

You can eventually learn how to create and design either the rough or finished ads with no educational or profession background in copywriting or art thanks to a wide variety of computer software design programs.

Do you have a product that you're ready to sell? Now is the time to find out the best angles to use and the tricks of the trade to putting money in your pocket through an in-house agency

3. Boosting Your Business

Do you have a mail-order business? Maybe you sell clothing, camping supplies, or information through ads to the mail order trade or on the Internet. Perhaps you've run classified ads for years and are ready to branch out into larger display advertisements.

Not only small home businesses but larger mail order companies and hundreds of major advertisers everywhere can set up in-house agencies under a variation of the company name get the agency discount. What used to set advertising agencies apart from internal or home operations is the appearance of the letterhead, correspondence and the ad form. All materials need to look sharp and professional and they rise to the quality level necessary to operate with relative acceptance from all concerned.

4. Begin With A Name

As stated in the last chapter, begin with a name for the ad agency you want to establish. It can be anything, but must be different from the name of the company that will be using the same office space. Then register the name with the county clerk. Check first to be sure you're not using a company name already in business.

Designing letterhead is easier than you think. You don't have to create an elaborate or clever logo, the initials of your company will do. You can choose your own custom logo and type style and produce your own materials such as brochures and flyers on your own computer, on-line or by working with a local printer.

Establishing your own ad agency is easy and the form you send in when you place ads is simple to produce. Just make that form and all of your materials look professional. Although there are no federal restrictions for in-house ad agencies, some publications may hesitate if you appear to pretending to have an agency. Make it real. And if your ad placement form looks as good as the rest, you'll have no problems.

5. The Ad Insertion Form

This book contains the following representation of a sample advertising insert order form and another example in the forms section. Just copy one of the forms and design a logo to be printed on top. You can choose a color combination and paper style for the forms so they appear professional. Then all you do is send in a copy of the completed form with your check and final ad artwork - and claim the appropriate discount(s).

The following will describe what the various terms on the insertion order form mean and how to fill them in. Space indicates what type of space you are buying: classified or display. If you want display space, indicate the size. Fill in the number of times you want the ad to be repeated. It will be run in the number of consecutive issues you indicate. Then fill in the actual dates of insertion for the ad. The position of an ad in a publication is an important factor in its success. Although you rarely can be guaranteed a certain position in the publication, ask for it anyway.

You may enhance your chances to at least obtain the next best placement position.

If you are running a short ad that will be printed by the publication, you can type out the copy in the instructions space at the bottom. The key designates the address code you'll use to analyze responses. For example, you can use a letter to indicate the name of the publication, and a number for the month of issue. Insert this key in the address, perhaps as a department division or suite number. When you get inquiries or orders with that key, you'll know which ad pulled the response.

Sample Standard Print Advertising Insert Form:

Advertising Agency _____ Date _____

Ad Enclosed From_____ Title_____

Address_____

Tel._____ Fax_____ E-mail_____

To the publisher of_____ Insert order number_____

Please publish advertising of_____

For (product)_____

Contracted advertising space to be ordered on dates _____through_____

Space_____ No Times _____ Dates of Insertion_____

Position _____Copy Key (copy attached) _____

Rate _____ Less agency commission of _____% on gross amount of_____

Prepay percentage agency discount _____% on net amount_____. Applicable. ___Yes ___No

Mail all invoices to:_____ Title_____

Accepted for publishing by _____ Title _____ Date _____

Sign and Return to:

Name_____ Title_____

Address_____Tel_____

6. How to Determine Rates

Every publication that solicits advertising has a rate-card. This card is available from the advertising coordinator, who is the contact for the publication and can be very helpful in assisting you. The best way to get a rate card is to write for one or call if the publication is in your city, or research on the Internet.

The rate-card has the general information you'll need for placing your ad. It should indicate the total circulation with a breakdown of subscriptions and newsstand buyers. Keep in mind that most publications have two to three readers for every one purchase.

The advertising rates may be broken down a number of ways, depending on how the publication sells space. Display rates may be sold by the column-inch or by lines. Or, they may be broken up into fractions such as a half-page or quarter-page. Some publications have a minimum size space ad, so keep this in mind when designing the ads for certain publications.

The rate-card will tell you the amount of discount you are entitled to as an ad agency. It will also give you the deadlines for placing the ads for the next issue and the issuance date, the actual day the magazine comes off press and goes to the newsstands and to subscribers.

If you have any questions concerning the type of space you need or the actual rate, just ask the advertising coordinator.

7. Your 15 % Discount

As an advertising agency, you are entitled to a fifteen percent discount on the ad space, unless the publication grants only lower discounts. The easiest way to subtract a 15% discount is to multiply the rate charge by .85. Immediately, you have the exact figure for placing the ad. To get back to the full price, multiply the amount by 17.65 percent.

Some publications realize that mail order businesses don't operate with a high capital for placing ads. Because of this, they may offer an additional discount for their display ads. To compute the fee for two discounts of 15 percent, simply multiply the total rate charge by .70 for the final amount.

Whether you are an ad agency or not, you are entitled to take a two percent discount for sending your check with the order of the publication's policy allows. This discount is offered to discourage billing and encourage pre-payment. To figure out the two percent cash discount, multiply the total rate charge by .98 after you have already taken the other appropriate discounts. That will give you the total you will pay for placing your ad.

8 Where to Place Ads

The rule of thumb for placing ads, especially for mail order, is to look through the publications catering to the same product you are selling, and do the same. Although advertisers are always looking for new and innovative ways to sell products, they usually stick with the proven ways of selling.

What are you selling? Where are the logical places these products are sold? Go there and place your ads where people will look for your products.

There is no reason you can't hit a successful ad campaign the first time but more often you'll find it necessary to spend some time testing different ads, different display sizes, and even different lead products. Testing is the name of the game and, if you're careful, you don't have to go for broke but can build a sound winner.

A number of significantly successful companies have made a fortune in return from advertising an appealing product and delivering a good deal. There is no reason why you can't too.

9. *Buying Space*

There are two types of advertising space in a publication - display space and classified ads. How you use ad space is entirely up to the type of appeal that will sell the product best and your budget.

Don't shortchange classifieds. A small, well-written classified ad can bring hundreds of responses on a continual basis. Often classifieds are used in a two-step approach of first placing an ad that has no price mentioned and soliciting the reader's response for free information. Then it is followed up with a sales letter or brochure - some sort of sales literature - that gives the pitch for the product.

Classifieds are the least expensive ad to place. People who run mail order businesses find them to be the best dollar-for-dollar investment in advertising. Look at the classifieds section of the publications you are planning to place ads in. If your product can be sold with a classified ad, you should start there.

If you have actual products to sell, display ads are your better bet. You'll probably need an illustration to show the product - something to catch the eye. You can also include a line or two about sending for a catalog.

10. *Display Ads*

Display advertising space is the area in a publication designated for companies to show their products and describe the benefits, appealing to consumers and potential buyers.

Display space comes in all sizes from full page to a smaller fraction. Since some publications don't have classified space, it may be your logical answer to place a small, one or two-inch ad. But if your ad is to be small and there is a classified section place it there - you'll save money and the ad will be seen by roughly the same amount of readers.

Your guideline for determining what size the ad should be is to decide what is going into the ad and what type of approach you plan to make. Some products need full one-page descriptions; some don't require a large space. You may be able to get by with a small, appealing ad that has a clear illustration.

If you have a limited budget, take out a smaller ad in a publication with a good reputation and a high circulation. Don't sacrifice a good pulling magazine for larger ad space in another publication. You have to consider the dollar-for-dollar response.

Other ways to save money are to advertise in the regional editions of publications and to buy remnant space that is the "leftover" space sometimes available just before the magazine goes to print. If you have a good working rapport with the publication, you might be able to place a low-cost ad at the last minute.

Depending on your product, you need to consider where you want your ad to appear in the publication. You'll most likely not require the prime spots such as the back cover, the first page or the inside covers.

But it has been proven that a right hand ad pulls better response than one on the left side of the publication. Ads placed closer to the front of the magazine pull better than those towards the back. Think about where you want the ad to show up and request it.

11. Keeping Records

How will you know if your ads are pulling the response you want? When you place different ads in different publications, you need to have a method to determine which ads are drawing the best results. To do this, you keep accurate records.

For each ad you place, you have an address key. Use a separate record sheet for each key. At the top of the sheet, put the pertinent information, such as the name and issue of the publication, the date of issue, the cost of the ad, and the information about the ad you placed.

The main body of the record sheet may be divided into the two categories of inquiries and orders. These in turn are separated into date received, number received, and running totals of inquiries, orders and sales.

The reason keeping records is important is two-fold. First, you must respond to any orders you receive without getting them mixed up. Second, you need to figure out which publications are bringing the highest responses.

Good records will indicate which headlines pull better, which size has a better draw, and which products out of a catalog have more appeal.

Testing is the best way to achieve results in advertising.

The major agencies do it, you can too.

12. Writing Copy

You've seen hundreds of ads in magazines, newspapers, and through the mail. Most of them are the same; most of them have similar products to sell. You read some of them because you're interested in the product and read some of them because they're interesting to read. Most of them just pass you by.

There are no best ways to describe a product or form an appeal for services. But there are proven methods of writing to catch a few people who didn't know about the product to read the ad and to get the people who are interested in the product to buy.

Your main concerns in creating ads are to get the reader's attention, sustain that attention, and push for action to buy. The longer you can hold interest, the greater number of people will respond.

Use short, simple sentences and paragraphs. Keep your writing concise and to the point. Rambling words and ideas will make the reader lose interest quickly. Always be relevant to what you are selling.

Subheads help cut copy into small and digestible pieces, such as we have done in this book. Use of italics, capital letters, bold face and oversized print can also help grab attention to the words.

Make the copy rewarding to read, the product appealing to have, and the offer too good to pass by, and you'll have plenty of business.

13. Choose An Appeal

What will put your product to best advantage? What can the reader gain? The headline is the stopper. It is the few words that will make the reader stop and look at the ad. Think of how your product can appeal to the readers you want to induce.

Questions: Can I manage to save, gain or accomplish something ordinary or special? Can I increase my finances, good health or general well-being? Can the product or service can help avoid worries, losses and mistakes. Or help decrease fears of poverty, illness in the family or the loss of a job?

The attitude you choose aims at the person's emotional state. It is the emotions that catch hold, then reason follows through to decide to read on or not. Consider the typical buyer you desire and go after that person. Use the words "you" or "your" or imply a direct connection with "we" and "our." Make the reader believe you are writing directly and honestly, offering the best available.

Consider a headline that uses "which one" or a comparative price. The choice alone entices you to read further. Or you might use an underdog approach such as I went wrong too, but will tell you how you can avoid it.

The headline that includes "how to" is always an appealing catcher. Invite the reader into your copy and then lead quickly into the main text of the ad.

14. Show the Advantages

Most ads placed by small in-house agencies don't solicit the national retail trade that large advertising companies handle. Instead, they offer an unusual product or service, a great price on close-out items, or products for the mail order consumer. More often than not, these ads will be short, concise, and stop not long after the headline. For many products, there's not much that needs to be said that a picture or drawing can't show.

But for those items that sell even better with copy, you'll need to think about the benefits you want to describe and the best ways to show these advantages.

You've caught the reader's attention with the headline.

Now hold it. Follow through with the facts that answer the headline. You have to convince the reader not only to want to have the product, but to want to buy it. Whatever you considered for the headline, study it again. What will this do for me? Why do I want to buy it? Is it less expensive than the other similar products? Is it the same but a newer model or a more efficient design?

Push the emotional appeal. How will this make me look better or feel better? What will my family and friends say and how will they react?

You might try to tap into the market of avoiding embarrassment, eliminating problems, minimizing risk. Will this help me enjoy my leisure? With the continued trend towards increasing leisure time and the many after work activities available to the public, people are looking for more and interesting things to do with spare time. Can your product tap into this?

Money is forever the great desire. Now more than ever people are seeking financial security and look for ways to save money, especially over the long run. Saving money and buying at a lower price are sound copy points. But they must be followed through with believable reasons and sound facts.

For example, ads for wood-burning stoves often appear in northern regional editions of publications, or magazines catering to homeowners. A small ad with a drawing of a wood burner may draw attention with a headline about saving heating costs. It can include an address to write for more information.

A larger space ad could include the advantages of a wood-burning stove over and above the savings on gas bills, such as efficiency, superb craftsmanship, quality of materials, or easy to install. Any benefits that sell the product can be used to appeal to the reader.

A still larger ad could have an "exploded" drawing of the inside of the stove, and might also include information about how it works, how it saves you money. it might mention the reputation of the company. But consider whether the cost of a larger ad will bring in the extra response to make it profitable.

15. Stick to Facts

Stick to the facts. And stay with the buying points. A potential customer may be sold on the concept or the idea but the important question is: will that person buy the product?

Endorsements and testimonials are effective ways to dramatize facts and back up the benefits of your product but don't use ones that seem transparent. They ring false. There are federal laws against misleading advertising, and officials do check up on and prosecute against fraud.

If you use an endorsement from a famous or popular person, that person should actually use the product. Any testimonials you use must be true, and the endorser must be available for verification.

Always aim for satisfaction. Self-respect, security and accomplishment are human aspects everyone strives for. And never talk down to the readers as though you know something they don't or you're better than they are. To you, the potential customer is potential gold.

16. Ask For Action

You've caught the reader's attention with a catchy headline. You've followed through with good copy that demonstrates benefits and appeals to the reader. Your ad design is graphically superior. Now, before you lose that interest, ask for an order.

You have to close the gap between reading the ad and acting upon impulse. The purpose of the ad is to make people buy. You have to tighten the desire to want into the desire to buy.

A money-back guarantee is the most useful tool in pressing action. It goes for the bottom line. What do I have to lose? And it affirms the quality of the product. If you are willing to back the claims you make with a full refund, you can get a hook into those borderline buyers.

If you give a time limit the product will be offered for sale, or mention a limited supply, or have a reduced price for a certain time, you'll increase the impulse to act. And that's what you're after. Appeal to the reader's sense of urgency and make your product totally desirable to have now.

17. Use of Illustrations

The major reason to use display space is to illustrate your product. Some items are difficult to sell without a photo or drawing and some illustrations work better with your product than others.

The illustration may be selling the only product you have, or you may want to use a lead illustration, something out of your product line that is particularly appealing. Then give the company's name and address for people to write for a free catalog.

Be particular about using photographs. Business owners should rarely insert their own photograph; it is sheer vanity and won't help to sell most products, the late Dave Thomas of Wendy's and Frank Perdue of chicken fame notwithstanding. And be very choosy about models for clothing or other wares. If necessary, use professionals or locals with a proven appeal and draw.

An advantage to photography is that you can picture your product in full, glowing color. But it's not usually that important. Considering the additional costs, it may not bring in the additional responses to make it worthwhile.

You can have your product pictured indoors or out. But consider the size of the ad, and get rid of extraneous visual matter in the background. You are aiming for a clear, appealing view of what you have to offer, and you want the reader to buy that product.

When using photographs, always go for top quality. You can find dozens of excellent professional photographers from the yellow pages and at the photo supply stores. Look at the photographer's work and don't use a portrait-taker if you need an illustrator to sketch a product.

Can the photograph or product he converted or illustrated with art? Line drawings are beautiful ways to show off a product in a clear and direct manner. They can be simple-just an outline. Or they can be more elaborate.

Line art is easy to draw and reproduce. And usually it can show up a product to best advantage. There are no extras to detract attention.

Consider the simplest and most direct way to illustrate the products you want people to buy. Maybe you can try a layout with a photo and one with a simple drawing. What difference does it make?

What is the competition doing? When testing new ads, go with the tried and true. Don't try to be different. It is the sound and worthwhile that bring in the customers-time and time again.

18. *Working With Artists*

There are no special tricks to designing a good page and there is no great expense in having someone else do it. The key is to get it right and return on the investment will soon be obvious.

The best way to find an artist to draw line art, design and layout a page and paste up the ad is through a design studio. Or talk to individual designers and hire a freelancer. You can negotiate a very reasonable fee for design work but be certain to obtain the services of a professional.

Work directly with the artist to ensure that your objectives are well communicated. And be sure you are satisfied with the final work. You both have something to say but let the product speak the loudest.

19. Doing Layouts

You don't need to hire a designer to do the layout for your ad. You are capable of doing it yourself - after all, you know the product best. Consider what you want to say. You need to make it different from the other ads but don't try to win design awards.

The ad must be interesting to look at and should have a feeling of movement and action. That movement is not necessarily in the illustration but it is in the placement of the illustration and copy within the ad so flow will be in easy and appealing movements.

You need to consider where the illustration will be located and its relation to the headline and body text. Perhaps you wish to show the product in use or maybe the illustration is intended as just a simple product photo of illustration.

A rule of thumb in layout is to use contrast. The most obvious contrast is the black print on white paper. Use that white space. Although it's not apparent, the white space is as important in the visual appeal as the illustration and type.

Don't try for too much symmetry. The unusual or irregular catches the eye more readily. The illustration works hand in hand with the headline to grab readers' attention.

Be simple and direct. Don't push too much copy into a small area, crowding the illustration. If you don't have room, cut copy or reduce the illustration.

You can use any size and style type you want for the ad. But don't get carried away. You shouldn't use a special typeface unless it helps sell the product. And, never use a headline type that's hard to read.

Using different sizes of type help point out the benefits of the product. Bold or italicized type will bring more visual appeal to the ad.

If you find that the illustration is too big for the ad space you want to use, you can reduce it to a smaller size or crop out portions not absolutely necessary. A "bleed" photo runs straight off the page. Check with the advertising coordinator first to be sure the publication will do bleeds.

A good way to do a rough layout is a pencil-sketching placement of the type and illustration, and lines to indicate body copy and the name of the company. Try different pencil layouts until you're satisfied you have the product at its best appeal.

20. Camera-Ready Copy

Most publications require final artwork for display ads. Camera-ready copy means that it's ready to be made into the films that printers need for reproduction. Computer-generated discs with final artwork are now used by most printers and provide a simplified method of doing this.
Final artwork should-not be a photocopy of a drawing but the original drawing or a photo-stat of

the original. The latter might need to be reduced or enlarged to fit the layout.

If you are using a photograph, it should be a professional quality print. Any areas that need to be cropped should be indicated with a red grease pencil that won't harm the surface of the photo--don't cut the photo.

If you are using color photography, you may need to have color separations made before you submit the ad. This is a process whereby the color in the photo is separated into its four elements of red, yellow, blue and black. The advertising coordinator will be able to tell you what you need, and a local printer can help you with the separations.

If you have no experience in pasting up layouts, you'll need to get a professional. Why make a mistake so late in the game? Although it is a simple process of gluing the type and illustrations down with rubber cement, you need the correct tools to be sure everything is exactly straight.

21. Where to Go From Here

Setting up your own in-house advertising agency is easy. Placing ads and claiming your 15 percent discount is no problem. The challenge comes in writing appealing ads that are winners. The reward is selling products through those ads month after month, year after year.

At any stage of the advertising game you can call in professional advice. A freelance pro can offer sound, money-saving tips and be worth every dollar spent. Even if you commission the artwork and layout of the ad, you'll still save a bundle over ad agency costs.

If you have your own home business or if your company has expanded into advertising, there's no reason not to set up your own agency. There's no hassle, and the savings are great.

If you need specialized legal advice or assistance on this subject, the services of an attorney are recommended.

22. There are Options

After you've exhausted your look at forming an in-house public relations agency for a business or a consulting agency of your own, weigh it against the use of an existing agency.

There are of course many large, medium and small traditional, niche and boutique agencies that may better suit your needs and are a buffer to your attempting to do it all yourself, no easy chore in the best of situations.

Remember to match your needs against the nature, size and scope of the agencies you consider so you or your client doesn't get lost in the shuffle. Most agencies will claim that all clients are equal but few carry that through when the chips are down and their and resources and time are in demand. The loudest squeak - the major client - will get the oil.

Chapter Three

Selecting an Outside Agency

1. An Important Decision

Selecting a public relations agency to service the specific advertising and marketing needs of an employer or client is one of the most important decisions a PR employee or consultant will ever make or help to make. The agency of choice will have a major influence on the management team, on the marketing and sales department, and in the professional life of the associated PR practitioner. It will help to review and use the form at the end of this book during the process of selecting an outside public relations agency.

The investment of funds and trust in an agency will impact customers and clients, associates and employees, the management team and board members – literally everyone involved with the business or organization.

The practitioner, either an employee or consultant, should be the point-person to send requests for proposals (RFP's) to candidate agencies. An internal team consisting of the president and/or CEO, the marketing or sales director and any other appropriate decision-maker should join the practitioner on the selection team.

It is important that the PR practitioner be included in the management of the selected agency and in all of the PR and advertising activities of the employer or client, not only to insure continuity but also to protect the practitioner's own turf. Retaining (some) control is essential for the practitioner, but it should be done through cooperation and persuasion, not heavy handedness.

2. Considerations for Selection

A *full-service* agency may be chosen specifically for its public relations expertise, or for its mix of PR and advertising abilities. If desired, carefully screened freelancers can be plugged in for projects not handled by the agency of record, including for technical writing, ad production, graphic design, print spec, special events, research and surveys, *etc.*

These guidelines are for assistance in the important PR agency selection process:

1) Review the Custom Form@ titled 'Selecting An Agency', then create an agency evaluation committee and establish a decision-making process.

2) Evaluate the employer or client's current marketing communications plans, programs and budgets, and identify future needs.

3) Create a request-for-proposal (RFP) that asks for short *and* long-term PR and allied

marketing recommendations (suggested solutions) from outside agency applicants.

4) Invite reputable public relations agencies that are known to be strong in the employer or client's specific area of business or industry to submit proposals. They may include reputable PR or PR-advertising agencies.

5) Select three finalists for an in-depth interview with requests for multiple examples of their agency's work, client references and their proposal.

6) Attempt to screen out those agencies that appear to be incompatible according to the parameters established for the employer or client: too big or too small, too diverse or not diverse enough, too much a generalist or too much a specialist.

7) Review carefully for substance rather than style exactly what the agency specifically proposes to do and how they plan to do it.

8) Request from each agency its proposed monthly fee, advertising commission policies, marketing materials production costs and commissions, and its account management and billing policies.

9) Determine exactly who would serve as the agency representative and what his or her credentials are, who would handle other aspects of the account, and what are the technical and service capabilities within the agency.

10) The evaluation committee then would meet to review the candidates and make the selection based on the value of what the agency will bring to the table for an employer or client.

A PR Vignette:

A potential client was seeking public relations assistance to publicize a new upscale golf course and exclusive development. We were interested – what PR consultant wouldn't be?

When he declared that a previous consultant interviewee guaranteed front-page coverage in the largest newspaper in the state, we handed him a telephone and recommended that he immediately retain the services of such a wizard.

"What?" he asked incredulously.

When I explained that no one could *guarantee* coverage, he was taken aback.

Then I explained that we could provide the best *opportunity* for coverage.

We got the job.

This example proves two things: 1) sometimes client expectations must be tempered with reality and 2) sometimes people will stretch the truth a little too far in order to sign up a client. Just *don't* do it.

Section Seven

PRSA Public Relations
Society of America

Member Code of Ethics 2000

Approved by the PRSA Assembly
October, 2000

Letter from the PRSA Board of Directors

It is with enormous professional pleasure and personal pride that we, the Public Relations
Society of America Board of Directors put before you a new Public Relations Member Code of
Ethics for our Society. It is the result of two years of concentrated effort led by the Board of
Ethics and Professional Standards. Comments of literally hundreds and hundreds of members
were considered. There were focus groups at our 1999 national meeting in Anaheim, California.
We sought and received intensive advice and counsel from the Ethics Resource Center, our
outside consultants on the project. Additional recommendations were received from your Board
of Directors, PRSA staff, outside reviewers, as well as District and Section officers. Extensive
research involving analysis of numerous codes of conduct, ethics statements, and standards and
practices approaches was also carried out.

In fact, this Member Code of Ethics has been developed to serve as a foundation for discussion
of an emerging global Code of Ethics and Conduct for the practice of Public Relations.

This approach is dramatically different from that which we have relied upon in the past. You'll
find it different in three powerfully important ways:

1. Emphasis on enforcement of the Code has been eliminated. But, the PRSA Board of Directors retains the
   right to bar from membership or expel from the Society any individual who has been or is sanctioned by a
   government agency or convicted in a court of law of an action that is in violation of this Code.

2. The new focus is on universal values that inspire ethical behavior and performance.

3. Desired behavior is clearly illustrated by providing language, experience, and examples to help the
   individual practitioner better achieve important ethical and principled business objectives. This approach
   should help everyone better understand what the expected standards of conduct truly are.

Perhaps most important of all, the mission of the Board of Ethics and Professional Standards has now been substantially altered to focus primarily on education and training, on collaboration with similar efforts in other major professional societies, and to serve an advisory role to the Board on ethical matters of major importance.

The foundation of our value to our companies, clients and those we serve is their ability to rely on our ethical and morally acceptable behavior. Please review this new Member Code of Ethics in this context:

- Its Values are designed to inspire and motivate each of us every day to the highest levels of ethical practice.

- Its Code Provisions are designed to help each of us clearly understand the limits and specific performance required to be an ethical practitioner.

- Its Commitment mechanism is designed to ensure that every Society member understands fully the obligations of membership and the expectation of ethical behavior that are an integral part of membership in the PRSA.

This approach is stronger than anything we have ever had because:

- It will have a daily impact on the practice of Public Relations.

- There are far fewer gray areas and issues that require interpretation.

- It will grow stronger and be more successful than what we have had in the past through education, through training, and through analysis of behaviors.

The strength of the Code will grow because of the addition of precedent and the ethical experiences of other major professional organizations around the world.

Our new Code elevates our ethics, our values, and our commitment to the level they belong, at the very top of our daily practice of Public Relations.

PRSA Board of Directors

A Message from the PRSA Board of Ethics and Professional Standards

Our Primary Obligation

The primary obligation of membership in the Public Relations Society of America is the ethical practice of Public Relations.

The PRSA Member Code of Ethics is the way each member of our Society can daily reaffirm a commitment to ethical professional activities and decisions.

- The Code sets forth the principles and standards that guide our decisions and actions.

- The Code solidly connects our values and our ideals to the work each of us does every day.

- The Code is about what we should do, and why we should do it.

The Code is also meant to be a living, growing body of knowledge, precedent, and experience. It should stimulate our thinking and encourage us to seek guidance and clarification when we have questions about principles, practices, and standards of conduct.

Every member's involvement in preserving and enhancing ethical standards is essential to building and maintaining the respect and credibility of our profession. Using our values, principles, standards of conduct, and commitment as a foundation, and continuing to work together on ethical issues, we ensure that the Public Relations Society of America fulfills its obligation to build and maintain the framework for public dialogue that deserves the public's trust and support.

The Members of the 2000 Board of Ethics and Professional Standards:

Robert D. Frause, APR, Fellow PRSA
Chairman BEPS
Seattle, Washington

Kathy R. Fitzpatrick, APR
Gainesville, Florida

Linda Welter Cohen, APR
Tucson, Arizona

James R. Frankowiak, APR
Tampa, Florida

James E. Lukaszewski, APR, Fellow PRSA
White Plains, New York

Roger D. Buehrer, APR
Fellow PRSA
Las Vegas, Nevada

Jeffrey P. Julin, APR
Denver, Colorado

David M. Bicofsky, APR, Fellow PRSA
Teaneck, New Jersey

James W. Wyckoff, APR
New York, New York

The PRSA Assembly adopted this Code of Ethics in 2000. It replaces the Code of Professional Standards (previously referred to as the Code of Ethics) that was last revised in 1988. For further information on the Code, please contact the chair of the Board of Ethics through PRSA headquarters.

Preamble

Public Relations Society of America Member Code of Ethics 2000

- Professional Values
- Principles of Conduct
- Commitment and Compliance

This Code applies to PRSA members. The Code is designed to be a useful guide for PRSA members as they carry out their ethical responsibilities. This document is designed to anticipate and accommodate, by precedent, ethical challenges that may arise. The scenarios outlined in the Code provision are actual examples of misconduct. More will be added as experience with the Code occurs.

The Public Relations Society of America (PRSA) is committed to ethical practices. The level of public trust PRSA members seek, as we serve the public good, means we have taken on a special obligation to operate ethically.

The value of member reputation depends upon the ethical conduct of everyone affiliated with the Public Relations Society of America. Each of us sets an example for each other - as well as other professionals - by our pursuit of excellence with powerful standards of performance, professionalism, and ethical conduct.

Emphasis on enforcement of the Code has been eliminated. But, the PRSA Board of Directors retains the right to bar from membership or expel from the Society any individual who has been or is sanctioned by a government agency or convicted in a court of law of an action that is in violation of this Code.

Ethical practice is the most important obligation of a PRSA member. We view the Member Code of Ethics as a model for other professions, organizations, and professionals.

PRSA Member Statement of Professional Values

This statement presents the core values of PRSA members and, more broadly, of the public relations profession. These values provide the foundation for the Member Code of Ethics and set the industry standard for the professional practice of public relations. These values are the fundamental beliefs that guide our behaviors and decision-making process. We believe our professional values are vital to the integrity of the profession as a whole.

ADVOCACY

- We serve the public interest by acting as responsible advocates for those we represent.
- We provide a voice in the marketplace of ideas, facts, and viewpoints to aid informed public debate.

HONESTY

- We adhere to the highest standards of accuracy and truth in advancing the interests of those we represent and in communicating with the public.

EXPERTISE

- We acquire and responsibly use specialized knowledge and experience.

- We advance the profession through continued professional development, research, and education.

- We build mutual understanding, credibility, and relationships among a wide array of institutions and audiences.

INDEPENDENCE

- We provide objective counsel to those we represent.

- We are accountable for our actions.

LOYALTY

- We are faithful to those we represent, while honoring our obligation to serve the public interest.

FAIRNESS

- We deal fairly with clients, employers, competitors, peers, vendors, the media, and the general public.

- We respect all opinions and support the right of free expression.

PRSA Code Provisions

FREE FLOW OF INFORMATION

Core Principle

Protecting and advancing the free flow of accurate and truthful information is essential to serving the public interest and contributing to informed decision making in a democratic society.

Intent

- To maintain the integrity of relationships with the media, government officials, and the public.

- To aid informed decision-making.

Guidelines

A member shall:

- Preserve the integrity of the process of communication.

- Be honest and accurate in all communications.

- Act promptly to correct erroneous communications for which the practitioner is responsible.

- Preserve the free flow of unprejudiced information when giving or receiving gifts by ensuring that gifts are nominal, legal, and infrequent.

Examples of Improper Conduct Under this Provision:

- A member representing a ski manufacturer gives a pair of expensive racing skis to a sports magazine columnist, to influence the columnist to write favorable articles about the product.

- A member entertains a government official beyond legal limits and/or in violation of government reporting requirements.

COMPETITION

Core Principle

Promoting healthy and fair competition among professionals preserves an ethical climate while fostering a robust business environment.

Intent

- To promote respect and fair competition among public relations professionals.

- To serve the public interest by providing the widest choice of practitioner options.

Guidelines

A member shall:

- Follow ethical hiring practices designed to respect free and open competition without deliberately undermining a competitor.

- Preserve intellectual property rights in the marketplace.

Examples of Improper Conduct Under This Provision:

- A member employed by a "client organization" shares helpful information with a counseling firm that is competing with others for the organization's business.

- A member spreads malicious and unfounded rumors about a competitor in order to alienate the competitor's clients and employees in a ploy to recruit people and business.

DISCLOSURE OF INFORMATION

Core Principle

Open communication fosters informed decision making in a democratic society.

Intent

- To build trust with the public by revealing all information needed for responsible decision making.

Guidelines

A member shall:

- Be honest and accurate in all communications.

- Act promptly to correct erroneous communications for which the member is responsible.

- Investigate the truthfulness and accuracy of information released on behalf of those represented.

- Reveal the sponsors for causes and interests represented.

- Disclose financial interest (such as stock ownership) in a client's organization.

- Avoid deceptive practices.

Examples of Improper Conduct Under this Provision:

- Front groups: A member implements "grass roots" campaigns or letter-writing campaigns to legislators on behalf of undisclosed interest groups.

- Lying by omission: A practitioner for a corporation knowingly fails to release financial information, giving a misleading impression of the corporation's performance.

- A member discovers inaccurate information disseminated via a Web site or media kit and does not correct the information.

- A member deceives the public by employing people to pose as volunteers to speak at public hearings and participate in "grass roots" campaigns.

SAFEGUARDING CONFIDENCES

Core Principle

Client trust requires appropriate protection of confidential and private information.

Intent

- To protect the privacy rights of clients, organizations, and individuals by safeguarding confidential information.

Guidelines

A member shall:

- Safeguard the confidences and privacy rights of present, former, and prospective clients and employees.

- Protect privileged, confidential, or insider information gained from a client or organization.

- Immediately advise an appropriate authority if a member discovers that confidential information is being divulged by an employee of a client company or organization.

Examples of Improper Conduct Under This Provision:

- A member changes jobs, takes confidential information, and uses that information in the new position to the detriment of the former employer.

- A member intentionally leaks proprietary information to the detriment of some other party.

CONFLICTS OF INTEREST

Core Principle

Avoiding real, potential or perceived conflicts of interest builds the trust of clients, employers, and the publics.

Intent

- To earn trust and mutual respect with clients or employers.

- To build trust with the public by avoiding or ending situations that put one's personal or professional interests in conflict with society's interests.

Guidelines

A member shall:

- Act in the best interests of the client or employer, even subordinating the member's personal interests.

- Avoid actions and circumstances that may appear to compromise good business judgment or create a conflict between personal and professional interests.

- Disclose promptly any existing or potential conflict of interest to affected clients or organizations.

- Encourage clients and customers to determine if a conflict exists after notifying all affected parties.

Examples of Improper Conduct Under This Provision

- The member fails to disclose that he or she has a strong financial interest in a client's chief competitor.

- The member represents a "competitor company" or a "conflicting interest" without informing a prospective client.

ENHANCING THE PROFESSION

Core Principle

Public relations professionals work constantly to strengthen the public's trust in the profession.

Intent

- To build respect and credibility with the public for the profession of public relations.

- To improve, adapt and expand professional practices.

Guidelines

A member shall:

- Acknowledge that there is an obligation to protect and enhance the profession.

- Keep informed and educated about practices in the profession to ensure ethical conduct.

- Actively pursue personal professional development.

- Decline representation of clients or organizations that urge or require actions contrary to this Code.

- Accurately define what public relations activities can accomplish.

- Counsel subordinates in proper ethical decision-making.

- Require that subordinates adhere to the ethical requirements of the Code.

- Report ethical violations, whether committed by PRSA members or not, to the appropriate authority.

Examples of Improper Conduct Under This Provision:

- A PRSA member declares publicly that a product the client sells is safe, without disclosing evidence to the contrary.

- A member initially assigns some questionable client work to a non-member practitioner to avoid the ethical obligation of PRSA membership.

Rules and Guidelines

The following PRSA documents, available online at www.prsa.org provide detailed rules and guidelines to help guide your professional behavior. If, after reviewing them, you still have a question or issue, contact PRSA headquarters as noted below.

- PRSA Bylaws

- PRSA Administrative Rules

- Member Code of Ethics

QUESTIONS

The PRSA is here to help. If you have a serious concern or simply need clarification, please contact Kim Baldwin at (212) 460-1404.

PRSA Member Code of Ethics Pledge

I pledge:

To conduct myself professionally, with truth, accuracy, fairness, and responsibility to the public; To improve my individual competence and advance the knowledge and proficiency of the profession through continuing research and education; And to adhere to the articles of the Member Code of Ethics 2000 for the practice of public relations as adopted by the governing Assembly of the Public Relations Society of America. I understand and accept that there is a consequence for misconduct, up to and including membership revocation. And, I understand that those who have been or are sanctioned by a government agency or convicted in a court of law of an action that is in violation of this Code may be barred from membership or expelled from the Society.

(Signature/date)

The American Society of Newspaper Editors

Statement of Principles

ASNE's Statement of Principles was originally adopted in 1922 as the "Canons of Journalism." The document was revised and renamed "Statement of Principles" in 1975.

PREAMBLE. The First Amendment, protecting freedom of expression from abridgment by any law, guarantees to the people through their press a constitutional right, and thereby places on newspaper people a particular responsibility. Thus journalism demands of its practitioners not only industry and knowledge but also the pursuit of a standard of integrity proportionate to the journalist's singular obligation. To this end the American Society of Newspaper Editors sets forth this Statement of Principles as a standard encouraging the highest ethical and professional performance.

ARTICLE I - Responsibility. The primary purpose of gathering and distributing news and opinion is to serve the general welfare by informing the people and enabling them to make judgments on the issues of the time. Newspapermen and women who abuse the power of their professional role for selfish motives or unworthy purposes are faithless to that public trust. The American press was made free not just to inform or just to serve as a forum for debate but also to bring an independent scrutiny to bear on the forces of power in the society, including the conduct of official power at all levels of government.

ARTICLE II - Freedom of the Press. Freedom of the press belongs to the people. It must be defended against encroachment or assault from any quarter, public or private. Journalists must be constantly alert to see that the public's business is conducted in public. They must be vigilant against all who would exploit the press for selfish purposes.

ARTICLE III - Independence. Journalists must avoid impropriety and the appearance of impropriety as well as any conflict of interest or the appearance of conflict. They should neither accept anything nor pursue any activity that might compromise or seem to compromise their integrity.

ARTICLE IV - Truth and Accuracy. Good faith with the reader is the foundation of good journalism. Every effort must be made to assure that the news content is accurate, free from bias and in context, and that all sides are presented fairly. Editorials, analytical articles and commentary should be held to the same standards of accuracy with respect to facts as news reports. Significant errors of fact, as well as errors of omission, should be corrected promptly.

ARTICLE V - Impartiality. To be impartial does not require the press to be unquestioning or to refrain from editorial expression. Sound practice, however, demands a clear distinction for the reader between news reports and opinion. Articles that contain opinion or personal interpretation should be clearly identified.

ARTICLE VI - Fair Play. Journalists should respect the rights of people involved in the news, observe the common standards of decency and stand accountable to the public for the fairness and accuracy of their news reports. Persons publicly accused should be given the earliest opportunity to respond. Pledges of confidentiality to news sources must be honored at all costs, and therefore should not be given lightly. Unless there is clear and pressing need to maintain confidences, sources of information should be identified.

These principles are intended to preserve, protect and strengthen the bond of trust and respect between American journalists and the American people, a bond that is essential to sustain the grant of freedom entrusted to both by the nation's founders.

Home Page | Archive | Kiosk

Contact Craig Branson to comment on this site.

Section Eight

<u>Public Relations Custom Forms</u>@

1. Publicity Data Collection – for trade publications
2. Publicity Data Collection - for newspapers
3. Publicity Planning Calendar
4. Selecting Print and Broadcast Outlets
5. Public Relations Team Tasking
6. Publicity Return-On-Investment (ROI)
7. Planning the Media Conference
8. Letter or Media-Alert for a Conference
9. Case History Article
10. Public Relations Budget
11. Individual Print Outlet Evaluations
12. Media Comparisons – trade publications
13. Print Advertising Schedule
14. Newsletter Checklist
15. Special Event Checklist
16. Selecting an Outside Agency
17. Forming an Internal Agency
18. Establishing PR Resources
19. Advertising Budget
20. Ad Insert Order
21. Survey of Customer/Client Reading Preferences
22. Crisis-Problem Tracking – confidential
23. Crisis-Problem *Post Mortem*
24. PR Plan Tracking
25. Client/Employer PR Reporting

1) Publicity Data Collection
for trade publications

INFORMATION FROM:_____ TITLE:_____

1) PRODUCT / SERVICE INFORMATION:_____
_____
_____
(Use reverse side if necessary)

Check Appropriate Box:

☐ **new program** ⸱ ☐ **new service** ⸱ ☐ **new literature** ⸱ ☐ **new prices**

☐ **case history** ⸱ ☐ **new program** ⸱ ☐ **new organizations / associations**

2) EXECUTIVE / EMPLOYEE INFORMATION:_____
_____
_____
(Use reverse side if necessary)

Check Appropriate Box:

☐ **management news / opinion** ⸱ ☐ **promotion** ⸱ ☐ **award / recognition**

☐ **education /attendance** ⸱ ☐ **community relations activity** ☐ **other activity**

3) COMPANY NEWS INFORMATION:_____
_____
_____
(use reverse side if necessary)

Check Appropriate Box:

☐**client news** ☐ **community involvement** ☐ **speeches** ☐ **awards**

☐**financial news** ☐ **special event** ☐ **exhibits / shows**

COMMENTS:_____
_____

2) Publicity Data Collection
for newspapers

Main Topic:_____
_____
_____

Data Prepared by: _____**DATE:**_____

Photo Suggestion_____

Final Approvals by_____

BASIC INFORMATION

Who_____
_____
        (names and titles of personnel in the article)

What_____
_____
        (brief description of the subject of the article)

When_____
        (date and time of the activity)

Where_____
        (location in detail)

Why_____
        (purpose of the activity)

ADDITIONAL INFORMATION_____
_____
_____
        (use reverse side, if necessary)

3) Publicity Planning Calendar

Category:	Capsule Description:
Company News	
Sale/Promotion	_____
Vendor/Supplier News	_____
Member News	_____
Government Relations	_____
Major Contract	_____
VIP Visit	_____
Merger/Acquisition	_____
Reception/Party/Picnic	_____
Grand Opening	_____
Retirement Event	_____
Awards Event	_____
Organizations	_____
Exhibits/Shows	_____
Other	_____
Personnel News	
Promotion	_____
Award	_____
New Hire	_____
Retirement	_____
Management Opinion	_____
Management Change	_____
Community Activity	_____
Seminar/Education	_____
Unusual Hobby/Sports	_____
Other	_____
Product News	
Pricing	_____
Improvement	_____
New Application/Use	_____
Technical Data	_____
New Literature/Logo	_____
Manufacturing/Design	_____
Technical Data	_____
Case History	_____
Other	_____

Continue description on reverse side.

Prepared By: _____ Date:_____

4) Selecting Print and Broadcast Outlets

Client__ Employer__ Name:_____

Project:_____

Timeline: Start date:_____ Completion date:_____

PR Point-Person:_____ Client/Emp. Pt. Person:_____

Newspaper/Magazine selections in order of importance:

1-Publication:_____ Contact:_____ Tel._____

2-Publication:_____ Contact:_____ Tel._____

3-Publication:_____ Contact:_____ Tel._____

4-Publication:_____ Contact:_____ Tel._____

5-Publication:_____ Contact:_____ Tel._____

6-Publication:_____ Contact:_____ Tel._____

7-Publication:_____ Contact:_____ Tel._____

8-Publication:_____ Contact:_____ Tel._____

9-Publication:_____ Contact:_____ Tel._____

10-Publication:_____ Contact:_____ Tel._____

Radio Stations in order of importance:

1-Station:_____ Contact:_____ Tel._____

2-Station:_____ Contact:_____ Tel._____

3-Station:_____ Contact:_____ Tel._____

4-Station:_____ Contact:_____ Tel._____

5-Station:_____ Contact:_____ Tel._____

Cable-TV and National TV Stations in order of importance

1-Station:_____ Contact:_____ Tel._____

2-Station:_____ Contact:_____ Tel._____

3-Station:_____ Contact:_____ Tel._____

4-Station:_____ Contact:_____ Tel._____

Use reverse side for additional outlets.

5) Public Relations Team Tasking

Public Relations Team

Name	Title	Telephone	e-mail

Agency Name_____ Agency Rep_____ Tel._____

Public Relations Point-Person/Tasking Assignments

Planning/Management _____
Publicity Preparation _____
Publicity Servicing _____
Photography _____
Special Events _____
Community Relations _____
Printed Material-writing _____
Printed Materials-design _____
Direct Mail _____
Research _____
Newsletters _____
Crisis-Problem Mgmt. _____
Advertising _____
Budgets/Controls _____

Public Relations Mission Statement

_____
_____
_____

Public Relations Primary Objectives

1) _____
2) _____
3) _____

Scheduled Projects   *Budget*

Project 1_____ $_____
Project 2_____ $_____
Project 3_____ $_____

@2002PratherGroup

6) Publicity Return-On-Investment (ROI)

Explanation: A quantitative analysis of the return-on-investment for publicity within your public relations program simply requires that you track and measure all of the actual placements in newspapers, magazines or trade journals. A critical look at the qualitative worth of those outlets is equally important: what are each publication's clout, reputation and credibility among your publics of interest. In short, are you helping to influence important markets? Are you making things *sell* better or *seem* better? The value of the publicity that the PR practitioner generates must first be analyzed before she or he can defend its positive effects to a client or employer.

This quantitative analysis can also be applied to publicity and PSA airtime on radio, cable-TV or network TV, but that is much harder to translate into meaningful statistics. The fact that you gain the airtime is really what is important and your deduction that it has qualitative as well as monetary value is a case that can be simply made to your client or employer.

Publicity Value Tracking Form for Print Media:

Follow these four procedures to compare your publicity placement space to advertising buy space in order to determine its net quantitative value:

1) Obtain the rate cards for each publication in which your publicity appears.
2) Measure in total inches the pace devoted to your publicity, including the headline, article and photo(s) in each publication.
3) Calculate what the cost would be for buying that same amount display advertising space in each publication.
4) Add the individual amounts to reach the total quantitative value of the placements.

*Publicity Placed for*_____ *Dates*_____

Publication	Publicity Inches	Relative Ad Cost	Publicity Value
1.			
2.			
3.			
4.			
5.			
6			
7.			
8.			
9.			
10.			
11.			
12.			

(Continue on reverse side if necessary.)

TOTALS: No. of Outlets_____. Total Inches_____. Dollar Value Compared to Ad Buys_____

@2002PratherGroup

7) Planning the Media Conference

Date of Event _____ Time _____ Place _____

Client/Employer _____

Purpose of Event _____

Host _____ Spokesperson _____

Internal Attendees/Responsibilities:

Name	*Title*	*Responsibilities*
1-		
2-		
3-		
4-		
5-		
6-		

Materials for Handout _____

Reception Food/Beverage _____

Media Invitees:

Name	*Title*	*Outlet*	*Tel. No.*
1-			
2-			
3-			
5-			
6-			
7-			
8-			
9-			
10-			
11-			
12-			

(Use reverse side if necessary.)   @2002PratherGroup

8) Letter or Media Alert for a Conference

Explanation: It is important to invite all appropriate newspaper and magazine editors, reporters and columnists as well as broadcast news directors and reporters to any media conference or event within their coverage areas. The letter or media-alert will provide at the very least notice of an important media event. It also gives the practitioner an opportunity to host and possibly bond with key media members. Conversely, if you do not invite a media member who is then scooped you will have established a bad precedent and created bad blood for both you and your client or employer.

It is also vital to service your publicity material to those outlets that choose not to attend or are unable to attend the media conference. Timing is everything, so do not get the material to an outlet until the deadline for advance publication has passed but not too late to assure timely placement. Disadvantages to media not in attendance include not being able to report executive comments, inability to ask questions and lack of first-person perspective of a significant event.

The following form is to collect information for the letter or media-alert and can be serviced via fax, e-mail or mail. An advance phone call alerting the contact about the event and that a letter or alert is coming is also good PR protocol. Adding in a personal note such as "Hi, hope to see you!" to the media-alert or letter adds a personal touch and is also appropriate. PR practitioners should collect this information and then prepare a succinct letter or media-alert to print and broadcast media members that she or he and the client or employer hope will attend.

Information for Letter or Media-Alert

To: Name   Title   Date

Outlet Name   Address

Re: Conference Theme

Location   Date   Time-from   to

Purpose of Conference

From: Client/Employer Business Name

Location

Products or Services (brief)

CEO/President

Conference Host   Spokesperson

Photography Opportunities

Radio/TV Sound System   TV Lighting

Other Information

For Additional Information: Title   Tel.

@2002PratherGroup

258

9) Case History Article
data collection form - *confidential*

Explanation. This information is to be used for a case history article that will document: 1-the original need of the client, 2-the solutions offered and 3-the results obtained. Approvals will be obtained from the client prior to publication. Where appropriate, photos and other artwork will accompany the article. Placement will be in a publication of value.

Information for business:

Business Name: _____ Title: _____ Extension: _____

Department: _____

_____ Description of Product or Service: _____

_____

_____

_____

Attach pertinent information on product or service. Use reverse side or attach additional information.

Information for organization:

Organization Name: _____

Address: _____

Contact's Name: _____ Title: _____ Tel: _____

History: _____

_____

Case History Information:

1) The Need: _____

_____

2) The Solutions: _____

_____

3) The Results: _____

_____

_____

_____

259

10) Public Relations Budget

ACTIVITY   sub-Totals

Agency Fees (if applicable)

Agency Expenses (if applicable)

Internal Expenses

PR Support Advertising*

Direct Mail for PR*

Photography

Graphics

Special Events

Printed Materials Costs

Promotional Items

Publicity Reproduction

Postage/Distribution Costs

Expenses - travel/entertainment/miscellaneous

Other (specify)

(* - or insert in advertising budget.)

TOTAL

Prepared By   Date

11) Individual Print Outlet Evaluations

PUBLICATION _____

AD REP _____ TEL. _____

ADDRESS _____ . _____

DATE(S) PUBLISHED _____

CIRCULATION _____ PUBLICATION TYPE _____ FREQUENCY _____

TOTAL INQUIRIES _____ By Inquiry Card _____ By Tel _____ By Fax _____ By Mail _____

TOTAL ADVERTISING COST _____ For Placement _____ For Production _____

COST PER INQUIRY _____ - divide the total advertising costs by the number of inquiries. ____

SALES FROM ADVERTISING IN DOLLARS _____ Attach results for products/services sold. ____

ADVERTISING RETURN-ON-INVESTMENT (ROI) RATIO* _____ to 1 _____

*- to calculate the ROI ratio, divide sales from ads in dollars by the total ad costs and insert as the first number.

EVALUATION:

_____
_____
_____
_____
_____
_____
_____
_____
_____

Information Compiled By_____

Date_____

12) **Media Comparisons**
for Trade Publications

PUBLICATION AD SIZE DATE CIRC. INQUIRIES *GROSS REVENUES

1-_____

          Ad Rates:_____ Cost per Thousand:_____

2 -_____

          Ad Rates:_____ Cost per Thousand:_____

3-_____

          Ad Rates:_____ Cost per Thousand:_____

4 -_____

          Ad Rates:_____ Cost per Thousand:_____

5 -_____

          Ad Rates:_____ Cost per Thousand:_____

6 -_____

          Ad Rates:_____ Cost per Thousand:_____

7 -_____

          Ad Rates:_____ Cost per Thousand:_____

*- indicates total of gross revenues from sales resulting from the ad.

13) Print Media Advertising Schedule

Print Outlets - *information gathering form*

COMPANY_____   FOR MONTHS ___ to ___ . PAGE ___ of ___ .

PUBLICATION	Jan	Feb	Mar	Apr	May	June	July	Aug	Sept	Oct	Nov	Dec
Name:	A											
Circ:	B											
Publishing Date:	C											
Closing:	D											
Rate:	E											
No. of Times:	F											
Contract:	G											
Key Code*:	H											
Special Issue:	I											

PUBLICATION	Jan	Feb	Mar	Apr	May	June	July	Aug	Sept	Oct	Nov	Dec
NAME:	A											
Circ:	B											
Publ. Date:	C											
Closing:	D											
Rate:	E											
No. Times:	F											
Contract:	G											
Key Code*:	H											
Special Issue:	I											

PUBLICATION	Jan	Feb	Mar	Apr	May	June	July	Aug	Sept	Oct	Nov	Dec
NAME:	A											
Circ:	B											
Publ. Date:	C											
Closing:	D											
Rate:	E											
No. Times:	F											
Contract:	G											
Key Code*:	H											
Special Issue:	I											

PUBLICATION	Jan	Feb	Mar	Apr	May	June	July	Aug	Sept	Oct	Nov	Dec
NAME:	A											
Circ:	B											
Publ. Date:	C											
Closing:	D											
Rate:	E											
No. Times:	F											
Contract:	G											
Key Code*:	H											
Special Issue:	I											

NOTE: Enter information under the month for monthly trade publications. Indicate dates for other publications.

LETTER CODE: A - size, B - color(s), C - key number*, D - IO number, E - miscellaneous, F - cost, G - contract information, H - Rep's Name, I - Special Issue name, if applicable.

*KEY CODE: 1 - new product or service, 2 - inquiry generator ad, 3 - institutional ad.

14) Newsletter Checklist

Newsletter Name_____ **Editor**_____

Newsletter Format
___2 pages ___4 pages ___8 pages ___16 pages ___24-pages___other

___1 color ___2 color ___4 color ___uncoated stock ___plain stock

Newsletter Frequency
Monthly___ Bi-Monthly___ Semi-Annually___ Annually___

Newsletter Publication Dates
_____

Newsletter Themes
Issue dated_____ Issue dated_____
Issue dated_____ Issue dated_____

Committee Names
Assignments_____ Articles/Features_____ Photography_____
Editing_____ Personals_____ Letters_____
Design/Layout_____ Printing_____ Distribution_____
Other_____

Circulation Figures
Total Circulation_____ For Mailing_____ For Pick Up_____ Electronic_____
Notes:_____

Contents for Issue of_____
News Stories_____
Case Histories_____
Features_____
Interviews_____
Management Column_____
Opinions and Editorial_____
Briefs_____
Personals_____
Photographs and Graphics_____

Notes_____

Deadlines for copy and materials_____ for final approvals_____

15) Special Event Checklist

Name/Description of Promotion: _____

Hosted/Sponsored By: _____

Expected Attendance: _____ Total Invitees: _____ Years Run: _____

Date(s): _____

Time(s): _____

Location(s): _____

Chairperson: _____ Tel: _____

Committee Members: _____

_____

Event Objectives: _____

_____

Total Budget: _____ Advertising: _____ Materials: _____ Menu: _____ Site: _____ Miscellaneous: _____

Notes: _____

Committee Leaders For –

Advertising: _____ Publicity: _____

Print Materials: _____ Accounting: _____

Invitations: _____ Lists: _____

Mailings: _____ Follow-Up: _____

Menu: _____ Giveaways: _____

Site Management: _____ Set-Up: _____

Photography: _____ Hosts/Hostesses: _____

Break-Down: _____ Clean-Up: _____

Post-Event Summary: _____ Responses: _____

Timeline –

Publicity/Photography Deadline: _____ Submission Deadline: _____

Media Coverage Request By: _____ Site Preparation Deadline: _____

Materials Deadline: _____ Distribution Deadline: _____

Invitation Planning/Printing _____ Mail Deadline: _____

Ad Production Deadline: _____ Ad Placement Deadline: _____

Ad Print Outlets: _____

Ad Broadcast Outlets: _____

Ad Schedules: _____

Date of Next Meeting: _____ Prepared By: _____ Date: _____

Notes: _____

_____

_____

_____

(use reverse side, if necessary)   @2002PratherGroup

265

16) Selecting an Outside PR Agency
evaluation form

To be filled in by the internal public relations employee or consultant:

Advertising Objectives
_____

Annual Advertising Budget _____ Previous Year _____

Evaluate Current Ad Program as: Effective _____ Adequate _____ Ineffective _____

Evaluate Competitors' Ads as: Effective _____ Adequate _____ Ineffective _____

Advertising Chain-Of-Command: _____

Agency Evaluation Committee: _____

To be filled in by the selection committee for each of three bidding agencies. Attach notes or further information.

1) AGENCY_____ Lead Contact:_____ Tel._____

Size: ☐ small   ☐ medium   ☐ large. Compatibility: ☐ good   ☐ fair   ☐ poor

Knowledge of the Industry: ☐ good   ☐ fair   ☐ poor   ☐ capability of learning

Client Base: ☐ good   ☐ fair   ☐ poor. References: ☐ good   ☐ fair   ☐ poor

Presentation: ☐ good   ☐ fair   ☐ poor. Proposals: ☐ good   ☐ fair   ☐ poor

Style: ☐ good   ☐ fair   ☐ poor. Meeting Objectives: ☐ good   ☐ fair   ☐ poor

Hourly Rate_____ Management Fee_____ Commission Structure_____

Expense Policies_____Billing Policy_____

Rating from 1-to-10: _____creativity _____graphics _____placement skill _____client relations

Rating Total Agency One___ Comments_____

2) AGENCY_____ Lead Contact:_____ Tel._____

Size: ☐ small   ☐ medium   ☐ large. Compatibility: ☐ good   ☐ fair   ☐ poor

Knowledge of the Industry: ☐ good   ☐ fair   ☐ poor   ☐ capability of learning

Client Base: ☐ good   ☐ fair   ☐ poor. References: ☐ good   ☐ fair   ☐ poor

Presentation: ☐ good   ☐ fair   ☐ poor. Proposals: ☐ good   ☐ fair   ☐ poor

Style: ☐ good   ☐ fair   ☐ poor. Meeting Objectives: ☐ good   ☐ fair   ☐ poor

Hourly Rate_____ Management Fee_____ Commission Structure_____

Expense Policies_____Billing Policy_____

Rating from 1-to-10: _____creativity _____graphics _____placement skill _____client relations

Rating Total Agency Two___ Comments_____

3) AGENCY_____ Lead Contact:_____ Tel._____

Size: ☐ small   ☐ medium   ☐ large. Compatibility: ☐ good   ☐ fair   ☐ poor

Knowledge of the Industry: ☐ good   ☐ fair   ☐ poor   ☐ capability of learning

Client Base: ☐ good   ☐ fair   ☐ poor. References: ☐ good   ☐ fair   ☐ poor

Presentation: ☐ good   ☐ fair   ☐ poor. Proposals: ☐ good   ☐ fair   ☐ poor

Style: ☐ good   ☐ fair   ☐ poor. Meeting Objectives: ☐ good   ☐ fair   ☐ poor

Hourly Rate_____ Management Fee_____ Commission Structure_____

Expense Policies_____Billing Policy_____

Rating from 1-to-10: _____creativity _____graphics ____placement _____client relations

Rating Total Agency Three___ Comments_____

17) Forming an Internal PR Agency
action checklist

Advertising Director:_____ Title:_____ Tel._____

Committee Members:_____

Copywriters:_____

Photography:_____ Placement:_____

Budget Manager:_____ Analysis:_____

Internal Agency Name:_____

Advertising Objectives:_____

_____

Annual Advertising Budget_____ Quarterly: 1st:____ 2nd:____ 3rd:____ 4th:____

Print Outlets Review:

Name -	Rates -	Circ. -	Rep -
Name -	Rates -	Circ. -	Rep -
Name -	Rates -	Circ. -	Rep -
Name -	Rates -	Circ. -	Rep -
Name -	Rates -	Circ. -	Rep -
Name -	Rates -	Circ. -	Rep -

(attach print calendar)

Broadcast Outlets Review:

Name -	Rates -	Reach -	Rep -
Name -	Rates -	Reach -	Rep -
Name -	Rates -	Reach -	Rep -

(attach broadcast calendar)

Point Persons for Other Marketing Communications Programs:

direct mail	telemarketing	public relations
print materials	newsletters	community rel.

Payment Guidelines:

1) Deduct standard agency commission of 15 percent from appropriate advertising bills.

2) Deduct two percent for pre-payment where applicable and indicated.

3) Use Insert Order form when placing advertising.

4) Use letterhead of internal agency in all communications.

18) Establishing PR Resources

The public relations practitioner who wishes to form a consulting agency or serve as a one-person operation must examine available resources that will allow him or her to offer viable and professional services. Then the practitioner must quickly learn how to assemble a team of professionals that can affordably and cost-efficiently provide the services that will be needed to fulfill missions and compete in the marketplace against established agencies, boutique agencies and a myriad of consulting competitors. The PR employee for a business or organization who is managing an internal agency often must reach out for additional resources, too.

Following is a form that can be employed when interviewing select professionals in virtually any discipline: writing, technical writing, photography, graphic design, printing, advertising, *etc.*

Resource: Photography

Name _____ Affiliation (if any) _____

Address _____ Tel. _____ e-Mail _____

Specialty _____

Experience _____

References _____

Special Abilities or Talents _____

Rates and/or fees _____

Payment Policy _____

Partners or Associates (if any) _____

Their Experience _____

Ratings from 1-to-10:

Demeanor _____ Appearance _____ Professionalism _____ Compatibility _____

Summary _____
_____
_____

19) Advertising Budget
quarterly/annual

ACTIVITY	Total	1st Q	2nd Q	3rd Q	4th Q
Print Advertising Placement					
Print Advertising Production					
Broadcast Advt. Placement					
Broadcast Advertising Production					
Agency Fees (if applicable)					
Agency Expenses (if applicable)					
Public Relations Support Advt.					
Direct Mail					
Telemarketing					
Other Expenses (specify)					
Miscellaneous Expenses (specify)					

(If appropriate, also credit appropriate ad budget items to or from the Public Relations Budget)

QUARTERLY TOTALS _____ _____ _____ _____

ANNUAL TOTAL_____

Prepared by_____ Date_____

20) Advertising Insert Order Form
placement form

INSERT ORDER NO._____Date Submitted_____ By_____

Publication_____Circulation_____

Address_____Rep._____ Tel._____

Ad Enclosed ☐ Ad to Follow ☐ Ad Copy to Follow ☐ Ad Copy Written Below ☐

Display ☐ Classified Display ☐ Classified ☐ ROP ☐ Request_____

Additional Instructions_____

_____

Insertion Dates_____

Ad Size_____ Ad Description: 1-color ☐ 2-color ☐ 4-color ☐ Bleed ☐

Ad Cost_____ Less SAC_____ Less Discount (if applicable)

Total Due_____ Submitted in Advance_____ Bill Balance of_____

Advertising copy below or attached:

_____
_____
_____
_____
_____
_____
_____
_____

Please promptly forward tear sheets to:

Name_____ Title_____
Agency/Company_____
Address_____
Submitted by (print)_____ Date_____
Signature_____ Tel._____

21) **Survey of Customer/Client Reading Preferences**

Dear _____   Date _____

In order for us to determine the most effective venues in which to advertise on your behalf, we wish to analyze your specific industry-related reading preferences and their influence on you.

By identifying the trade and consumer media that you consider effective for general information, publicity and advertising, we can assure they these outlets are integrated into our master lists for both advertising and publicity placements. Our objective is to finalize a media action plan that will reach and favorably influence your target publics of interest in the most comprehensive and effective manner possible.

Please sequence your selections and rankings by number in order of importance on the form below and return the survey to the undersigned at your earliest convenience with our sincere thanks in advance.

PRIMARY INDUSTRY PUBLICATIONS OF IMPORTANCE TO YOU:

1) Publication - _____   Read Frequently ☐ Read Infrequently ☐

2) Publication - _____   Read Frequently ☐ Read Infrequently ☐

3) Publication - _____   Read Frequently ☐ Read Infrequently ☐

4) Publication - _____   Read Frequently ☐ Read Infrequently ☐

5) Publication - _____   Read Frequently ☐ Read Infrequently ☐

6) Publication - _____   Read Frequently ☐ Read Infrequently ☐

(Please use reverse side to list recommended personal contacts and for additional listings.)

Indicate by number the publications you read thoroughly_____ those you scan_____

Please enter the numbers of publications that have been effective for:

information_____ inquiries_____ sales_____ publicity_____ advertising_____

Please rate from 1-to-10 the importance to you of the following (10 is best):

product advertising___ service advertising___ publicity   _____

Survey competed by _____ Title _____ Date _____
Signature _____
Please return to: _____

271

22) Crisis-Problem Tracking - confidential

1-Describe the nature or cause of the crisis or problem:_____

_____
(continue on reverse side if necessary)

2-Describe damages to facilities or property, injuries or fatalities:_____

_____

3-What caused the situation?_____

_____

4-Who first identified the crisis or problem and to whom?_____

5-Who does it affect internally and how?_____

_____

6-Who does it affect externally and how?_____

_____

7-What date and time did it occur or become known?_____

8-Where did the situation arise or occur?_____

9-Who knows about this situation among management and employees?_____

_____

10-Is the media aware of this situation?   11-Is the public aware of the situation; how?

_____   _____

What action if any has already been taken in response to the situation?

_____

What actions are necessary to deal with the situation now and in the immediate future?

_____

Rapid Response Action Team Members will be:_____

_____

The spokesperson will be:_____   Committee meeting date and time:_____

Confirm your attendance to:_____

Circulated by:_____   Return completed form ASAP to:_____

Completed by:_____   Date:_____

23) Crisis-Problem *Post Mortem* Analysis

1-What was the final resolution of the crisis or problem?_____
_____
_____
_____
_____

2-What are the short-term and long-term effects?_____
_____
_____
_____

3-What policies, procedures or controls need to be changed because of the situation?_____
_____
_____

4-What was handled well and/or what could have been handled better?_____
_____
_____

5-Describe the media response?_____

6-Describe the employee response?_____

7-Describe the customer or client response?_____

8-Was the company response plan timely, effective and comprehensive? Explain._____
_____

9-Who was effective in responding and how?_____
_____

10-Comments:_____
_____
_____
_____
_____
_____
_____

Circulated by:_____   Return ASAP to:_____

Completed by:_____   Date:_____

24) Public Relations Plan Tracking

The PR plan attached is for: client_____ employer_____ business____ non-profit organization_____

Name:_____ Main Contact:_____ Title:_____ Tel._____

The PR point-person managing the plan is:_____

Others on the PR team are:_____

The objectives of the plan are to:

    Increase sales and profits. Explain:_____

    Introduce-launch a product or service. Explain:_____

    Deal with a crisis or problem. Explain:_____

    Other. Explain:_____

The techniques to be employed will include the following:

    Publicity. Explain:_____

    Promotion. Explain:_____

    Advertising. Explain:_____

    Printed Materials. Explain:_____

    Direct Mail. Explain:_____

    Special Events. Explain:_____

    Other. Explain:_____

The plan timeline is: Beginning:_____ Completion:_____

Circulated to all concerned by:_____ Date:_____

25) Client/Employer PR Reporting

It is vitally important for the public relations practitioner to report on all activities and efforts undertaken on behalf of the client or employer on a regular basis, monthly, quarterly, annually. A systematic reporting process will memorialize and track these activities and efforts, provide documentation of the value of PR to the paying client or employer, and represent a flow of work that can be checked and crosschecked as time elapses on a project or program.

During the reporting process, the PR pro generally discovers that she or he has actually done much more for the client of employer than first comes to mind. Checking daily calendars and taking copious notes will help when it comes time to commit the report to paper. The attachment of clips, communications and other pertinent materials will bolster the presentations.

Following is a sample form for reporting PR activities and efforts.

Public Relations Report for (Month)

Report By: _____ To: _____ Date _____

Public Relations Activities (dates) _____ to _____

Publicity in Newspapers _____
_____
_____

Publicity in Magazines _____
_____

Publicity on Radio/TV _____
_____

Promotion _____
Results _____

Special Event _____
Results _____

Newsletter (attached) Role _____

Printed Material (attached) Role _____

Media Relations (explanation) _____

Summary _____

Thank you for sharing my world of public relations . . .

Jack J. Prather, 2002
Newton, N.J.